TABL

C000100367

FOREWORD by MICHAEL USLAN & ROBERT KLEIN

It was the 1960's.

Stan Lee, Jack Kirby and Steve Ditko became overnight "number-one-with-a-bullpen" success stories as the Marvel super-hero style took the comic book world by storm. By January 1966, the ultra-camp Pop-Art exaggeration of Batman on TV exploded across America's culturally "vast wasteland," imbuing art, design, and clothing styles with new Pop sensibilities-along with assorted "Pows," "Zaps," and "Whams!" These were wild times! Super-heroes were "in" and everybody jumped on the bandwagon. Charlton, Dell/Gold Key, Tower, ACG, Harvey and others leaped into the super-hero business, hoping to emulate not only DC's prosperity, but especially Marvel's torrid success in the changing marketplace. And then, it was Archie Comics Group's turn...

Archie Publications did not start with a blank slate, and its proud super-hero history was an important additional ingredient in the mix. While Archie ultimately became their mainstay, MLJ Comics (originally named for publishers Morris Coyne, Louis Silberkleit, and John Goldwater) initially published a long list of super-heroes. Archie's success eclipsed the first hero to drape himself in a flag, The Shield, and pushed that red-white-and-blue crusader right out of "PEP COMICS." The Black Hood, the pulpish costumed detective, was evicted by Jughead from the pages of "TOP-NOTCH COMICS," turning that title into "LAUGH COMICS" instead. And lest we forget, Steel Sterling (the original "Man of Steel," long before that other guy from Krypton adopted the name), was usurped from his throne in "JACKPOT COMICS" by Archie and the Riverdale gang. These were great action-adventure characters, too long gone from the comics scene by 1965.

MLJ (eventually changing its corporate name to Archie Comics Group, but maintaining Radio Comics as its corporate entity publishing any non-Archie books) had previously attempted to bring back their super-heroes prior to 1965, when the Silver Age of Comics was still in gestation (circa 1959). Archie had turned to Joe Simon to bring back a revamped Shield (in "The DOUBLE LIFE OF PRIVATE STRONG") and to start up a second new book, "THE ADVENTURES OF THE FLY,"

both featuring artwork by the legendary team of Joe Simon & Jack Kirby in what would be their last work together for decades.

The Fly buzzed through 30 issues, battling Spider Spry and a variety of other early-60's style aliens, robots and super-villains. Along the way, Fly-Girl, his female counterpart, joined the fray, as did The Comet (an old MLJ hero re-designed in a Peter Maxx-styled rainbow helmet for the Pop 60's). Every so often, a now red-hooded Black Hood showed up to teach judo lessons to comic book readers who might be tiring of getting sand kicked in their faces on local beaches. As part of the Radio Comics/Archie Adventure Line, the publisher added "THE ADVENTURES OF THE JAGUAR" (an animal kingdom version of The Fly), "YOUNG DR. MASTERS" (a Dr. Kildare-type soap opera), and its own unique version of "THE SHADOW" in black and blue leotards, a cape and mask.

It was in the pages of "THE SHADOW" #5, where the first teaser ad featuring The Fly (now renamed Fly-Man) appeared. Although his comic had been discontinued many months before, it was clear that he was being revamped, with new powers, a new look and a new name. The last panel of the ad referred to a mysterious trio who would change everything. How true that would prove to be!

The mystery was solved in "FLY-MAN" #31, on sale a few months later. The mystery trio turned out to be three super-heroes from the past: what appeared to be the original 1940 Shield; The Black Hood, now with his original black hood but suddenly caped and riding a mechanical, flying rocking horse; and The Comet (not the original from "PEP COMICS" #1, but an alien ruler of the Planet Altrox). Besides the title change, a new artist was clearly at the helm. Paul Reinman's art was recognizable from his Marvel Comics work on Ant-Man, Iron Man, and those other super-teams, the X-Men and Avengers. Clearly, Archie was out to emulate everything Marvel. The Fly was renamed Fly-Man to sound more like Spider-Man. His powers were now a combination of Spidey's, Ant-Man's, and Giant-Man's. Soon, the entire Archie Adventure Line would be

rechristened as the more Marvelous sounding, Mighty Comics Group. There was a new writing style, too-campy/corny, long-winded dialogue often simply describing the action drawn in the panel, lots of purple prose. It would be several issues before the world at large was told who the writer was. In a take-off on the name of Marvel's Stan Lee, the writing credit was attributed to "Jerry Ess." It was Jerry Siegel, the creator of Superman! Shocked readers were bowled over!

There was lots of action in the stories, especially fights among the heroes on the team. The heroes seemed to spend more time brawling with each other than battling the villains, playing up (way, way up) the Marvel theme of heroes who don't always get along. Although villainous Spider Spry named their team The Mighty Crusaders in "FLY-MAN" #31, it took them until "MIGHTY CRUSADERS" #1, seven months later, before they would agree on this name. These guys had a hard time coming to a consensus. This is probably the only team in comics history named by the bad guy.

Reading this stuff over the summer of 1965 was great for kids of that era. Where else could they find a mosquito saving the day... an intelligent mosquito from ancient Atlantis endowed with Thrust Power Vision, no less? It was High Camp and not a bit self-conscious.

The letter columns were filled with continuing calls to bring back more of the MLJ characters (and yes, it's true...one of those fan letters was from one Michael Uslan), and so it was done. "FLY-MAN" #33 revived the 1940's Hangman, now capeless and with a magic rope, and the Golden Age Wizard, re-costumed and totally different from the original. In an unexpected twist, they were revived by Archie... as villains.

These stories are a memory of a time long past, when Iran and Iraq were America's friends, Lyndon Johnson was President, and Adam West was Batman. Come with us now, Mighty Reader, back to where comics didn't take themselves so seriously, where the villains snarled as they bragged about their schemes, and where it was still OK for super-heroes to talk with insects.

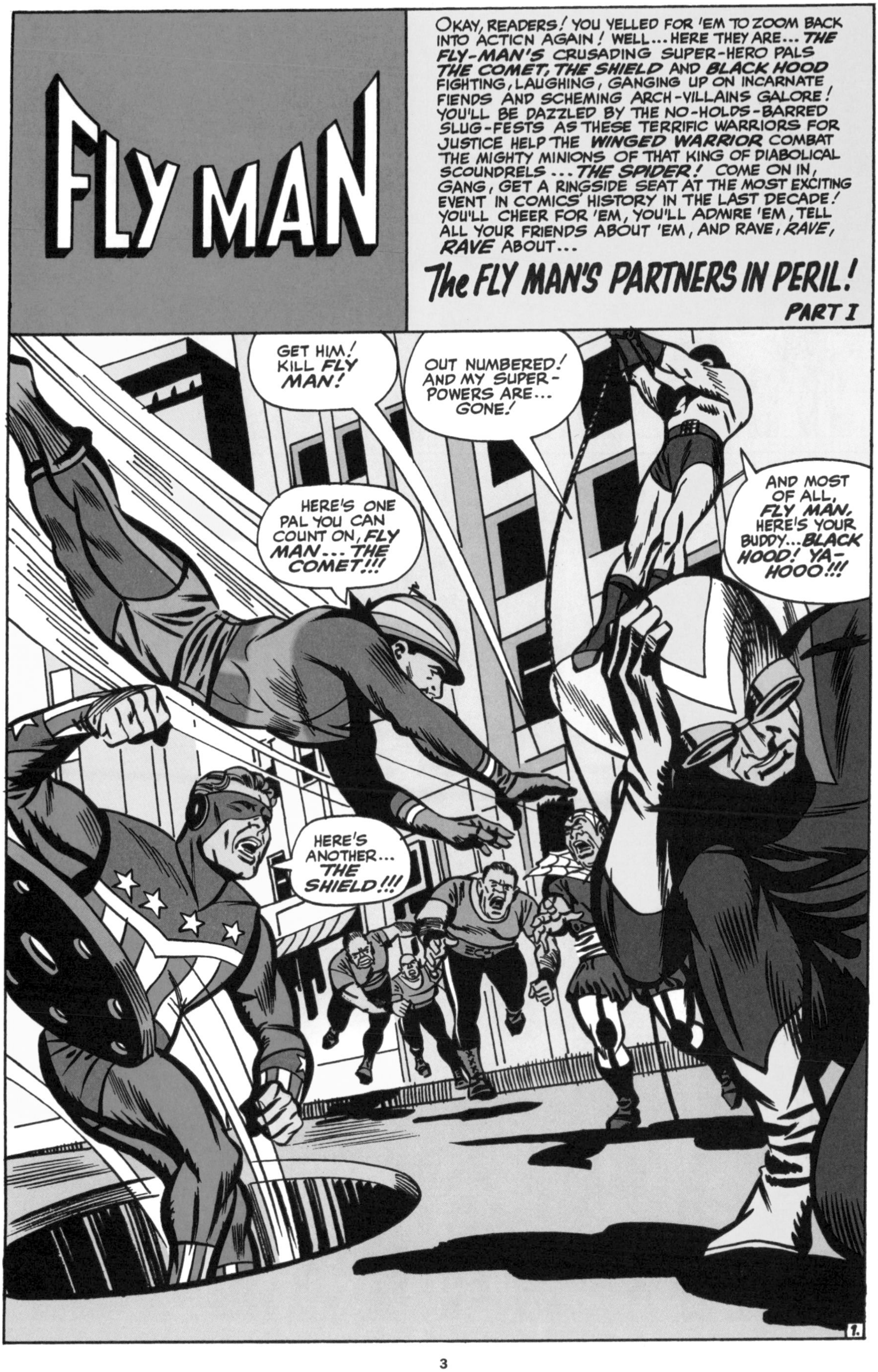
FLY MAN
OKAY, READERS! YOU YELLED FOR 'EM TO ZOOM BACK INTO ACTION AGAIN! WELL... HERE THEY ARE... THE FLY-MAN'S CRUSADING SUPER-HERO PALS THE COMET, THE SHIELD AND BLACK HOOD FIGHTING, LAUGHING, GANGING UP ON INCARNATE FIENDS AND SCHEMING ARCH-VILLAINS GALORE! YOU'LL BE DAZZLED BY THE NO-HOLDS-BARRED SLUG-FESTS AS THESE TERRIFIC WARRIORS FOR JUSTICE HELP THE WINGED WARRIOR COMBAT THE MIGHTY MINIONS OF THAT KING OF DIABOLICAL SCOUNDRELS ... THE SPIDER! COME ON IN, GANG, GET A RINGSIDE SEAT AT THE MOST EXCITING EVENT IN COMICS' HISTORY IN THE LAST DECADE! YOU'LL CHEER FOR 'EM, YOU'LL ADMIRE 'EM, TELL ALL YOUR FRIENDS ABOUT 'EM, AND RAVE, RAVE, RAVE ABOUT...
The FLY MAN'S PARTNERS IN PERIL!
PART I
GET HIM! KILL FLY MAN!
OUT NUMBERED! AND MY SUPER-POWERS ARE... GONE!
HERE'S ONE PAL YOU CAN COUNT ON, FLY MAN... THE COMET!!!
AND MOST OF ALL, FLY MAN, HERE'S YOUR BUDDY... BLACK HOOD! YA-HOOO!!!
HERE'S ANOTHER... THE SHIELD!!!
1.

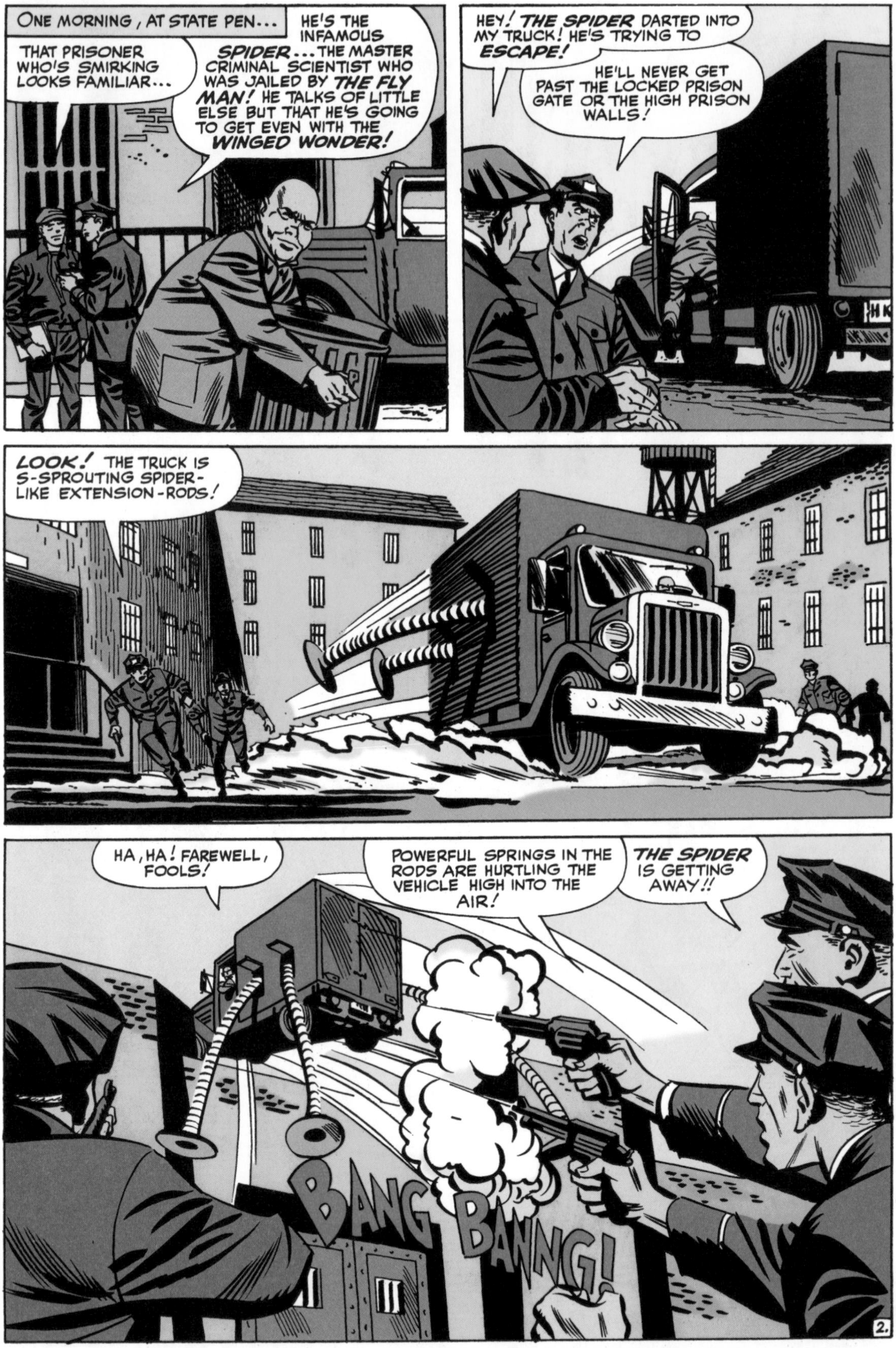

ONE MORNING, AT STATE PEN...
THAT PRISONER WHO'S SMIRKING LOOKS FAMILIAR...
HE'S THE INFAMOUS SPIDER... THE MASTER CRIMINAL SCIENTIST WHO WAS JAILED BY THE FLY MAN! HE TALKS OF LITTLE ELSE BUT THAT HE'S GOING TO GET EVEN WITH THE WINGED WONDER!
HEY! THE SPIDER DARTED INTO MY TRUCK! HE'S TRYING TO ESCAPE!
HE'LL NEVER GET PAST THE LOCKED PRISON GATE OR THE HIGH PRISON WALLS!
LOOK! THE TRUCK IS S-SPROUTING SPIDER-LIKE EXTENSION-RODS!
HA, HA! FAREWELL, FOOLS!
POWERFUL SPRINGS IN THE RODS ARE HURTLING THE VEHICLE HIGH INTO THE AIR!
THE SPIDER IS GETTING AWAY!!
BANG BANNG!
2.

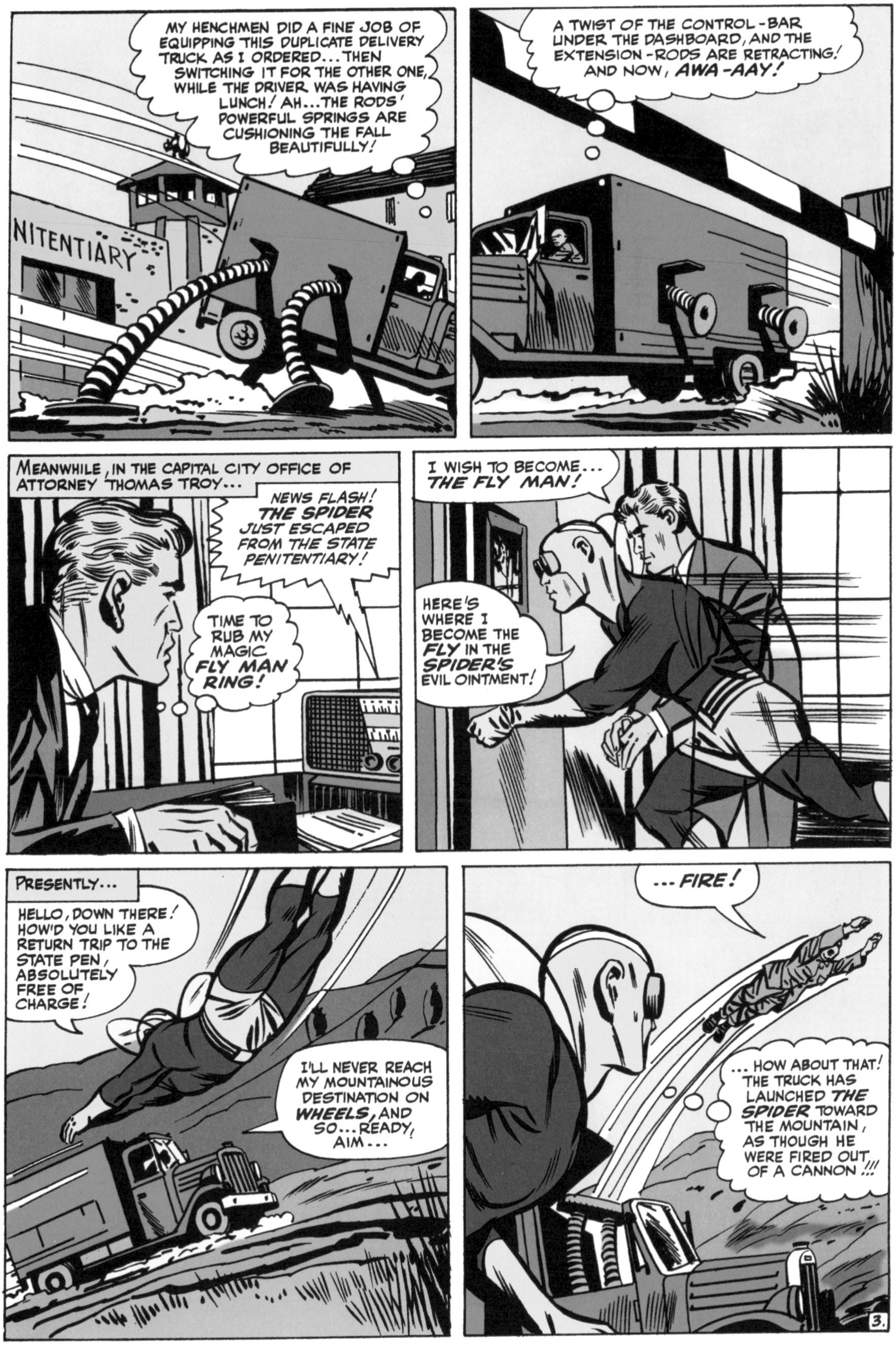
MY HENCHMEN DID A FINE JOB OF EQUIPPING THIS DUPLICATE DELIVERY TRUCK AS I ORDERED... THEN SWITCHING IT FOR THE OTHER ONE, WHILE THE DRIVER WAS HAVING LUNCH! AH... THE RODS' POWERFUL SPRINGS ARE CUSHIONING THE FALL BEAUTIFULLY!
NITENTIARY
A TWIST OF THE CONTROL-BAR UNDER THE DASHBOARD, AND THE EXTENSION-RODS ARE RETRACTING! AND NOW, AWA-AAY!
MEANWHILE, IN THE CAPITAL CITY OFFICE OF ATTORNEY THOMAS TROY...
NEWS FLASH! THE SPIDER JUST ESCAPED FROM THE STATE PENITENTIARY!
TIME TO RUB MY MAGIC FLY MAN RING!
I WISH TO BECOME... THE FLY MAN!
HERE'S WHERE I BECOME THE FLY IN THE SPIDER'S EVIL OINTMENT!
PRESENTLY...
HELLO, DOWN THERE! HOW'D YOU LIKE A RETURN TRIP TO THE STATE PEN, ABSOLUTELY FREE OF CHARGE!
I'LL NEVER REACH MY MOUNTAINOUS DESTINATION ON WHEELS, AND SO... READY, AIM...
...FIRE!
...HOW ABOUT THAT! THE TRUCK HAS LAUNCHED THE SPIDER TOWARD THE MOUNTAIN, AS THOUGH HE WERE FIRED OUT OF A CANNON!!!
3.

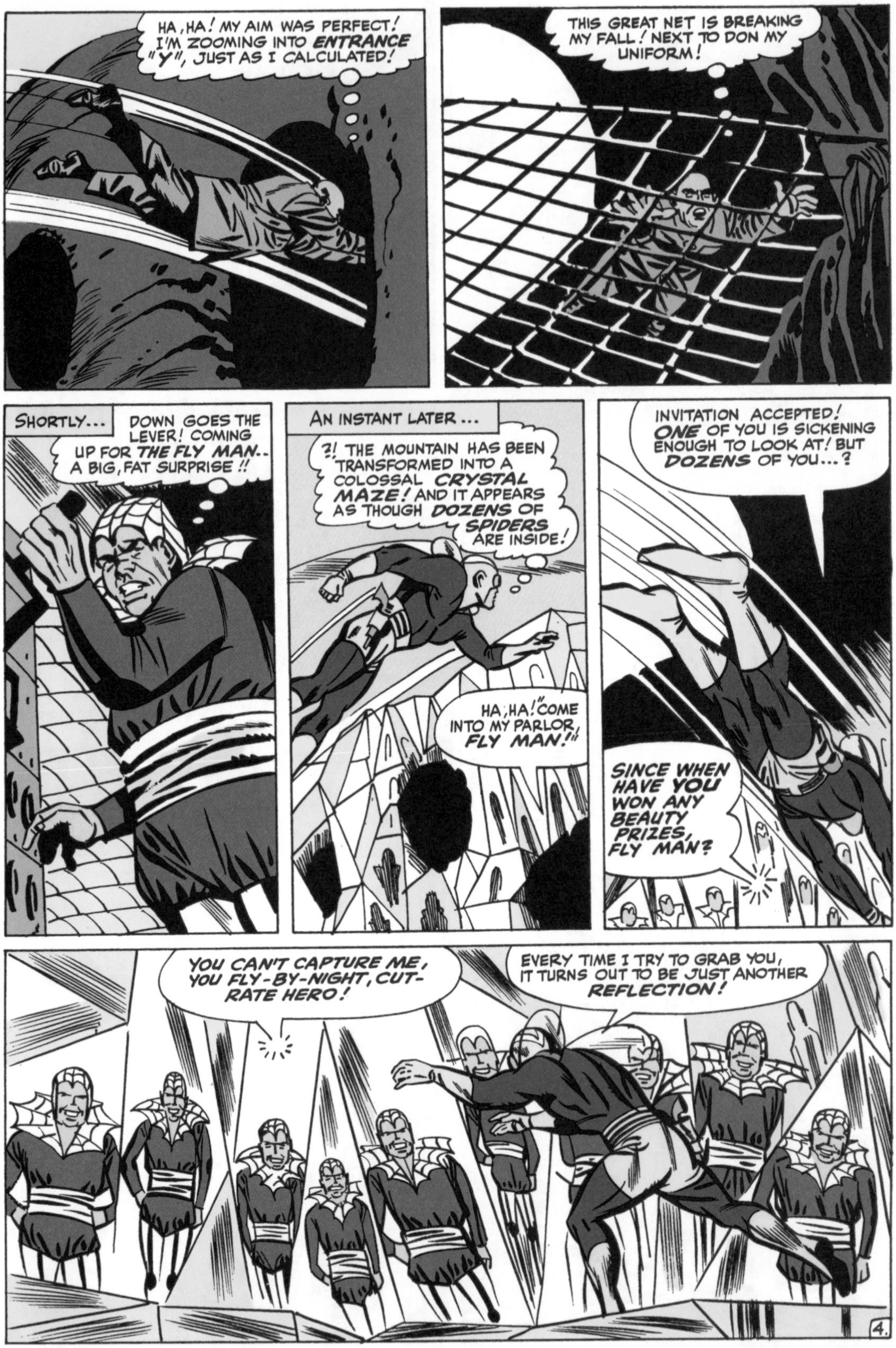
HA, HA! MY AIM WAS PERFECT! I'M ZOOMING INTO ENTRANCE "Y", JUST AS I CALCULATED!
THIS GREAT NET IS BREAKING MY FALL! NEXT TO DON MY UNIFORM!
SHORTLY...
DOWN GOES THE LEVER! COMING UP FOR THE FLY MAN.. A BIG, FAT SURPRISE!!
AN INSTANT LATER...
?! THE MOUNTAIN HAS BEEN TRANSFORMED INTO A COLOSSAL CRYSTAL MAZE! AND IT APPEARS AS THOUGH DOZENS OF SPIDERS ARE INSIDE!
HA, HA! "COME INTO MY PARLOR, FLY MAN!"
INVITATION ACCEPTED! ONE OF YOU IS SICKENING ENOUGH TO LOOK AT! BUT DOZENS OF YOU...?
SINCE WHEN HAVE YOU WON ANY BEAUTY PRIZES, FLY MAN?
YOU CAN'T CAPTURE ME, YOU FLY-BY-NIGHT, CUT-RATE HERO!
EVERY TIME I TRY TO GRAB YOU, IT TURNS OUT TO BE JUST ANOTHER REFLECTION!
4.

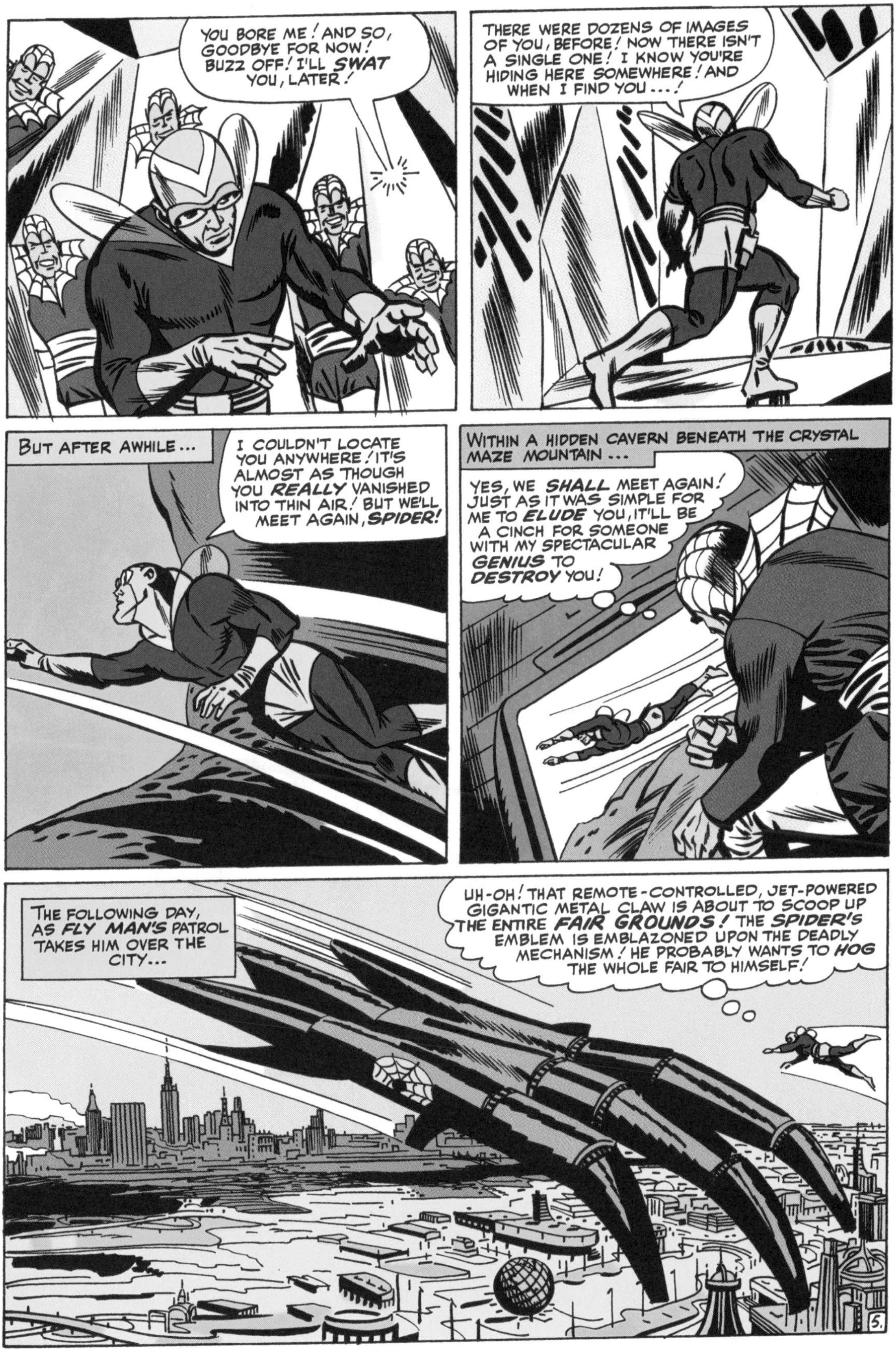
YOU BORE ME! AND SO, GOODBYE FOR NOW! BUZZ OFF! I'LL SWAT YOU, LATER!
THERE WERE DOZENS OF IMAGES OF YOU, BEFORE! NOW THERE ISN'T A SINGLE ONE! I KNOW YOU'RE HIDING HERE SOMEWHERE! AND WHEN I FIND YOU...!
BUT AFTER AWHILE...
I COULDN'T LOCATE YOU ANYWHERE! IT'S ALMOST AS THOUGH YOU REALLY VANISHED INTO THIN AIR! BUT WE'LL MEET AGAIN, SPIDER!
WITHIN A HIDDEN CAVERN BENEATH THE CRYSTAL MAZE MOUNTAIN...
YES, WE SHALL MEET AGAIN! JUST AS IT WAS SIMPLE FOR ME TO ELUDE YOU, IT'LL BE A CINCH FOR SOMEONE WITH MY SPECTACULAR GENIUS TO DESTROY YOU!
THE FOLLOWING DAY, AS FLY MAN'S PATROL TAKES HIM OVER THE CITY...
UH-OH! THAT REMOTE-CONTROLLED, JET-POWERED GIGANTIC METAL CLAW IS ABOUT TO SCOOP UP THE ENTIRE FAIR GROUNDS! THE SPIDER'S EMBLEM IS EMBLAZONED UPON THE DEADLY MECHANISM! HE PROBABLY WANTS TO HOG THE WHOLE FAIR TO HIMSELF!
5.

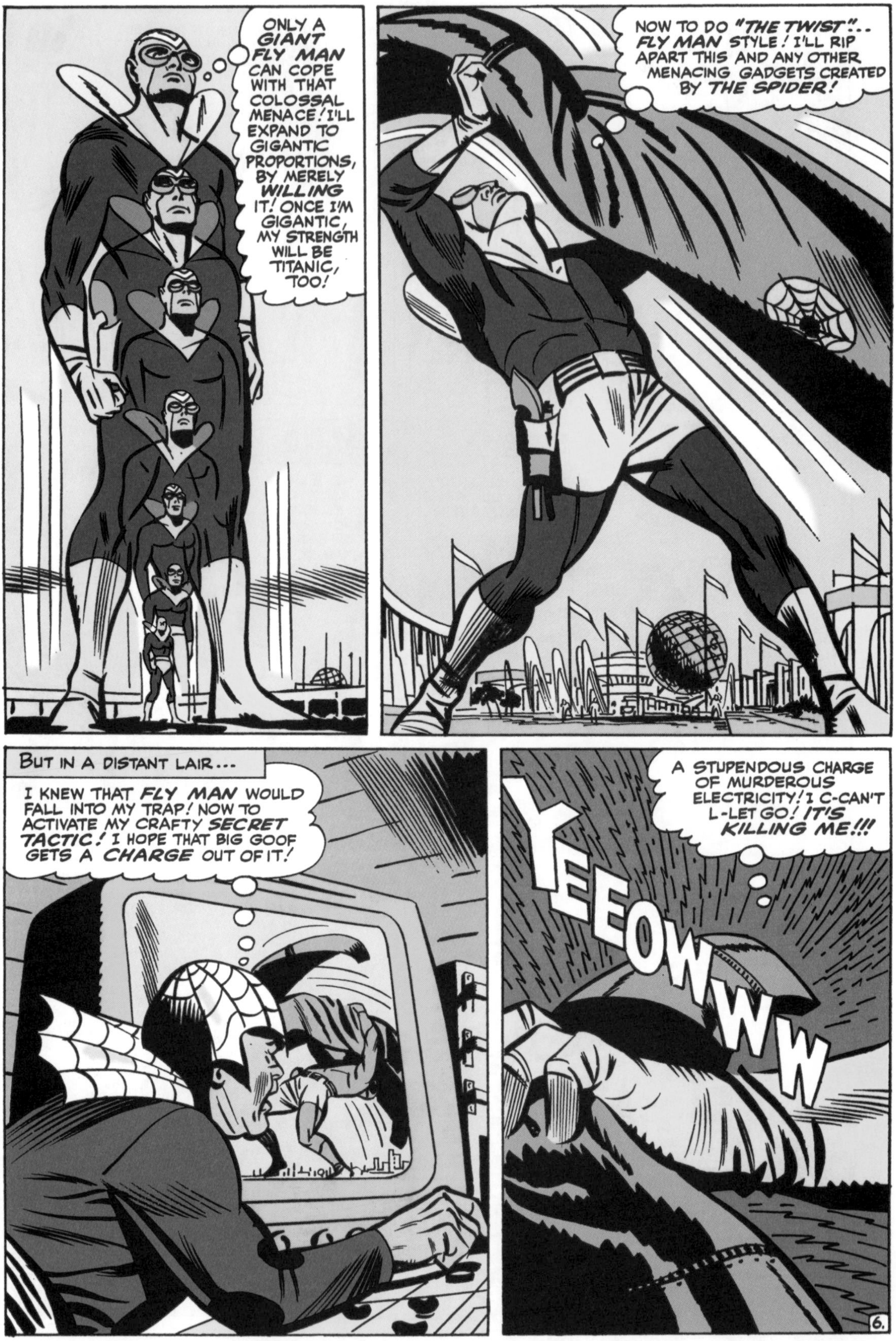
ONLY A GIANT FLY MAN CAN COPE WITH THAT COLOSSAL MENACE! I'LL EXPAND TO GIGANTIC PROPORTIONS, BY MERELY WILLING IT! ONCE I'M GIGANTIC, MY STRENGTH WILL BE TITANIC, TOO!
NOW TO DO "THE TWIST"... FLY MAN STYLE! I'LL RIP APART THIS AND ANY OTHER MENACING GADGETS CREATED BY THE SPIDER!
BUT IN A DISTANT LAIR...
I KNEW THAT FLY MAN WOULD FALL INTO MY TRAP! NOW TO ACTIVATE MY CRAFTY SECRET TACTIC! I HOPE THAT BIG GOOF GETS A CHARGE OUT OF IT!
A STUPENDOUS CHARGE OF MURDEROUS ELECTRICITY! I C-CAN'T L-LET GO! IT'S KILLING ME!!!
YEEOWWWW
6.

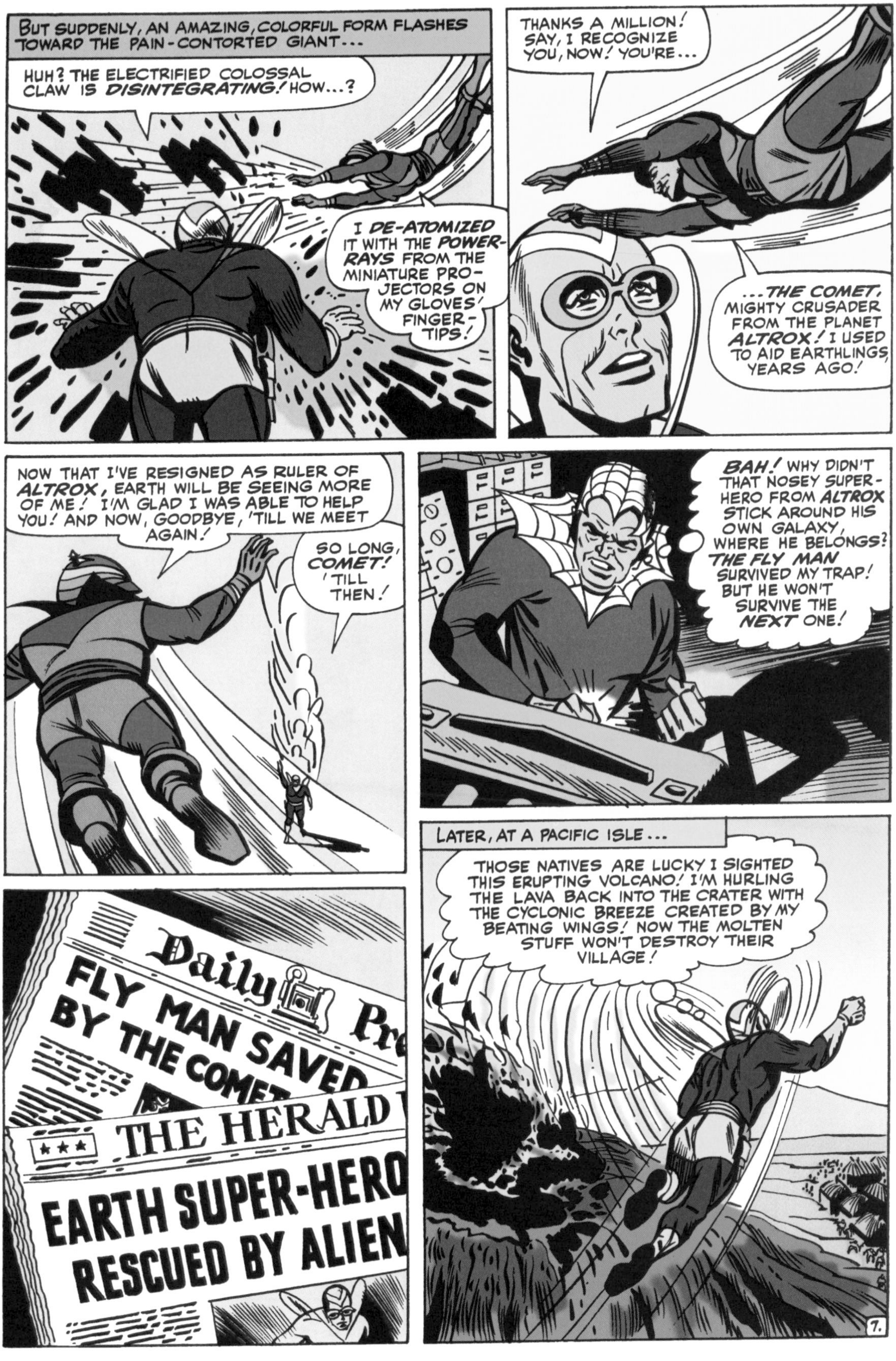

BUT SUDDENLY, AN AMAZING, COLORFUL FORM FLASHES TOWARD THE PAIN-CONTORTED GIANT...
HUH? THE ELECTRIFIED COLOSSAL CLAW IS DISINTEGRATING! HOW...?
I DE-ATOMIZED IT WITH THE POWER-RAYS FROM THE MINIATURE PROJECTORS ON MY GLOVES' FINGER-TIPS!
THANKS A MILLION! SAY, I RECOGNIZE YOU, NOW! YOU'RE...
...THE COMET, MIGHTY CRUSADER FROM THE PLANET ALTROX! I USED TO AID EARTHLINGS, YEARS AGO!
NOW THAT I'VE RESIGNED AS RULER OF ALTROX, EARTH WILL BE SEEING MORE OF ME! I'M GLAD I WAS ABLE TO HELP YOU! AND NOW, GOODBYE, 'TILL WE MEET AGAIN!
SO LONG, COMET! 'TILL THEN!
BAH! WHY DIDN'T THAT NOSEY SUPER-HERO FROM ALTROX STICK AROUND HIS OWN GALAXY, WHERE HE BELONGS? THE FLY MAN SURVIVED MY TRAP! BUT HE WON'T SURVIVE THE NEXT ONE!
Daily Pre
FLY MAN SAVED BY THE COMET
THE HERALD
EARTH SUPER-HERO RESCUED BY ALIEN
LATER, AT A PACIFIC ISLE...
THOSE NATIVES ARE LUCKY I SIGHTED THIS ERUPTING VOLCANO! I'M HURLING THE LAVA BACK INTO THE CRATER WITH THE CYCLONIC BREEZE CREATED BY MY BEATING WINGS! NOW THE MOLTEN STUFF WON'T DESTROY THEIR VILLAGE!
7.

MEANWHILE, AT A PARTY GIVEN AT THE VAN PYLE MANSION...

I'M "BOPPO, THE MIGHTY"!

I'M "FLIPSY, THE TERRIFIC"!

AND I'M "BASHER, THE DYNAMIC"! HAND OVER YOUR VALUABLES, FOLKS, AND YOU'LL LIVE TO TELL YOUR RITZY CHUMS ALL ABOUT IT!

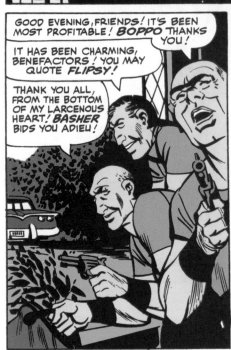

GOOD EVENING, FRIENDS! IT'S BEEN MOST PROFITABLE! BOPPO THANKS YOU!

IT HAS BEEN CHARMING, BENEFACTORS! YOU MAY QUOTE FLIPSY!

THANK YOU ALL, FROM THE BOTTOM OF MY LARCENOUS HEART! BASHER BIDS YOU ADIEU!

BUT AS THE ACROBATIC THIEVES EXIT, THEY ARE OBSERVED BY A FLY...

MUST TELEPATHICALLY TIP-OFF MY NOBLE FRIEND, THE FLY MAN, ABOUT THESE SINISTER HAPPENINGS!

RETURNING TO THE UNITED STATES, THE WINGED WONDER ZIPS ALONG ON THE ATHLETIC CROOKS' TRAIL...

TURN LEFT AT THE NEXT CORNER, FLY MAN!

WILL DO! CALLING ALL INSECTS! KEEP REPORTING THE WHERE-ABOUTS OF THAT CAR!

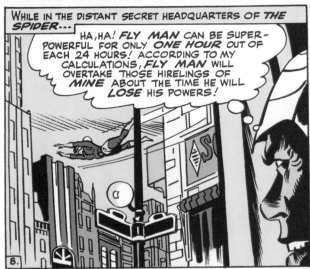

WHILE IN THE DISTANT SECRET HEADQUARTERS OF THE SPIDER...

HA, HA! FLY MAN CAN BE SUPER-POWERFUL FOR ONLY ONE HOUR OUT OF EACH 24 HOURS! ACCORDING TO MY CALCULATIONS, FLY MAN WILL OVERTAKE THOSE HIRELINGS OF MINE ABOUT THE TIME HE WILL LOSE HIS POWERS!

8.

FLY MAN WILL BE NO MATCH FOR BOPPO, FLIPSY AND BASHER! THEY'LL SQUASH HIM OUT OF EXISTENCE! AND I WILL BE REVENGED.. REVENGED!!!

END OF PART I

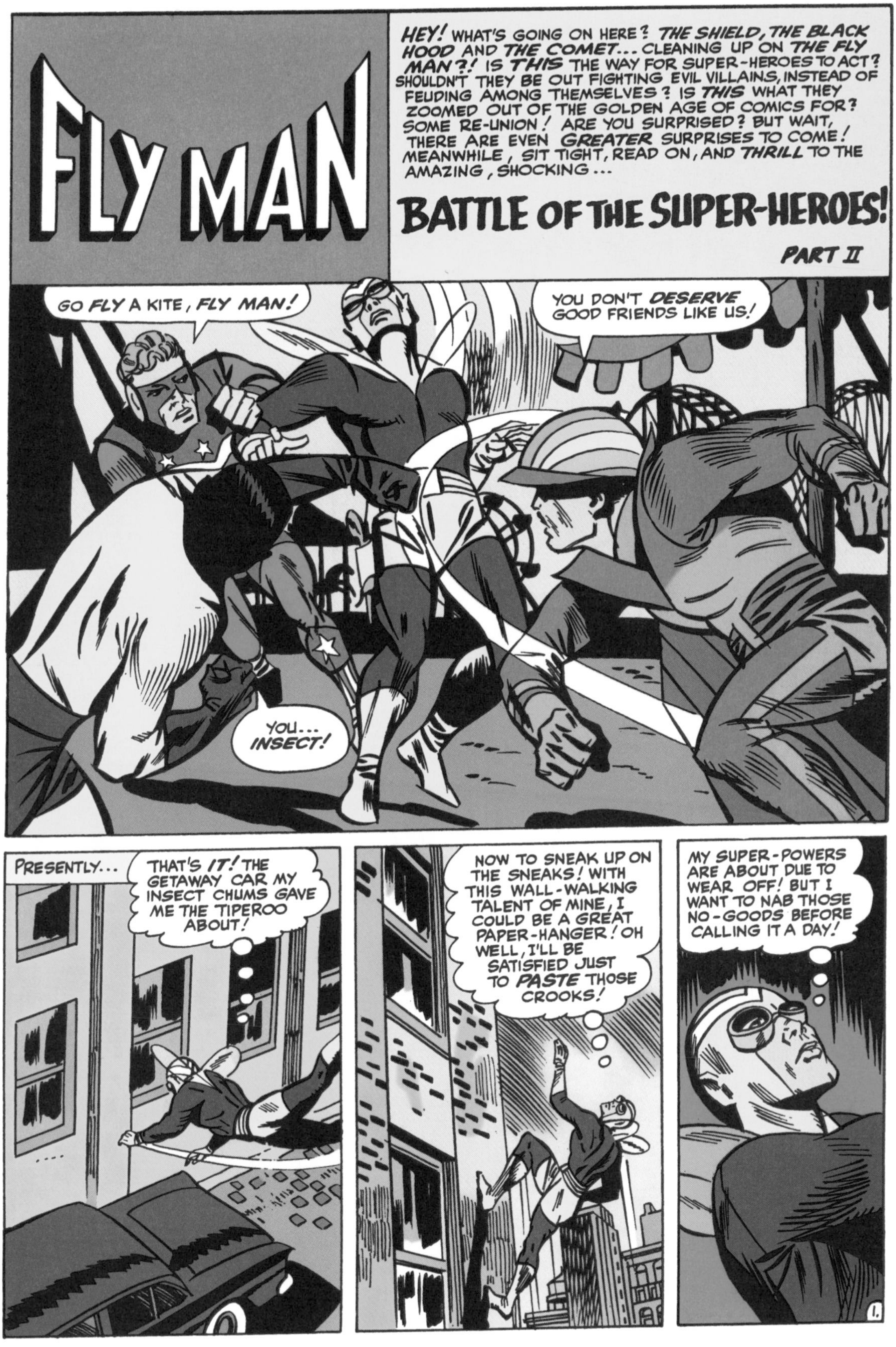
FLY MAN
HEY! WHAT'S GOING ON HERE? THE SHIELD, THE BLACK HOOD AND THE COMET... CLEANING UP ON THE FLY MAN?! IS THIS THE WAY FOR SUPER-HEROES TO ACT? SHOULDN'T THEY BE OUT FIGHTING EVIL VILLAINS, INSTEAD OF FEUDING AMONG THEMSELVES? IS THIS WHAT THEY ZOOMED OUT OF THE GOLDEN AGE OF COMICS FOR? SOME RE-UNION! ARE YOU SURPRISED? BUT WAIT, THERE ARE EVEN GREATER SURPRISES TO COME! MEANWHILE, SIT TIGHT, READ ON, AND THRILL TO THE AMAZING, SHOCKING...
BATTLE OF THE SUPER-HEROES!
PART II
GO FLY A KITE, FLY MAN!
YOU DON'T DESERVE GOOD FRIENDS LIKE US!
YOU... INSECT!
PRESENTLY...
THAT'S IT! THE GETAWAY CAR MY INSECT CHUMS GAVE ME THE TIPEROO ABOUT!
NOW TO SNEAK UP ON THE SNEAKS! WITH THIS WALL-WALKING TALENT OF MINE, I COULD BE A GREAT PAPER-HANGER! OH WELL, I'LL BE SATISFIED JUST TO PASTE THOSE CROOKS!
MY SUPER-POWERS ARE ABOUT DUE TO WEAR OFF! BUT I WANT TO NAB THOSE NO-GOODS BEFORE CALLING IT A DAY!
1.

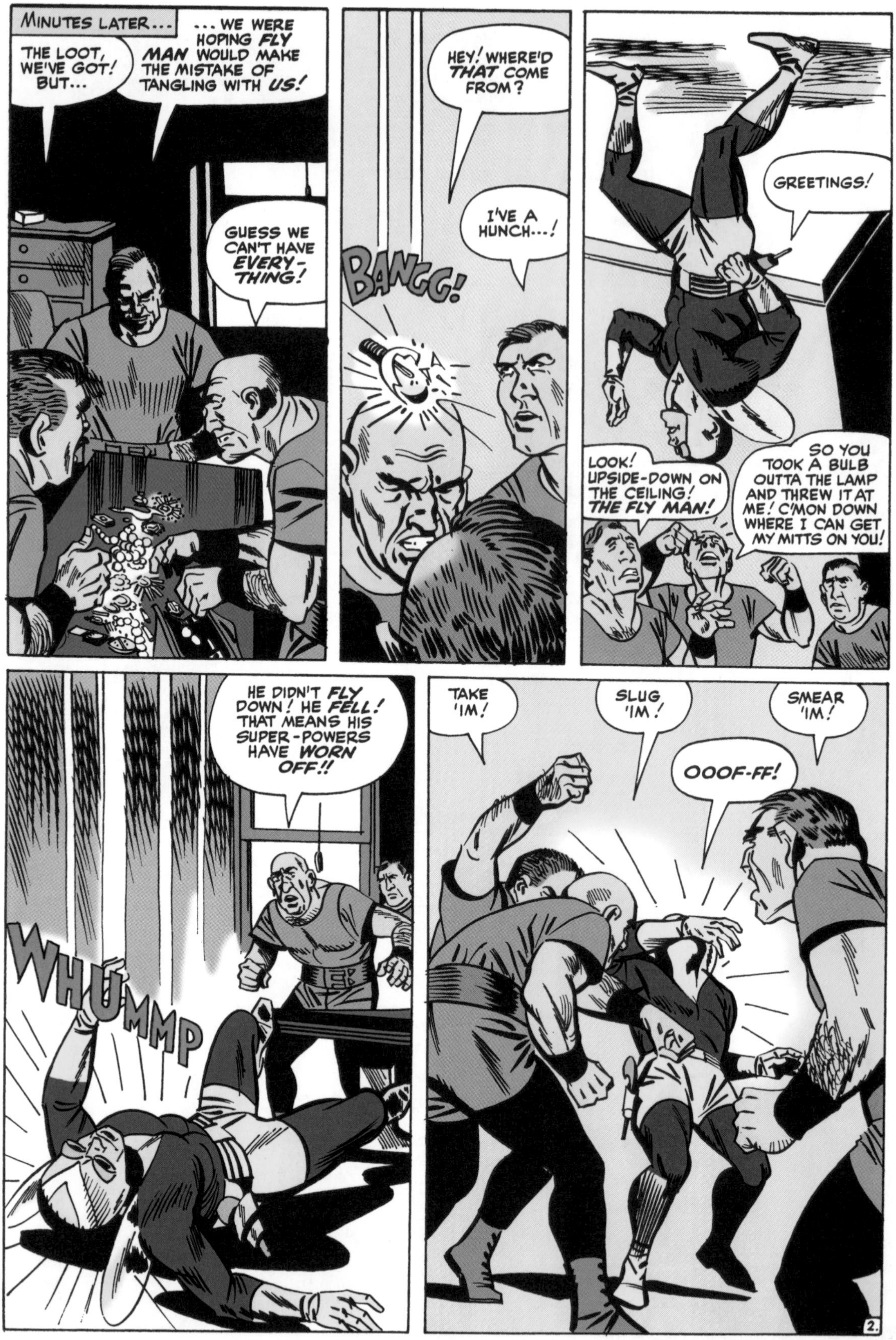
MINUTES LATER...
THE LOOT, WE'VE GOT! BUT...
...WE WERE HOPING FLY MAN WOULD MAKE THE MISTAKE OF TANGLING WITH US!
GUESS WE CAN'T HAVE EVERY-THING!
HEY! WHERE'D THAT COME FROM?
I'VE A HUNCH...!
BANGG!
GREETINGS!
LOOK! UPSIDE-DOWN ON THE CEILING! THE FLY MAN!
SO YOU TOOK A BULB OUTTA THE LAMP AND THREW IT AT ME! C'MON DOWN WHERE I CAN GET MY MITTS ON YOU!
HE DIDN'T FLY DOWN! HE FELL! THAT MEANS HIS SUPER-POWERS HAVE WORN OFF!!
WHUMMP
TAKE 'IM!
SLUG 'IM!
SMEAR 'IM!
OOOF-FF!
2.

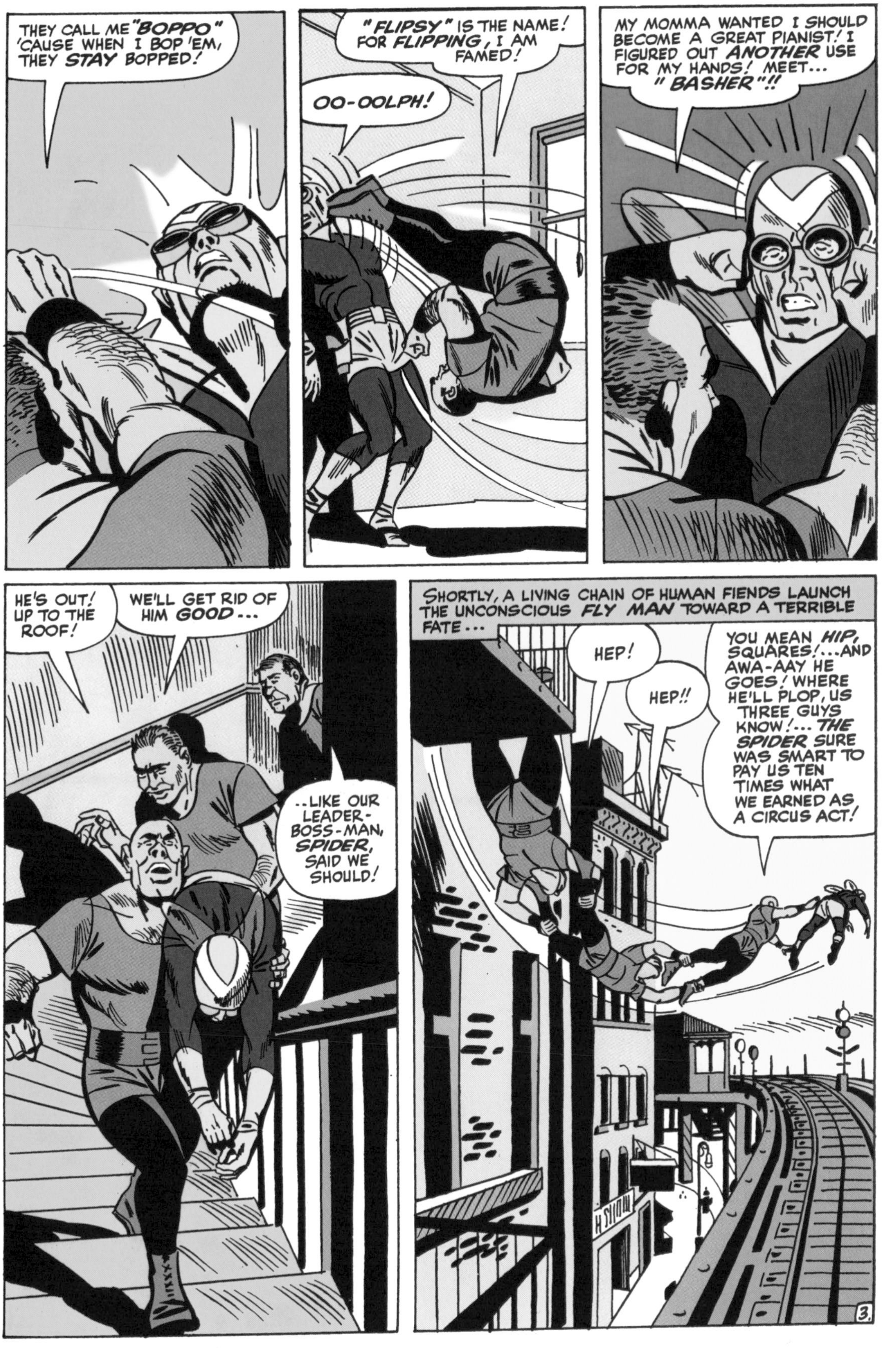
THEY CALL ME "BOPPO" 'CAUSE WHEN I BOP 'EM, THEY STAY BOPPED!
"FLIPSY" IS THE NAME! FOR FLIPPING, I AM FAMED!
OO-OOLPH!
MY MOMMA WANTED I SHOULD BECOME A GREAT PIANIST! I FIGURED OUT ANOTHER USE FOR MY HANDS! MEET... "BASHER"!!
HE'S OUT! UP TO THE ROOF!
WE'LL GET RID OF HIM GOOD...
..LIKE OUR LEADER-BOSS-MAN, SPIDER, SAID WE SHOULD!
SHORTLY, A LIVING CHAIN OF HUMAN FIENDS LAUNCH THE UNCONSCIOUS FLY MAN TOWARD A TERRIBLE FATE...
HEP!
HEP!!
YOU MEAN HIP, SQUARES!...AND AWA-AAY HE GOES! WHERE HE'LL PLOP, US THREE GUYS KNOW!... THE SPIDER SURE WAS SMART TO PAY US TEN TIMES WHAT WE EARNED AS A CIRCUS ACT!
3.

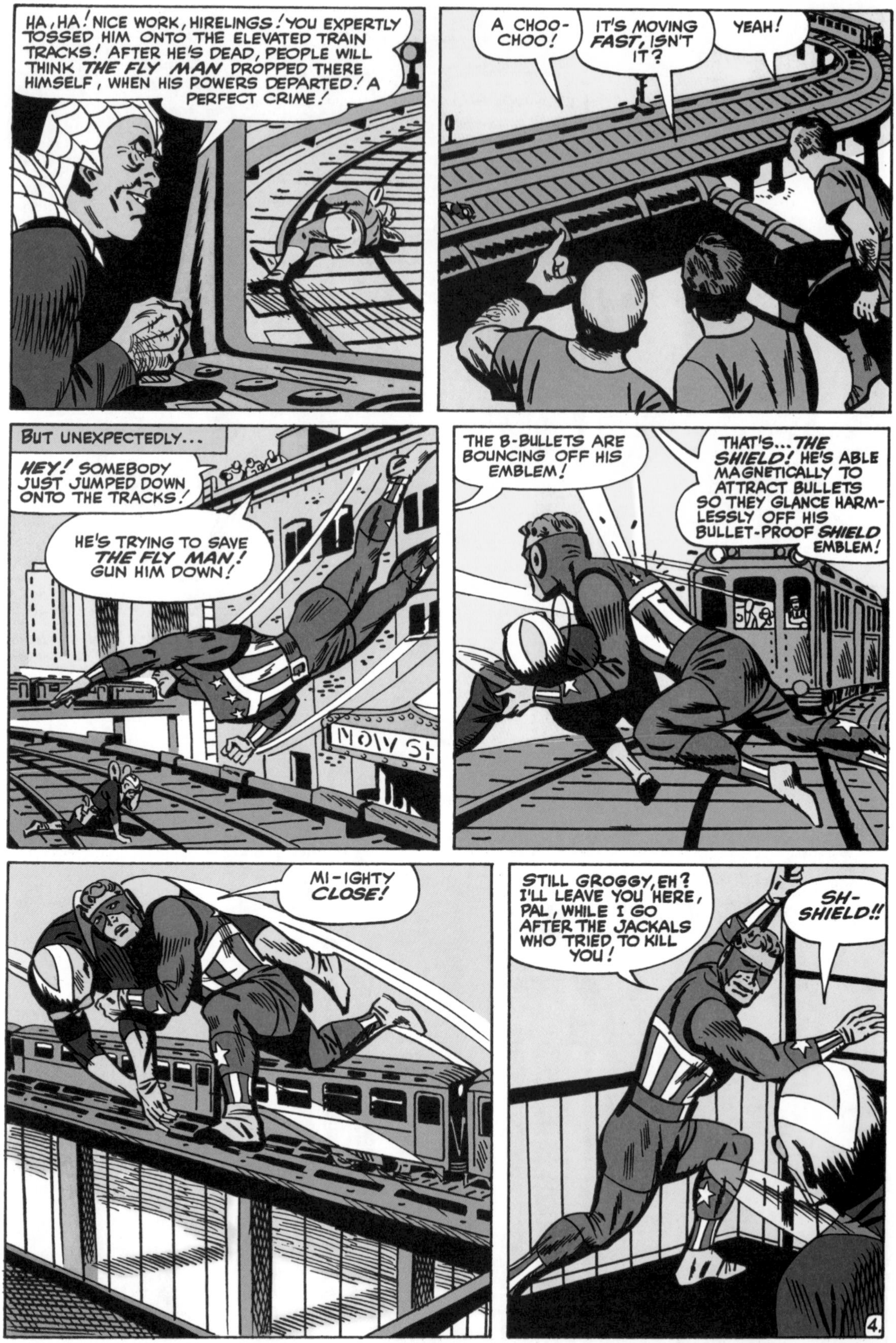
HA, HA! NICE WORK, HIRELINGS! YOU EXPERTLY TOSSED HIM ONTO THE ELEVATED TRAIN TRACKS! AFTER HE'S DEAD, PEOPLE WILL THINK THE FLY MAN DROPPED THERE HIMSELF, WHEN HIS POWERS DEPARTED! A PERFECT CRIME!
A CHOO-CHOO!
IT'S MOVING FAST, ISN'T IT?
YEAH!
BUT UNEXPECTEDLY...
HEY! SOMEBODY JUST JUMPED DOWN ONTO THE TRACKS!
HE'S TRYING TO SAVE THE FLY MAN! GUN HIM DOWN!
NOW SH
THE B-BULLETS ARE BOUNCING OFF HIS EMBLEM!
THAT'S... THE SHIELD! HE'S ABLE MAGNETICALLY TO ATTRACT BULLETS SO THEY GLANCE HARMLESSLY OFF HIS BULLET-PROOF SHIELD EMBLEM!
MI-IGHTY CLOSE!
STILL GROGGY, EH? I'LL LEAVE YOU HERE, PAL, WHILE I GO AFTER THE JACKALS WHO TRIED TO KILL YOU!
SH-SHIELD!!
4.

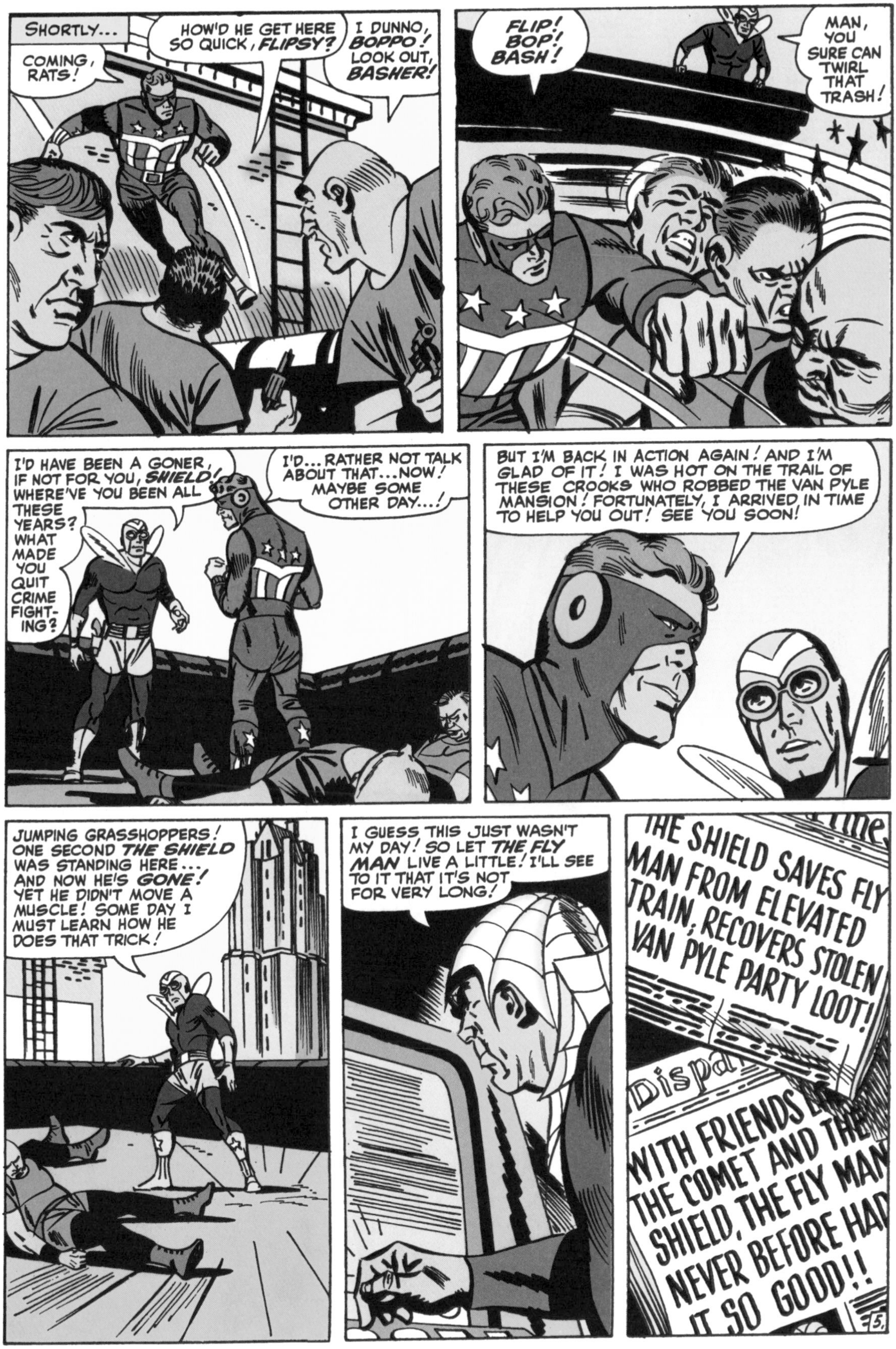
SHORTLY...
HOW'D HE GET HERE SO QUICK, FLIPSY?
I DUNNO, BOPPO! LOOK OUT, BASHER!
COMING, RATS!
FLIP! BOP! BASH!
MAN, YOU SURE CAN TWIRL THAT TRASH!
I'D HAVE BEEN A GONER, IF NOT FOR YOU, SHIELD! WHERE'VE YOU BEEN ALL THESE YEARS? WHAT MADE YOU QUIT CRIME FIGHTING?
I'D... RATHER NOT TALK ABOUT THAT... NOW! MAYBE SOME OTHER DAY...!
BUT I'M BACK IN ACTION AGAIN! AND I'M GLAD OF IT! I WAS HOT ON THE TRAIL OF THESE CROOKS WHO ROBBED THE VAN PYLE MANSION! FORTUNATELY, I ARRIVED IN TIME TO HELP YOU OUT! SEE YOU SOON!
JUMPING GRASSHOPPERS! ONE SECOND THE SHIELD WAS STANDING HERE... AND NOW HE'S GONE! YET HE DIDN'T MOVE A MUSCLE! SOME DAY I MUST LEARN HOW HE DOES THAT TRICK!
I GUESS THIS JUST WASN'T MY DAY! SO LET THE FLY MAN LIVE A LITTLE! I'LL SEE TO IT THAT IT'S NOT FOR VERY LONG!
THE SHIELD SAVES FLY MAN FROM ELEVATED TRAIN; RECOVERS STOLEN VAN PYLE PARTY LOOT!
WITH FRIENDS LIKE THE COMET AND THE SHIELD, THE FLY MAN NEVER BEFORE HAD IT SO GOOD!!
5

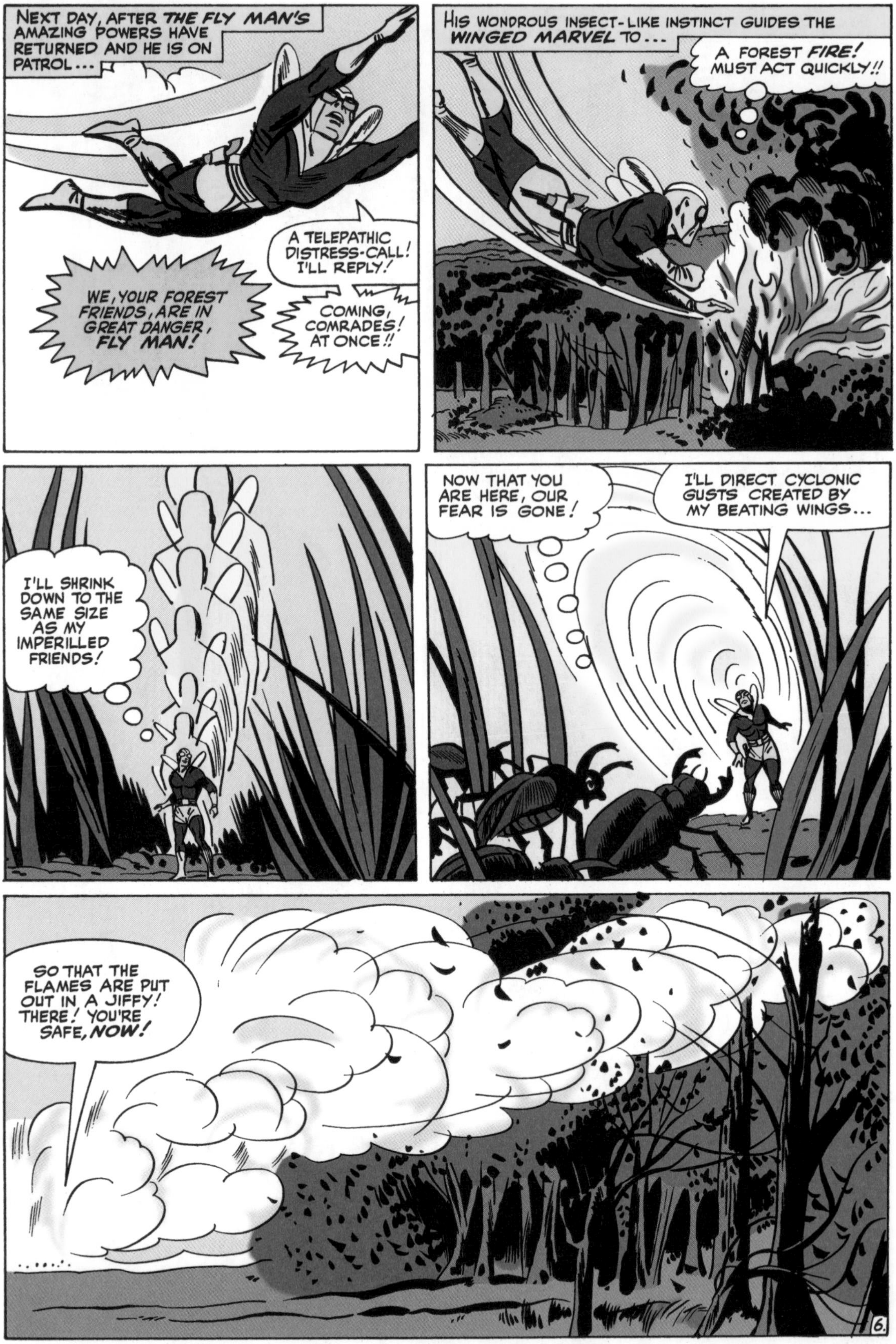
NEXT DAY, AFTER THE FLY MAN'S AMAZING POWERS HAVE RETURNED AND HE IS ON PATROL...
A TELEPATHIC DISTRESS-CALL! I'LL REPLY!
WE, YOUR FOREST FRIENDS, ARE IN GREAT DANGER, FLY MAN!
COMING, COMRADES! AT ONCE!!
HIS WONDROUS INSECT-LIKE INSTINCT GUIDES THE WINGED MARVEL TO...
A FOREST FIRE! MUST ACT QUICKLY!!
I'LL SHRINK DOWN TO THE SAME SIZE AS MY IMPERILLED FRIENDS!
NOW THAT YOU ARE HERE, OUR FEAR IS GONE!
I'LL DIRECT CYCLONIC GUSTS CREATED BY MY BEATING WINGS...
SO THAT THE FLAMES ARE PUT OUT IN A JIFFY! THERE! YOU'RE SAFE, NOW!
6.

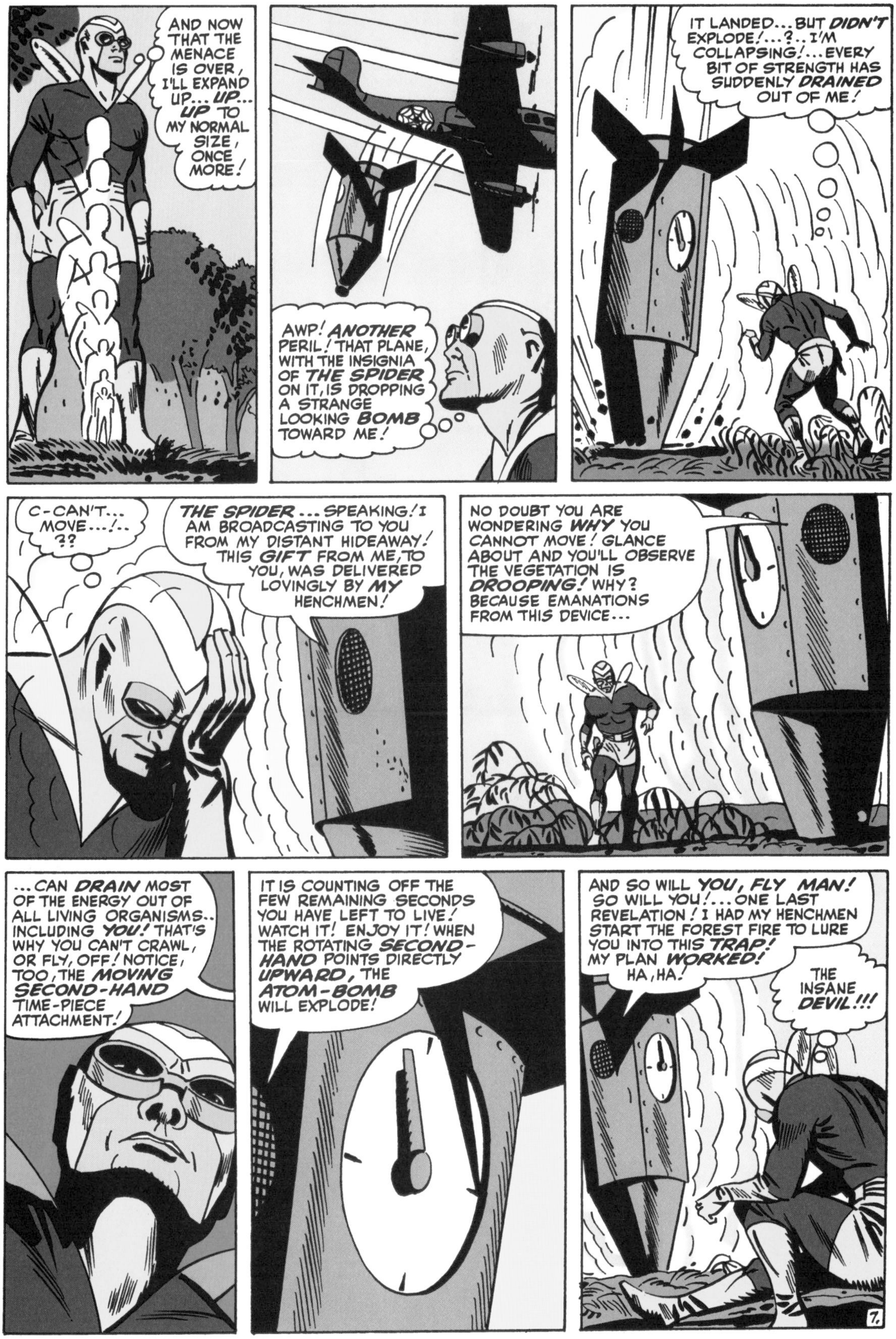
AND NOW THAT THE MENACE IS OVER, I'LL EXPAND UP... UP... UP TO MY NORMAL SIZE, ONCE MORE!
AWP! ANOTHER PERIL! THAT PLANE, WITH THE INSIGNIA OF THE SPIDER ON IT, IS DROPPING A STRANGE LOOKING BOMB TOWARD ME!
IT LANDED... BUT DIDN'T EXPLODE!...?.. I'M COLLAPSING!... EVERY BIT OF STRENGTH HAS SUDDENLY DRAINED OUT OF ME!
C-CAN'T... MOVE...!.. ??
THE SPIDER... SPEAKING! I AM BROADCASTING TO YOU FROM MY DISTANT HIDEAWAY! THIS GIFT FROM ME, TO YOU, WAS DELIVERED LOVINGLY BY MY HENCHMEN!
NO DOUBT YOU ARE WONDERING WHY YOU CANNOT MOVE! GLANCE ABOUT AND YOU'LL OBSERVE THE VEGETATION IS DROOPING! WHY? BECAUSE EMANATIONS FROM THIS DEVICE...
...CAN DRAIN MOST OF THE ENERGY OUT OF ALL LIVING ORGANISMS.. INCLUDING YOU! THAT'S WHY YOU CAN'T CRAWL, OR FLY, OFF! NOTICE, TOO, THE MOVING SECOND-HAND TIME-PIECE ATTACHMENT!
IT IS COUNTING OFF THE FEW REMAINING SECONDS YOU HAVE LEFT TO LIVE! WATCH IT! ENJOY IT! WHEN THE ROTATING SECOND-HAND POINTS DIRECTLY UPWARD, THE ATOM-BOMB WILL EXPLODE!
AND SO WILL YOU, FLY MAN! SO WILL YOU!... ONE LAST REVELATION! I HAD MY HENCHMEN START THE FOREST FIRE TO LURE YOU INTO THIS TRAP! MY PLAN WORKED! HA, HA!
THE INSANE DEVIL!!!
7.

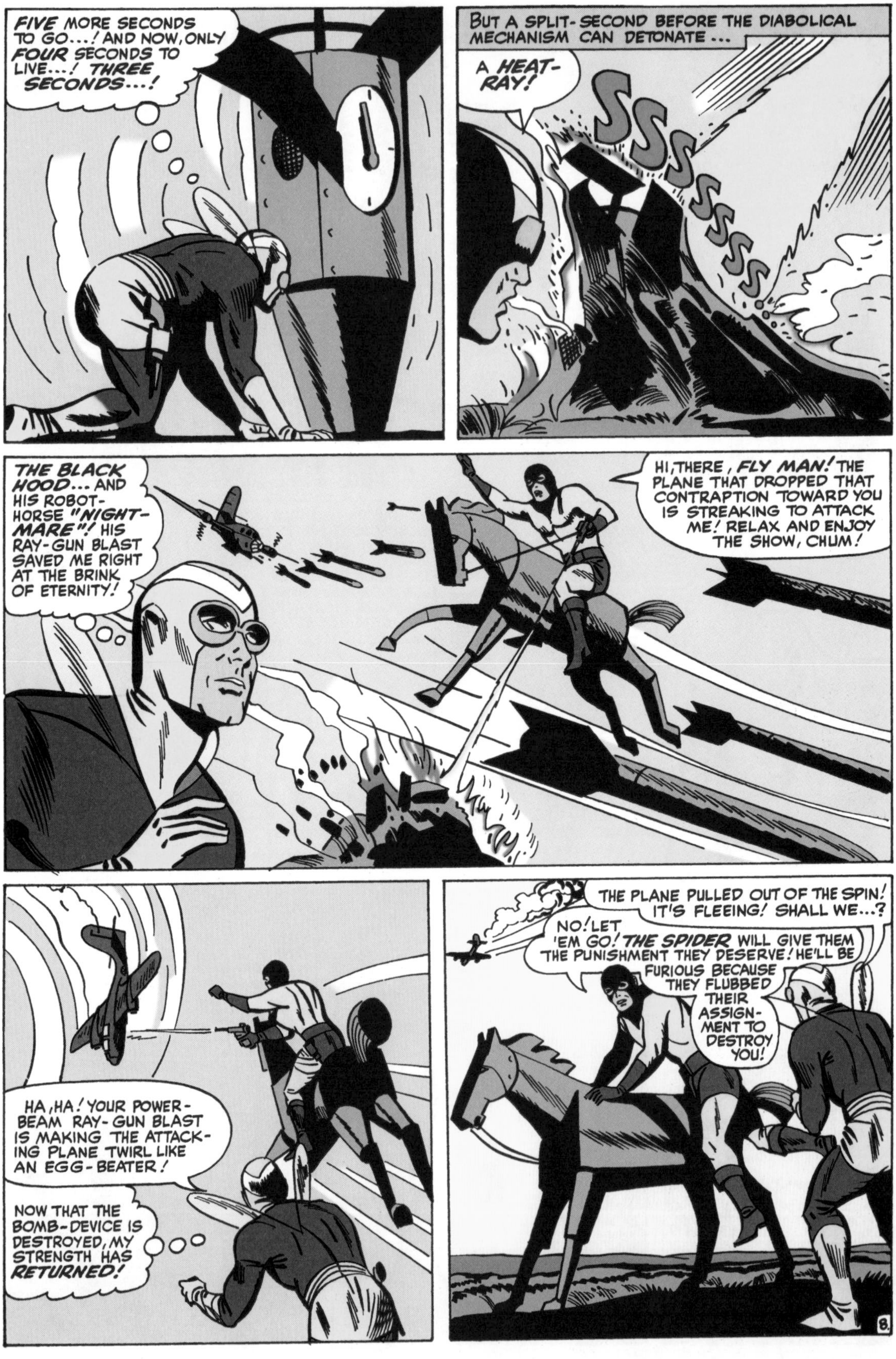
FIVE MORE SECONDS TO GO...! AND NOW, ONLY FOUR SECONDS TO LIVE...! THREE SECONDS...!
BUT A SPLIT-SECOND BEFORE THE DIABOLICAL MECHANISM CAN DETONATE...
A HEAT-RAY!
SSSSSSSSS
THE BLACK HOOD... AND HIS ROBOT-HORSE "NIGHT-MARE"! HIS RAY-GUN BLAST SAVED ME RIGHT AT THE BRINK OF ETERNITY!
HI, THERE, FLY MAN! THE PLANE THAT DROPPED THAT CONTRAPTION TOWARD YOU IS STREAKING TO ATTACK ME! RELAX AND ENJOY THE SHOW, CHUM!
HA, HA! YOUR POWER-BEAM RAY-GUN BLAST IS MAKING THE ATTACKING PLANE TWIRL LIKE AN EGG-BEATER!
NOW THAT THE BOMB-DEVICE IS DESTROYED, MY STRENGTH HAS RETURNED!
THE PLANE PULLED OUT OF THE SPIN! IT'S FLEEING! SHALL WE...?
NO! LET 'EM GO! THE SPIDER WILL GIVE THEM THE PUNISHMENT THEY DESERVE! HE'LL BE FURIOUS BECAUSE THEY FLUBBED THEIR ASSIGNMENT TO DESTROY YOU!
8

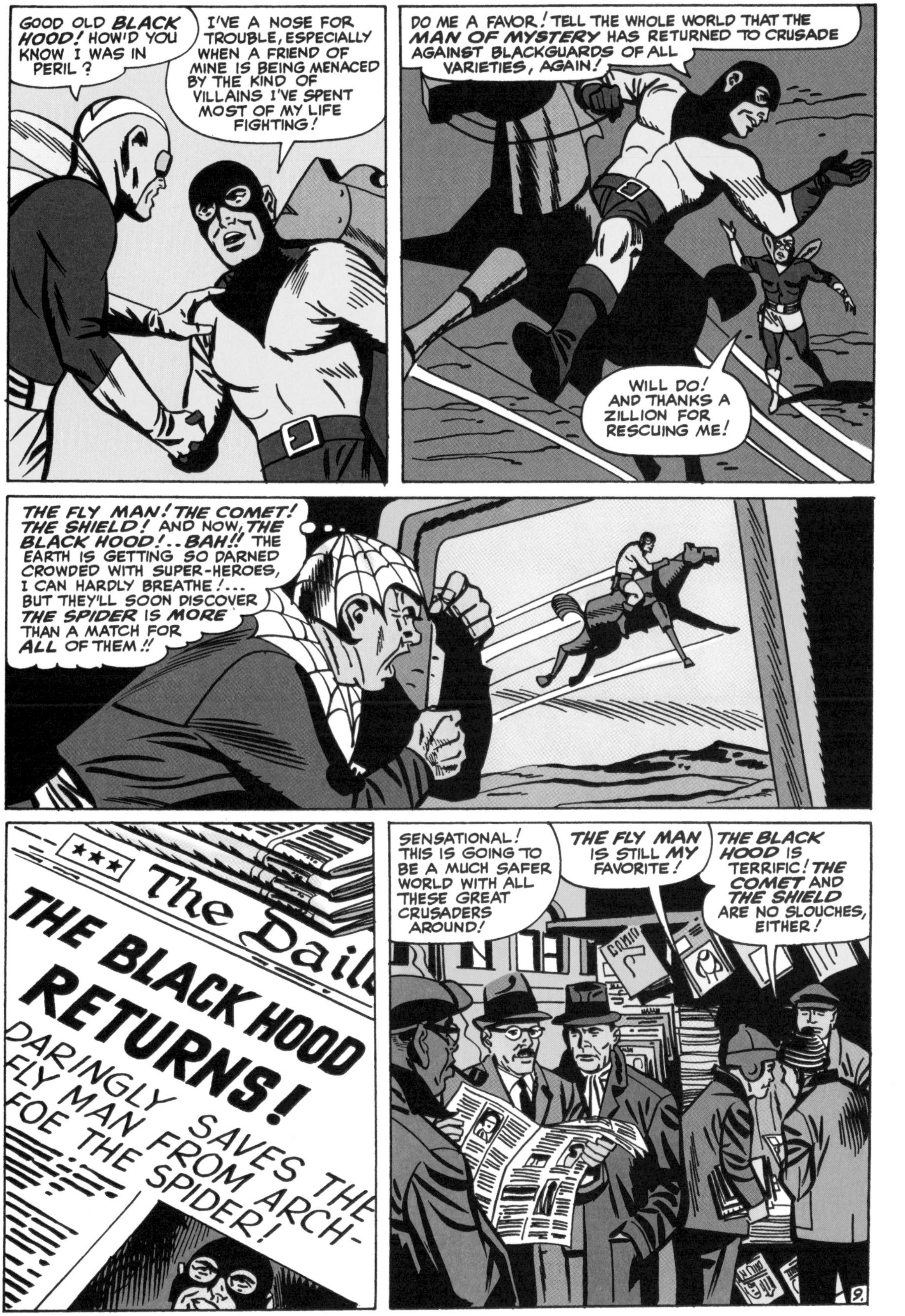
GOOD OLD BLACK HOOD! HOW'D YOU KNOW I WAS IN PERIL?
I'VE A NOSE FOR TROUBLE, ESPECIALLY WHEN A FRIEND OF MINE IS BEING MENACED BY THE KIND OF VILLAINS I'VE SPENT MOST OF MY LIFE FIGHTING!
DO ME A FAVOR! TELL THE WHOLE WORLD THAT THE MAN OF MYSTERY HAS RETURNED TO CRUSADE AGAINST BLACKGUARDS OF ALL VARIETIES, AGAIN!
WILL DO! AND THANKS A ZILLION FOR RESCUING ME!
THE FLY MAN! THE COMET! THE SHIELD! AND NOW, THE BLACK HOOD!..BAH!! THE EARTH IS GETTING SO DARNED CROWDED WITH SUPER-HEROES, I CAN HARDLY BREATHE!... BUT THEY'LL SOON DISCOVER THE SPIDER IS MORE THAN A MATCH FOR ALL OF THEM!!
The Daily
THE BLACK HOOD RETURNS!
DARINGLY SAVES THE FLY MAN FROM ARCH-FOE THE SPIDER!
SENSATIONAL! THIS IS GOING TO BE A MUCH SAFER WORLD WITH ALL THESE GREAT CRUSADERS AROUND!
THE FLY MAN IS STILL MY FAVORITE!
THE BLACK HOOD IS TERRIFIC! THE COMET AND THE SHIELD ARE NO SLOUCHES, EITHER!
9.

NEXT DAY, HIGH IN THE SKY...

THIS-A-WAY, SUPER-HEROES! FORM..."THE MIGHTY CRUSADERS"!

UP THERE! CLOUD-LETTERS...A MESSAGE!

AND SUPER-HEROES ARE ANSWERING THE FANTASTIC SUMMONS! THERE GOES FLY MAN! AND BLACK HOOD AND THE COMET, TOO!

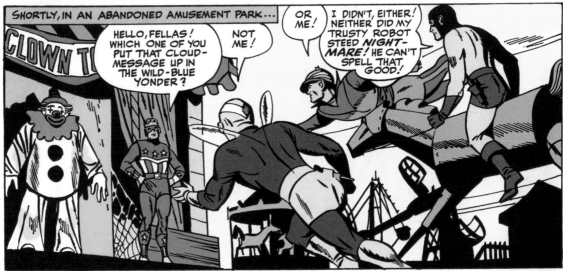

SHORTLY, IN AN ABANDONED AMUSEMENT PARK...

HELLO, FELLAS! WHICH ONE OF YOU PUT THAT CLOUD-MESSAGE UP IN THE WILD-BLUE YONDER?

NOT ME!

OR ME!

I DIDN'T, EITHER! NEITHER DID MY TRUSTY ROBOT STEED NIGHT-MARE! HE CAN'T SPELL THAT GOOD!

HM-MM! MAYBE THERE'S STILL ANOTHER SUPER-HERO LURKING AROUND! IF HE DID IT, HE MAY JOIN US SHORTLY!

WELL, WHOEVER DID IT, IT'S A GREAT IDEA...WE GUYS BANDING TOGETHER INTO AN INJUSTICE-FIGHTING GROUP!

YES! THE SPIDER'S WORLD-WIDE EVIL ORGANIZATION IS TOO POWERFUL, TOO COMPLEX, FOR JUST ONE OF US TO DEFEAT, ALONE! "THE MIGHTY CRUSADERS", EH? I'M FOR IT!

OBJECTION!!

10.

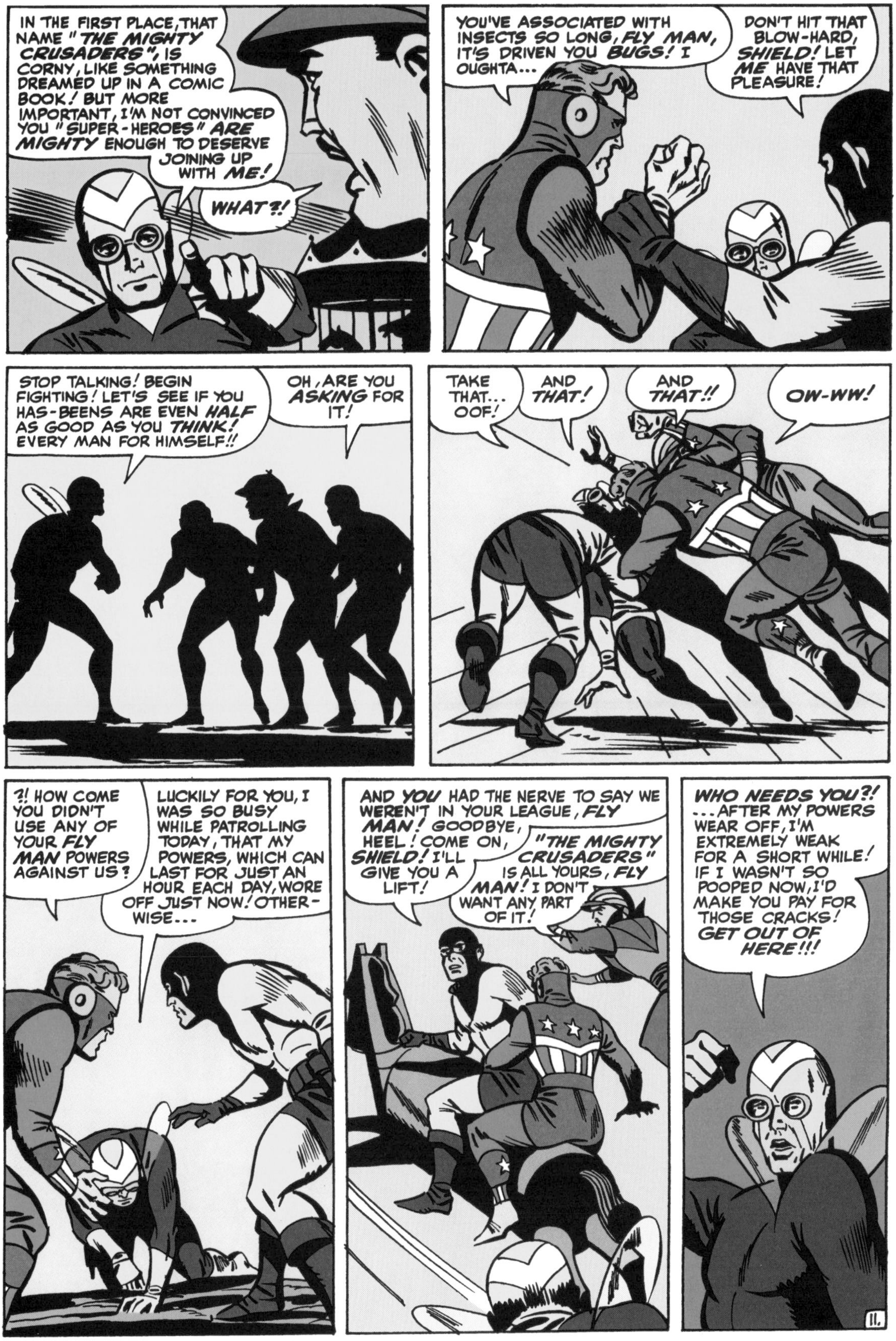
IN THE FIRST PLACE, THAT NAME "THE MIGHTY CRUSADERS", IS CORNY, LIKE SOMETHING DREAMED UP IN A COMIC BOOK! BUT MORE IMPORTANT, I'M NOT CONVINCED YOU "SUPER-HEROES" ARE MIGHTY ENOUGH TO DESERVE JOINING UP WITH ME!
WHAT?!
YOU'VE ASSOCIATED WITH INSECTS SO LONG, FLY MAN, IT'S DRIVEN YOU BUGS! I OUGHTA...
DON'T HIT THAT BLOW-HARD, SHIELD! LET ME HAVE THAT PLEASURE!
STOP TALKING! BEGIN FIGHTING! LET'S SEE IF YOU HAS-BEENS ARE EVEN HALF AS GOOD AS YOU THINK! EVERY MAN FOR HIMSELF!!
OH, ARE YOU ASKING FOR IT!
TAKE THAT... OOF!
AND THAT!
AND THAT!!
OW-WW!
?! HOW COME YOU DIDN'T USE ANY OF YOUR FLY MAN POWERS AGAINST US?
LUCKILY FOR YOU, I WAS SO BUSY WHILE PATROLLING TODAY, THAT MY POWERS, WHICH CAN LAST FOR JUST AN HOUR EACH DAY, WORE OFF JUST NOW! OTHERWISE...
AND YOU HAD THE NERVE TO SAY WE WEREN'T IN YOUR LEAGUE, FLY MAN! GOODBYE, HEEL! COME ON, SHIELD! I'LL GIVE YOU A LIFT!
"THE MIGHTY CRUSADERS" IS ALL YOURS, FLY MAN! I DON'T WANT ANY PART OF IT!
WHO NEEDS YOU?! ...AFTER MY POWERS WEAR OFF, I'M EXTREMELY WEAK FOR A SHORT WHILE! IF I WASN'T SO POOPED NOW, I'D MAKE YOU PAY FOR THOSE CRACKS! GET OUT OF HERE!!!
11.

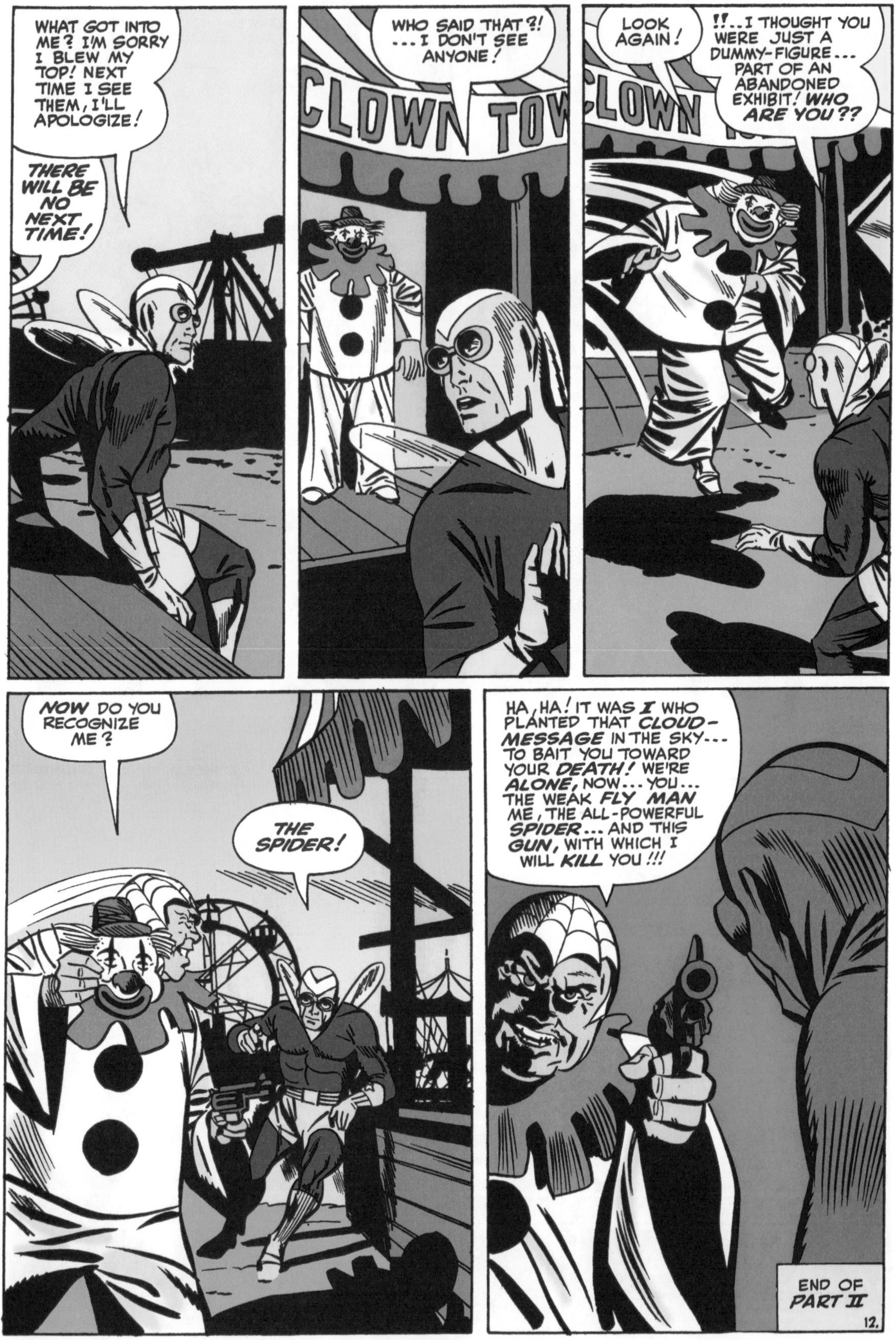
WHAT GOT INTO ME? I'M SORRY I BLEW MY TOP! NEXT TIME I SEE THEM, I'LL APOLOGIZE!
THERE WILL BE NO NEXT TIME!
WHO SAID THAT?! ... I DON'T SEE ANYONE!
CLOWN TOW
LOOK AGAIN!
!!.. I THOUGHT YOU WERE JUST A DUMMY-FIGURE... PART OF AN ABANDONED EXHIBIT! WHO ARE YOU??
CLOWN
NOW DO YOU RECOGNIZE ME?
THE SPIDER!
HA, HA! IT WAS I WHO PLANTED THAT CLOUD-MESSAGE IN THE SKY... TO BAIT YOU TOWARD YOUR DEATH! WE'RE ALONE, NOW... YOU... THE WEAK FLY MAN ME, THE ALL-POWERFUL SPIDER... AND THIS GUN, WITH WHICH I WILL KILL YOU!!!
END OF PART II
12.

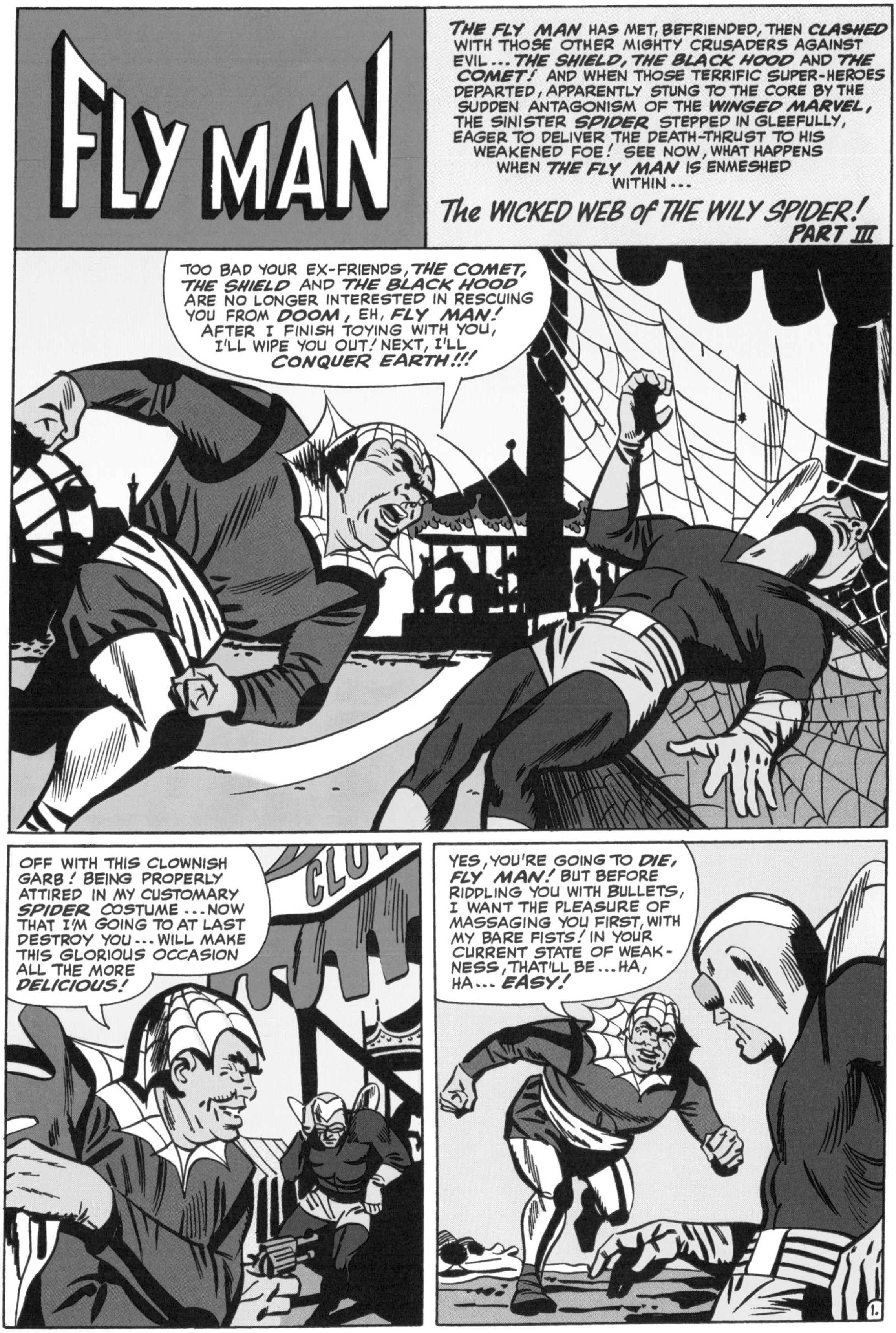
FLY MAN
THE FLY MAN HAS MET, BEFRIENDED, THEN CLASHED WITH THOSE OTHER MIGHTY CRUSADERS AGAINST EVIL... THE SHIELD, THE BLACK HOOD AND THE COMET! AND WHEN THOSE TERRIFIC SUPER-HEROES DEPARTED, APPARENTLY STUNG TO THE CORE BY THE SUDDEN ANTAGONISM OF THE WINGED MARVEL, THE SINISTER SPIDER STEPPED IN GLEEFULLY, EAGER TO DELIVER THE DEATH-THRUST TO HIS WEAKENED FOE! SEE NOW, WHAT HAPPENS WHEN THE FLY MAN IS ENMESHED WITHIN...
The WICKED WEB of THE WILY SPIDER! PART III
TOO BAD YOUR EX-FRIENDS, THE COMET, THE SHIELD AND THE BLACK HOOD ARE NO LONGER INTERESTED IN RESCUING YOU FROM DOOM, EH, FLY MAN! AFTER I FINISH TOYING WITH YOU, I'LL WIPE YOU OUT! NEXT, I'LL CONQUER EARTH!!!
OFF WITH THIS CLOWNISH GARB! BEING PROPERLY ATTIRED IN MY CUSTOMARY SPIDER COSTUME ... NOW THAT I'M GOING TO AT LAST DESTROY YOU ... WILL MAKE THIS GLORIOUS OCCASION ALL THE MORE DELICIOUS!
YES, YOU'RE GOING TO DIE, FLY MAN! BUT BEFORE RIDDLING YOU WITH BULLETS, I WANT THE PLEASURE OF MASSAGING YOU FIRST, WITH MY BARE FISTS! IN YOUR CURRENT STATE OF WEAK-NESS, THAT'LL BE ... HA, HA ... EASY!
1.

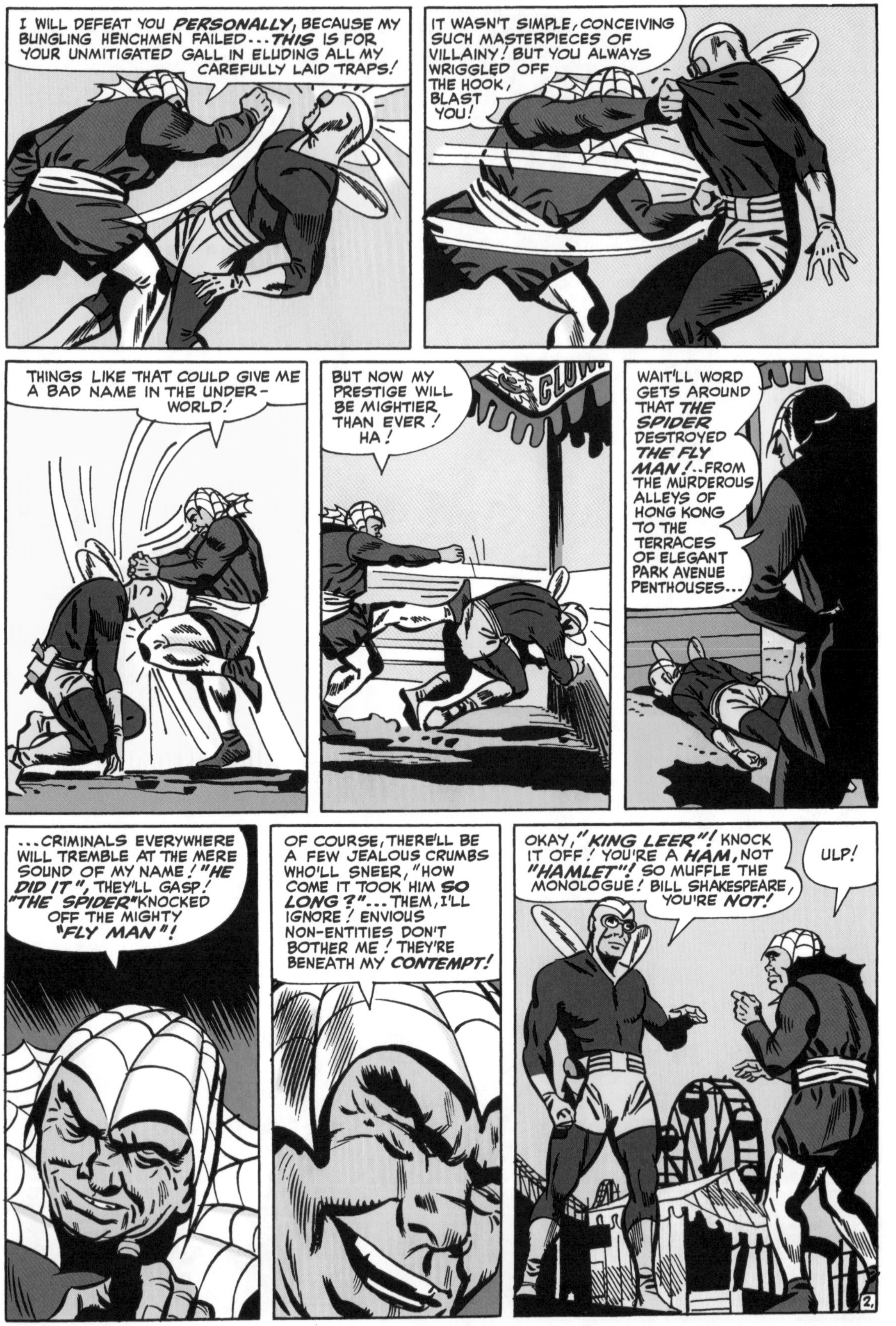
I WILL DEFEAT YOU PERSONALLY, BECAUSE MY BUNGLING HENCHMEN FAILED... THIS IS FOR YOUR UNMITIGATED GALL IN ELUDING ALL MY CAREFULLY LAID TRAPS!
IT WASN'T SIMPLE, CONCEIVING SUCH MASTERPIECES OF VILLAINY! BUT YOU ALWAYS WRIGGLED OFF THE HOOK, BLAST YOU!
THINGS LIKE THAT COULD GIVE ME A BAD NAME IN THE UNDER-WORLD!
BUT NOW MY PRESTIGE WILL BE MIGHTIER THAN EVER! HA!
WAIT'LL WORD GETS AROUND THAT THE SPIDER DESTROYED THE FLY MAN!..FROM THE MURDEROUS ALLEYS OF HONG KONG TO THE TERRACES OF ELEGANT PARK AVENUE PENTHOUSES...
...CRIMINALS EVERYWHERE WILL TREMBLE AT THE MERE SOUND OF MY NAME! "HE DID IT", THEY'LL GASP! "THE SPIDER" KNOCKED OFF THE MIGHTY "FLY MAN"!
OF COURSE, THERE'LL BE A FEW JEALOUS CRUMBS WHO'LL SNEER, "HOW COME IT TOOK HIM SO LONG?"... THEM, I'LL IGNORE! ENVIOUS NON-ENTITIES DON'T BOTHER ME! THEY'RE BENEATH MY CONTEMPT!
OKAY, "KING LEER"! KNOCK IT OFF! YOU'RE A HAM, NOT "HAMLET"! SO MUFFLE THE MONOLOGUE! BILL SHAKESPEARE, YOU'RE NOT!
ULP!
2.

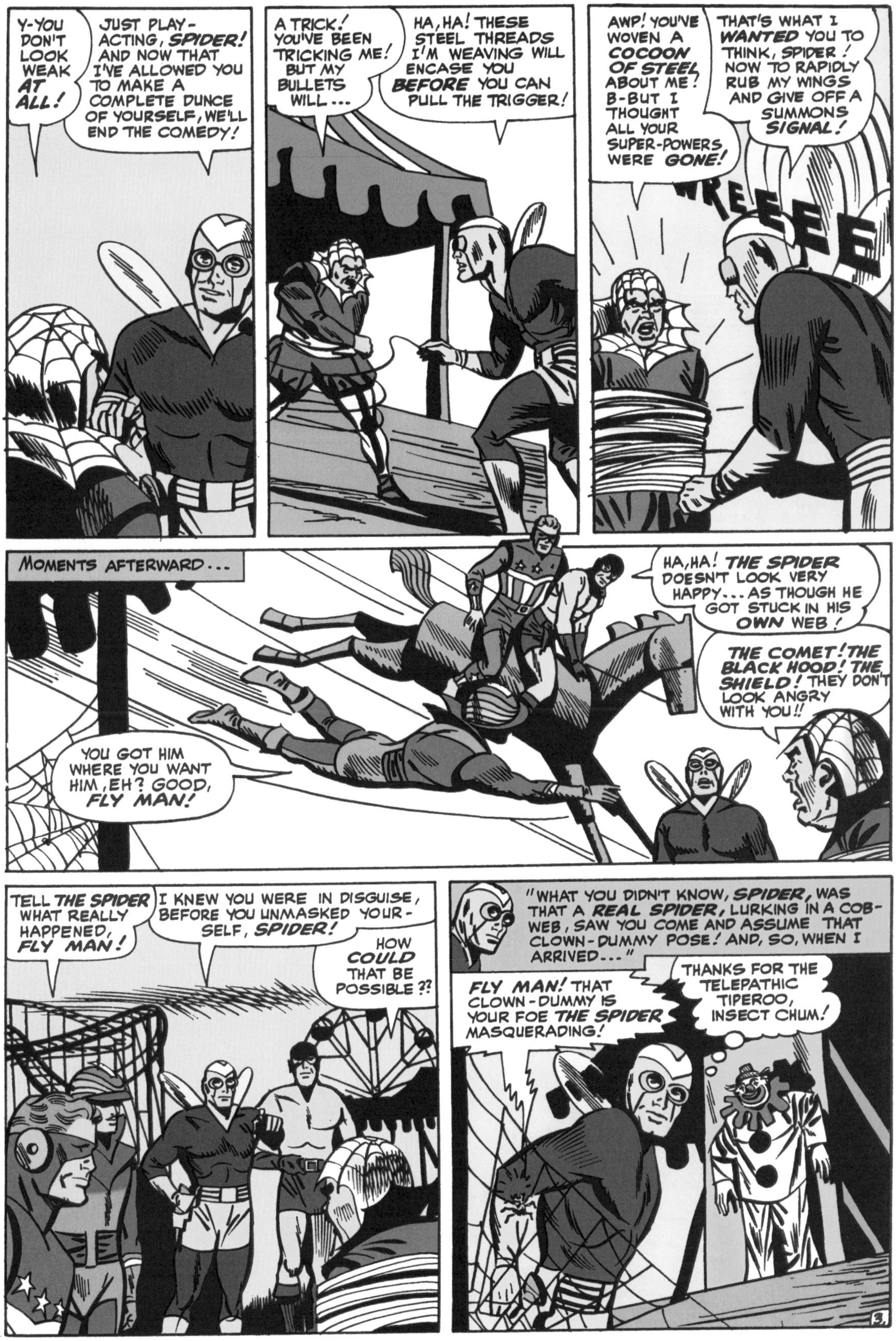
Y-YOU DON'T LOOK WEAK AT ALL!
JUST PLAY-ACTING, SPIDER! AND NOW THAT I'VE ALLOWED YOU TO MAKE A COMPLETE DUNCE OF YOURSELF, WE'LL END THE COMEDY!
A TRICK! YOU'VE BEEN TRICKING ME! BUT MY BULLETS WILL...
HA, HA! THESE STEEL THREADS I'M WEAVING WILL ENCASE YOU BEFORE YOU CAN PULL THE TRIGGER!
AWP! YOU'VE WOVEN A COCOON OF STEEL ABOUT ME! B-BUT I THOUGHT ALL YOUR SUPER-POWERS WERE GONE!
THAT'S WHAT I WANTED YOU TO THINK, SPIDER! NOW TO RAPIDLY RUB MY WINGS AND GIVE OFF A SUMMONS SIGNAL!
WREEEEE
MOMENTS AFTERWARD...
HA, HA! THE SPIDER DOESN'T LOOK VERY HAPPY... AS THOUGH HE GOT STUCK IN HIS OWN WEB!
THE COMET! THE BLACK HOOD! THE SHIELD! THEY DON'T LOOK ANGRY WITH YOU!!
YOU GOT HIM WHERE YOU WANT HIM, EH? GOOD, FLY MAN!
TELL THE SPIDER WHAT REALLY HAPPENED, FLY MAN!
I KNEW YOU WERE IN DISGUISE, BEFORE YOU UNMASKED YOURSELF, SPIDER!
HOW COULD THAT BE POSSIBLE ??
"WHAT YOU DIDN'T KNOW, SPIDER, WAS THAT A REAL SPIDER, LURKING IN A COBWEB, SAW YOU COME AND ASSUME THAT CLOWN-DUMMY POSE! AND, SO, WHEN I ARRIVED..."
FLY MAN! THAT CLOWN-DUMMY IS YOUR FOE THE SPIDER MASQUERADING!
THANKS FOR THE TELEPATHIC TIPEROO, INSECT CHUM!
3

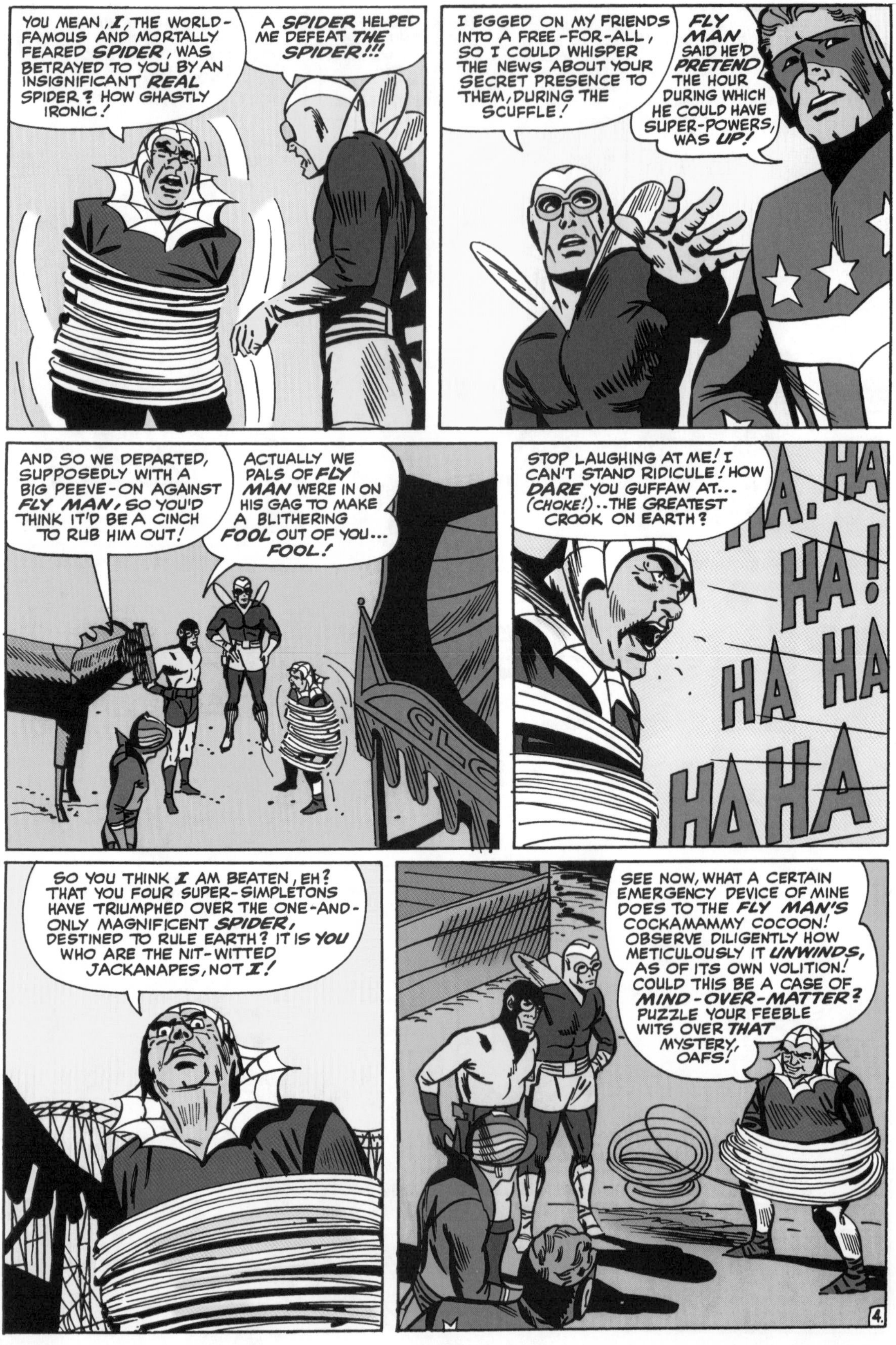

YOU MEAN, I, THE WORLD-FAMOUS AND MORTALLY FEARED SPIDER, WAS BETRAYED TO YOU BY AN INSIGNIFICANT REAL SPIDER? HOW GHASTLY IRONIC!
A SPIDER HELPED ME DEFEAT THE SPIDER!!!
I EGGED ON MY FRIENDS INTO A FREE-FOR-ALL, SO I COULD WHISPER THE NEWS ABOUT YOUR SECRET PRESENCE TO THEM, DURING THE SCUFFLE!
FLY MAN SAID HE'D PRETEND THE HOUR DURING WHICH HE COULD HAVE SUPER-POWERS, WAS UP!
AND SO WE DEPARTED, SUPPOSEDLY WITH A BIG PEEVE-ON AGAINST FLY MAN, SO YOU'D THINK IT'D BE A CINCH TO RUB HIM OUT!
ACTUALLY WE PALS OF FLY MAN WERE IN ON HIS GAG TO MAKE A BLITHERING FOOL OUT OF YOU... FOOL!
STOP LAUGHING AT ME! I CAN'T STAND RIDICULE! HOW DARE YOU GUFFAW AT... (CHOKE!)..THE GREATEST CROOK ON EARTH?
HA, HA HA! HA HA HA HA HA
SO YOU THINK I AM BEATEN, EH? THAT YOU FOUR SUPER-SIMPLETONS HAVE TRIUMPHED OVER THE ONE-AND-ONLY MAGNIFICENT SPIDER, DESTINED TO RULE EARTH? IT IS YOU WHO ARE THE NIT-WITTED JACKANAPES, NOT I!
SEE NOW, WHAT A CERTAIN EMERGENCY DEVICE OF MINE DOES TO THE FLY MAN'S COCKAMAMMY COCOON! OBSERVE DILIGENTLY HOW METICULOUSLY IT UNWINDS, AS OF ITS OWN VOLITION! COULD THIS BE A CASE OF MIND-OVER-MATTER? PUZZLE YOUR FEEBLE WITS OVER THAT MYSTERY, OAFS!
4.

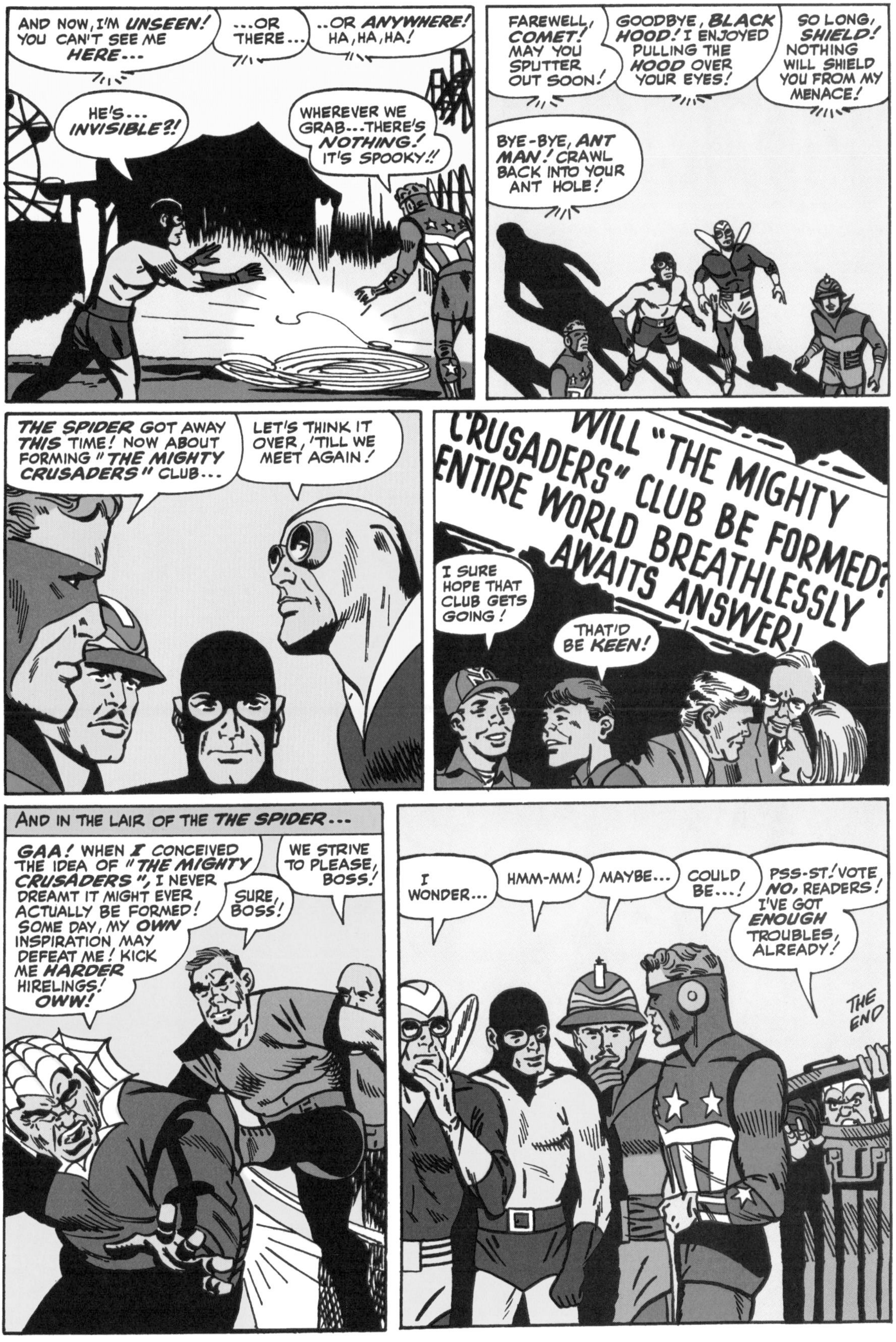
AND NOW, I'M UNSEEN! YOU CAN'T SEE ME HERE...
...OR THERE...
..OR ANYWHERE! HA, HA, HA!
HE'S... INVISIBLE?!
WHEREVER WE GRAB...THERE'S NOTHING! IT'S SPOOKY!!
FAREWELL, COMET! MAY YOU SPUTTER OUT SOON!
GOODBYE, BLACK HOOD! I ENJOYED PULLING THE HOOD OVER YOUR EYES!
SO LONG, SHIELD! NOTHING WILL SHIELD YOU FROM MY MENACE!
BYE-BYE, ANT MAN! CRAWL BACK INTO YOUR ANT HOLE!
THE SPIDER GOT AWAY THIS TIME! NOW ABOUT FORMING "THE MIGHTY CRUSADERS" CLUB...
LET'S THINK IT OVER, 'TILL WE MEET AGAIN!
WILL "THE MIGHTY CRUSADERS" CLUB BE FORMED? ENTIRE WORLD BREATHLESSLY AWAITS ANSWER!
I SURE HOPE THAT CLUB GETS GOING!
THAT'D BE KEEN!
AND IN THE LAIR OF THE THE SPIDER...
GAA! WHEN I CONCEIVED THE IDEA OF "THE MIGHTY CRUSADERS", I NEVER DREAMT IT MIGHT EVER ACTUALLY BE FORMED! SOME DAY, MY OWN INSPIRATION MAY DEFEAT ME! KICK ME HARDER HIRELINGS! OWW!
SURE, BOSS!
WE STRIVE TO PLEASE, BOSS!
I WONDER...
HMM-MM!
MAYBE...
COULD BE...!
PSS-ST! VOTE NO, READERS! I'VE GOT ENOUGH TROUBLES, ALREADY!
THE END

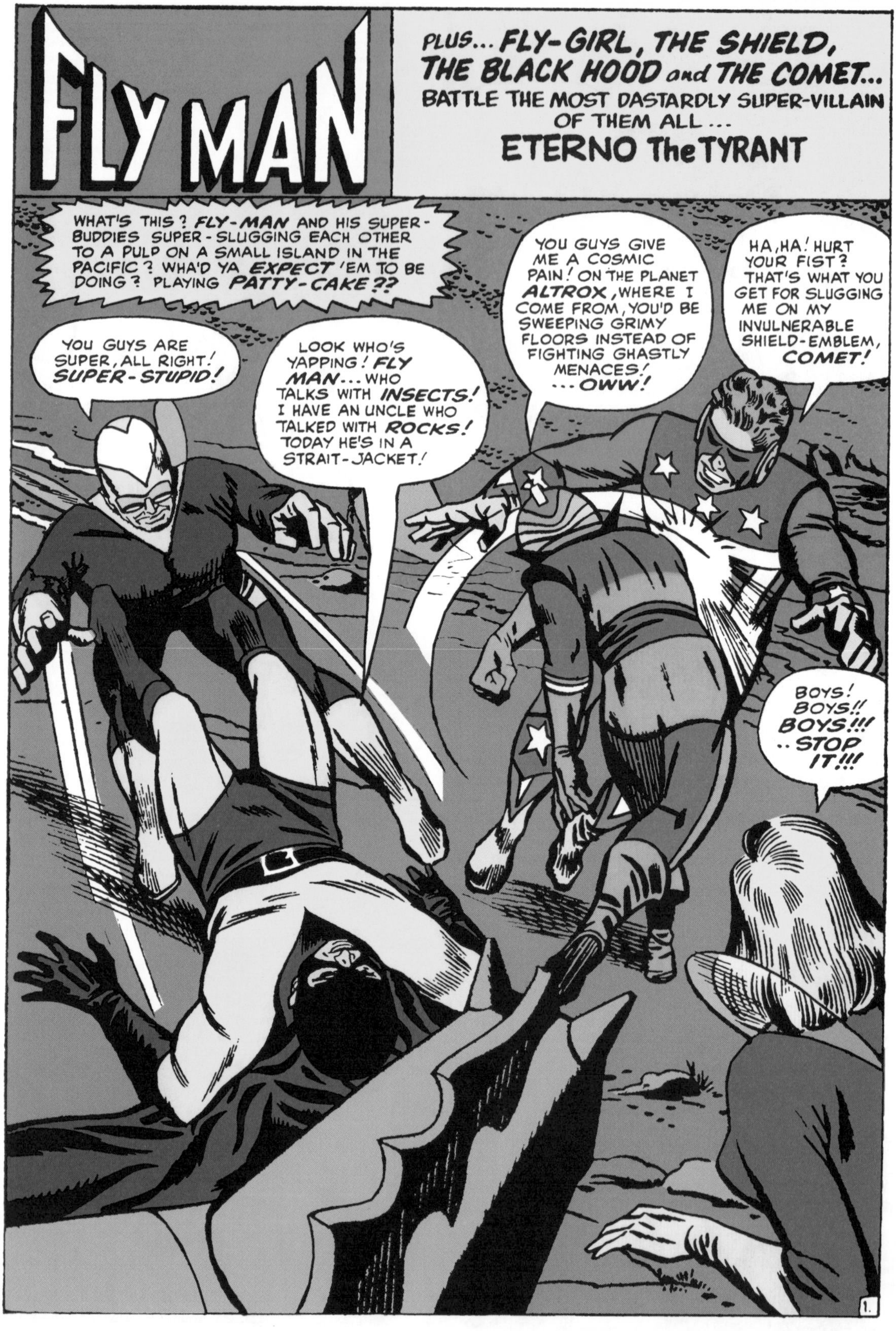
FLY MAN
PLUS... FLY-GIRL, THE SHIELD, THE BLACK HOOD and THE COMET... BATTLE THE MOST DASTARDLY SUPER-VILLAIN OF THEM ALL ...
ETERNO The TYRANT
WHAT'S THIS ? FLY-MAN AND HIS SUPER-BUDDIES SUPER-SLUGGING EACH OTHER TO A PULP ON A SMALL ISLAND IN THE PACIFIC ? WHA'D YA EXPECT 'EM TO BE DOING ? PLAYING PATTY-CAKE ??
YOU GUYS ARE SUPER, ALL RIGHT! SUPER-STUPID!
LOOK WHO'S YAPPING! FLY MAN... WHO TALKS WITH INSECTS! I HAVE AN UNCLE WHO TALKED WITH ROCKS! TODAY HE'S IN A STRAIT-JACKET!
YOU GUYS GIVE ME A COSMIC PAIN! ON THE PLANET ALTROX, WHERE I COME FROM, YOU'D BE SWEEPING GRIMY FLOORS INSTEAD OF FIGHTING GHASTLY MENACES! ...OWW!
HA, HA! HURT YOUR FIST? THAT'S WHAT YOU GET FOR SLUGGING ME ON MY INVULNERABLE SHIELD-EMBLEM, COMET!
BOYS! BOYS!! BOYS!!! ..STOP IT!!!
1.

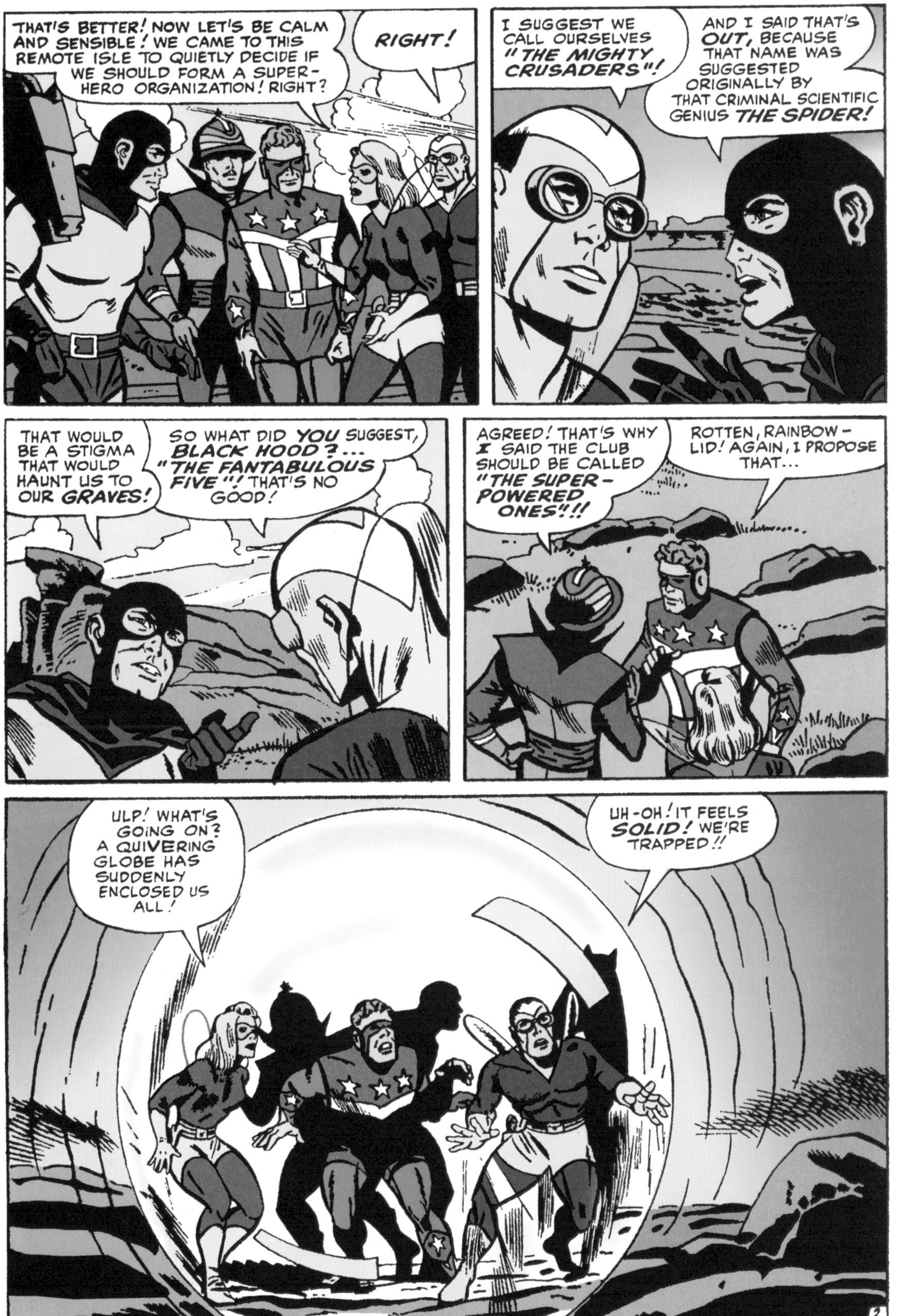

THAT'S BETTER! NOW LET'S BE CALM AND SENSIBLE! WE CAME TO THIS REMOTE ISLE TO QUIETLY DECIDE IF WE SHOULD FORM A SUPER-HERO ORGANIZATION! RIGHT?
RIGHT!
I SUGGEST WE CALL OURSELVES "THE MIGHTY CRUSADERS"!
AND I SAID THAT'S OUT, BECAUSE THAT NAME WAS SUGGESTED ORIGINALLY BY THAT CRIMINAL SCIENTIFIC GENIUS THE SPIDER!
THAT WOULD BE A STIGMA THAT WOULD HAUNT US TO OUR GRAVES!
SO WHAT DID YOU SUGGEST, BLACK HOOD?... "THE FANTABULOUS FIVE"! THAT'S NO GOOD!
AGREED! THAT'S WHY I SAID THE CLUB SHOULD BE CALLED "THE SUPER-POWERED ONES"!!!
ROTTEN, RAINBOW-LID! AGAIN, I PROPOSE THAT...
ULP! WHAT'S GOING ON? A QUIVERING GLOBE HAS SUDDENLY ENCLOSED US ALL!
UH-OH! IT FEELS SOLID! WE'RE TRAPPED!!
2

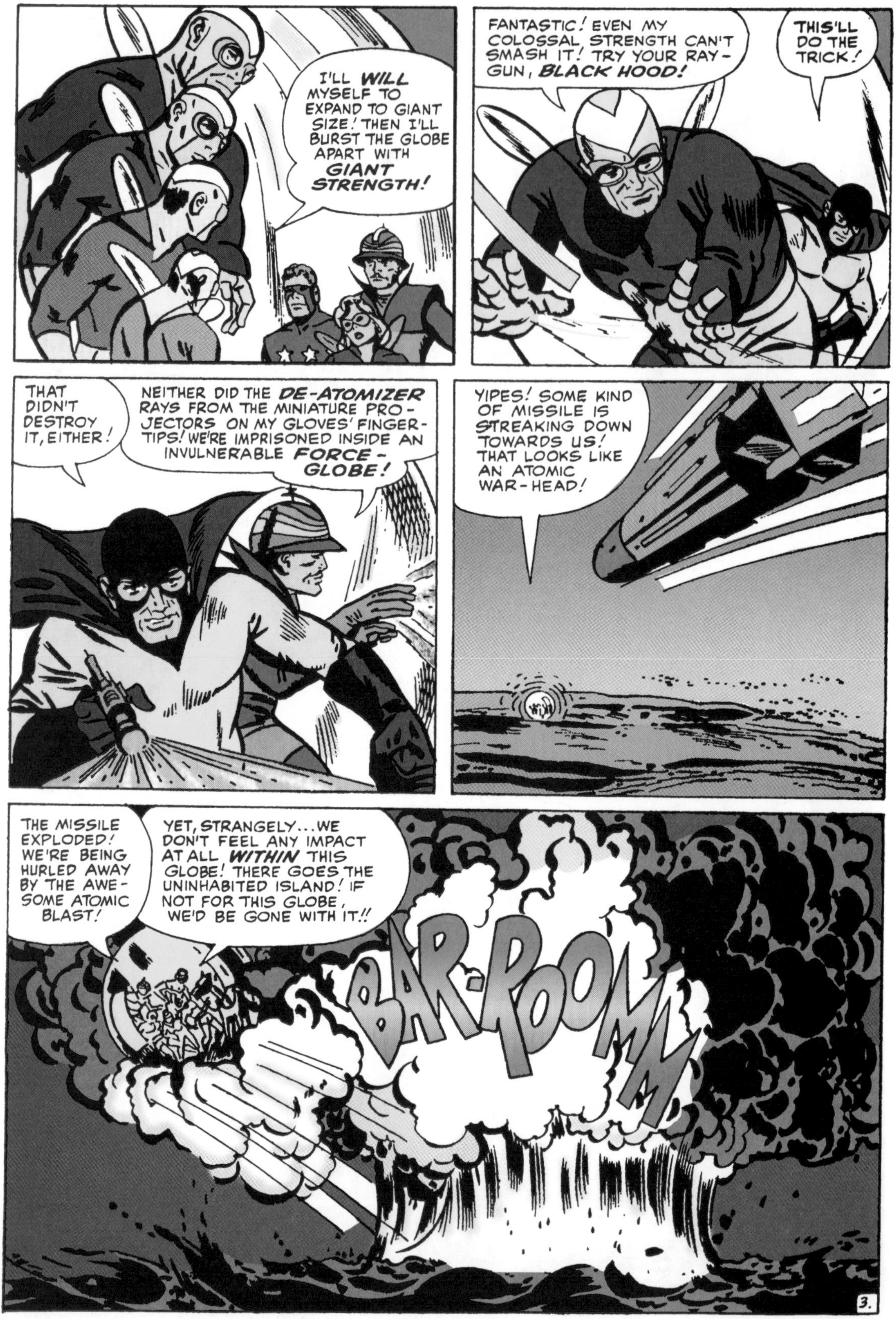
I'LL WILL MYSELF TO EXPAND TO GIANT SIZE! THEN I'LL BURST THE GLOBE APART WITH GIANT STRENGTH!
FANTASTIC! EVEN MY COLOSSAL STRENGTH CAN'T SMASH IT! TRY YOUR RAY-GUN, BLACK HOOD!
THIS'LL DO THE TRICK!
THAT DIDN'T DESTROY IT, EITHER!
NEITHER DID THE DE-ATOMIZER RAYS FROM THE MINIATURE PROJECTORS ON MY GLOVES' FINGER-TIPS! WE'RE IMPRISONED INSIDE AN INVULNERABLE FORCE-GLOBE!
YIPES! SOME KIND OF MISSILE IS STREAKING DOWN TOWARDS US! THAT LOOKS LIKE AN ATOMIC WAR-HEAD!
THE MISSILE EXPLODED! WE'RE BEING HURLED AWAY BY THE AWE-SOME ATOMIC BLAST!
YET, STRANGELY...WE DON'T FEEL ANY IMPACT AT ALL WITHIN THIS GLOBE! THERE GOES THE UNINHABITED ISLAND! IF NOT FOR THIS GLOBE, WE'D BE GONE WITH IT!!
BAR-ROOMM
3.

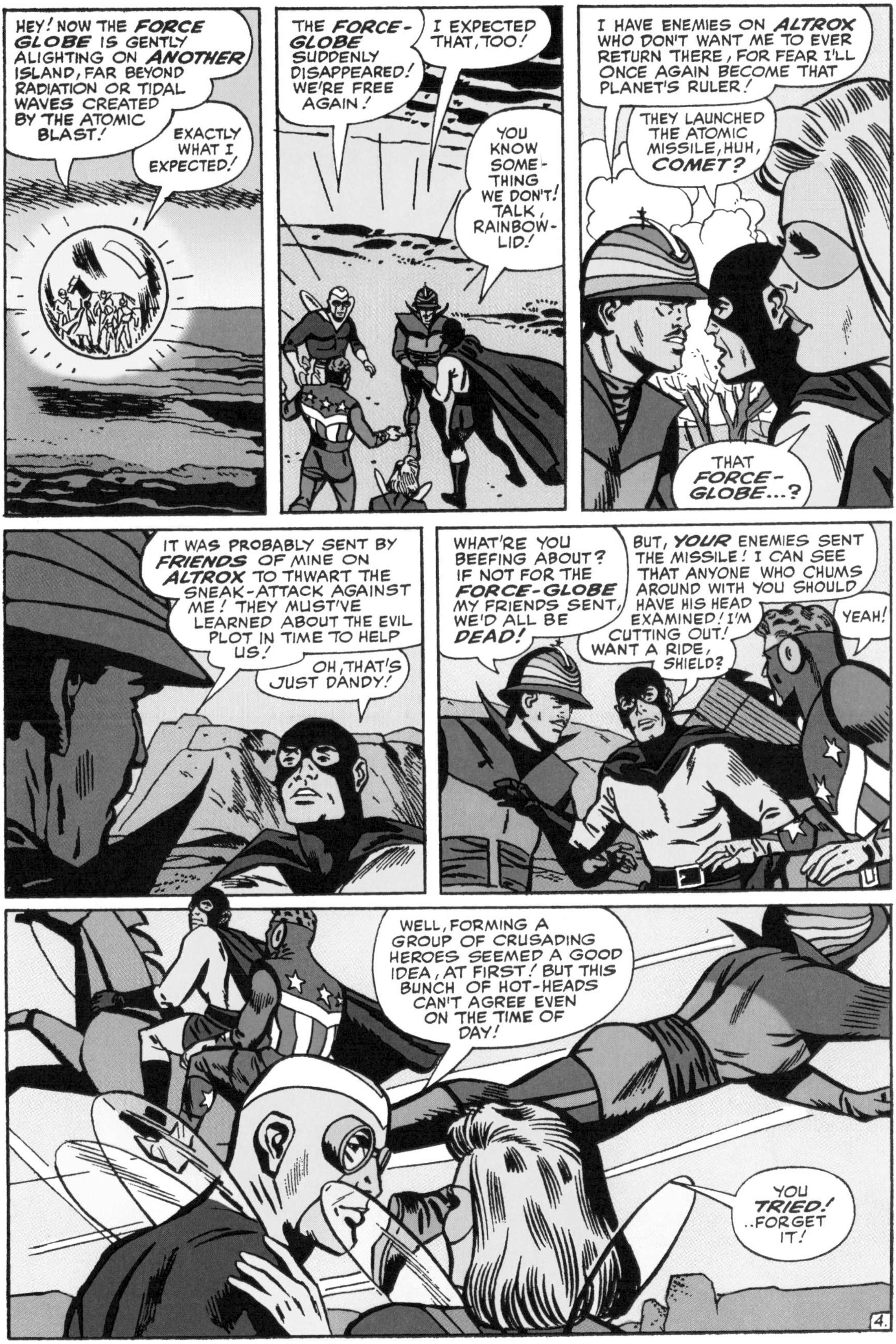
HEY! NOW THE FORCE GLOBE IS GENTLY ALIGHTING ON ANOTHER ISLAND, FAR BEYOND RADIATION OR TIDAL WAVES CREATED BY THE ATOMIC BLAST!
EXACTLY WHAT I EXPECTED!
THE FORCE-GLOBE SUDDENLY DISAPPEARED! WE'RE FREE AGAIN!
I EXPECTED THAT, TOO!
YOU KNOW SOME-THING WE DON'T! TALK, RAINBOW-LID!
I HAVE ENEMIES ON ALTROX WHO DON'T WANT ME TO EVER RETURN THERE, FOR FEAR I'LL ONCE AGAIN BECOME THAT PLANET'S RULER!
THEY LAUNCHED THE ATOMIC MISSILE, HUH, COMET?
THAT FORCE-GLOBE...?
IT WAS PROBABLY SENT BY FRIENDS OF MINE ON ALTROX TO THWART THE SNEAK-ATTACK AGAINST ME! THEY MUST'VE LEARNED ABOUT THE EVIL PLOT IN TIME TO HELP US!
OH, THAT'S JUST DANDY!
WHAT'RE YOU BEEFING ABOUT? IF NOT FOR THE FORCE-GLOBE MY FRIENDS SENT, WE'D ALL BE DEAD!
BUT, YOUR ENEMIES SENT THE MISSILE! I CAN SEE THAT ANYONE WHO CHUMS AROUND WITH YOU SHOULD HAVE HIS HEAD EXAMINED! I'M CUTTING OUT! WANT A RIDE, SHIELD?
YEAH!
WELL, FORMING A GROUP OF CRUSADING HEROES SEEMED A GOOD IDEA, AT FIRST! BUT THIS BUNCH OF HOT-HEADS CAN'T AGREE EVEN ON THE TIME OF DAY!
YOU TRIED! ..FORGET IT!
4.

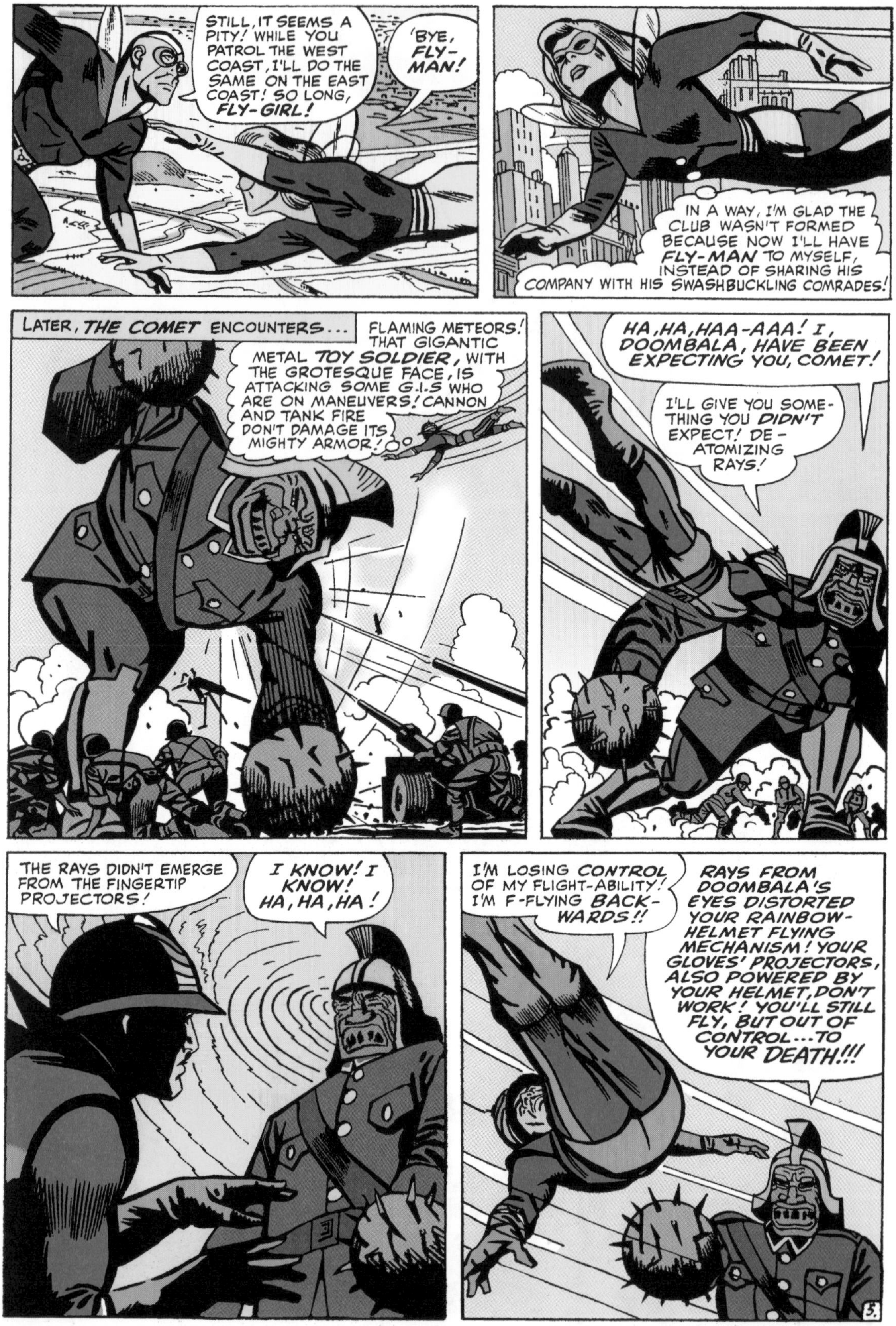
STILL, IT SEEMS A PITY! WHILE YOU PATROL THE WEST COAST, I'LL DO THE SAME ON THE EAST COAST! SO LONG, FLY-GIRL!
'BYE, FLY-MAN!
IN A WAY, I'M GLAD THE CLUB WASN'T FORMED BECAUSE NOW I'LL HAVE FLY-MAN TO MYSELF, INSTEAD OF SHARING HIS COMPANY WITH HIS SWASHBUCKLING COMRADES!
LATER, THE COMET ENCOUNTERS...
FLAMING METEORS! THAT GIGANTIC METAL TOY SOLDIER, WITH THE GROTESQUE FACE, IS ATTACKING SOME G.I.S WHO ARE ON MANEUVERS! CANNON AND TANK FIRE DON'T DAMAGE ITS MIGHTY ARMOR!
HA, HA, HAA-AAA! I, DOOMBALA, HAVE BEEN EXPECTING YOU, COMET!
I'LL GIVE YOU SOMETHING YOU DIDN'T EXPECT! DE-ATOMIZING RAYS!
THE RAYS DIDN'T EMERGE FROM THE FINGERTIP PROJECTORS!
I KNOW! I KNOW! HA, HA, HA!
I'M LOSING CONTROL OF MY FLIGHT-ABILITY! I'M F-FLYING BACKWARDS!!
RAYS FROM DOOMBALA'S EYES DISTORTED YOUR RAINBOW-HELMET FLYING MECHANISM! YOUR GLOVES' PROJECTORS, ALSO POWERED BY YOUR HELMET, DON'T WORK! YOU'LL STILL FLY, BUT OUT OF CONTROL...TO YOUR DEATH!!!
5.

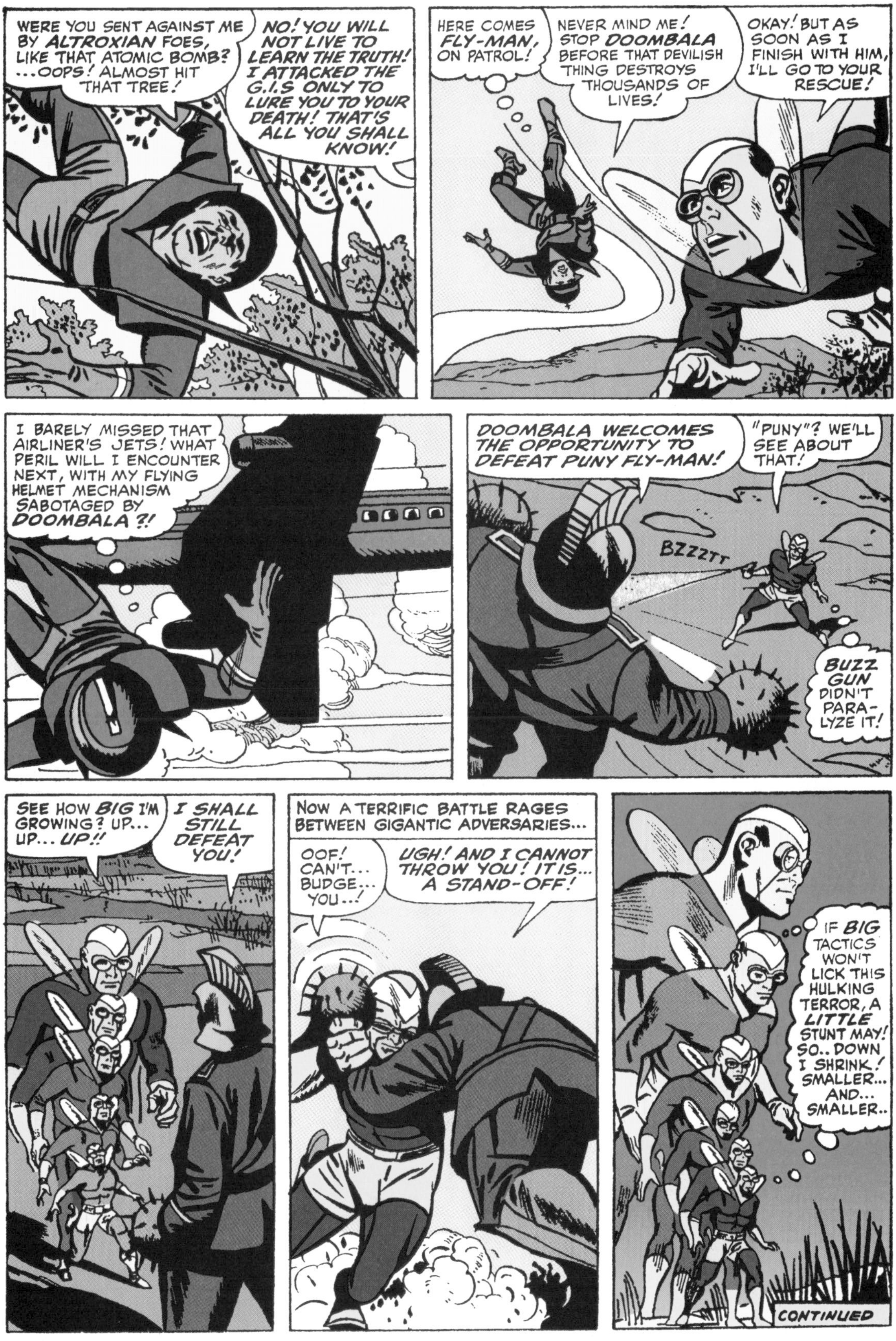
WERE YOU SENT AGAINST ME BY ALTROXIAN FOES, LIKE THAT ATOMIC BOMB? ...OOPS! ALMOST HIT THAT TREE!
NO! YOU WILL NOT LIVE TO LEARN THE TRUTH! I ATTACKED THE G.I.S ONLY TO LURE YOU TO YOUR DEATH! THAT'S ALL YOU SHALL KNOW!
HERE COMES FLY-MAN, ON PATROL!
NEVER MIND ME! STOP DOOMBALA BEFORE THAT DEVILISH THING DESTROYS THOUSANDS OF LIVES!
OKAY! BUT AS SOON AS I FINISH WITH HIM, I'LL GO TO YOUR RESCUE!
I BARELY MISSED THAT AIRLINER'S JETS! WHAT PERIL WILL I ENCOUNTER NEXT, WITH MY FLYING HELMET MECHANISM SABOTAGED BY DOOMBALA ?!
DOOMBALA WELCOMES THE OPPORTUNITY TO DEFEAT PUNY FLY-MAN!
"PUNY"? WE'LL SEE ABOUT THAT!
BZZZTT
BUZZ GUN DIDN'T PARA-LYZE IT!
SEE HOW BIG I'M GROWING? UP... UP... UP!!
I SHALL STILL DEFEAT YOU!
NOW A TERRIFIC BATTLE RAGES BETWEEN GIGANTIC ADVERSARIES...
OOF! CAN'T... BUDGE... YOU...!
UGH! AND I CANNOT THROW YOU! IT IS... A STAND-OFF!
IF BIG TACTICS WON'T LICK THIS HULKING TERROR, A LITTLE STUNT MAY! SO.. DOWN I SHRINK! SMALLER... AND... SMALLER..
CONTINUED

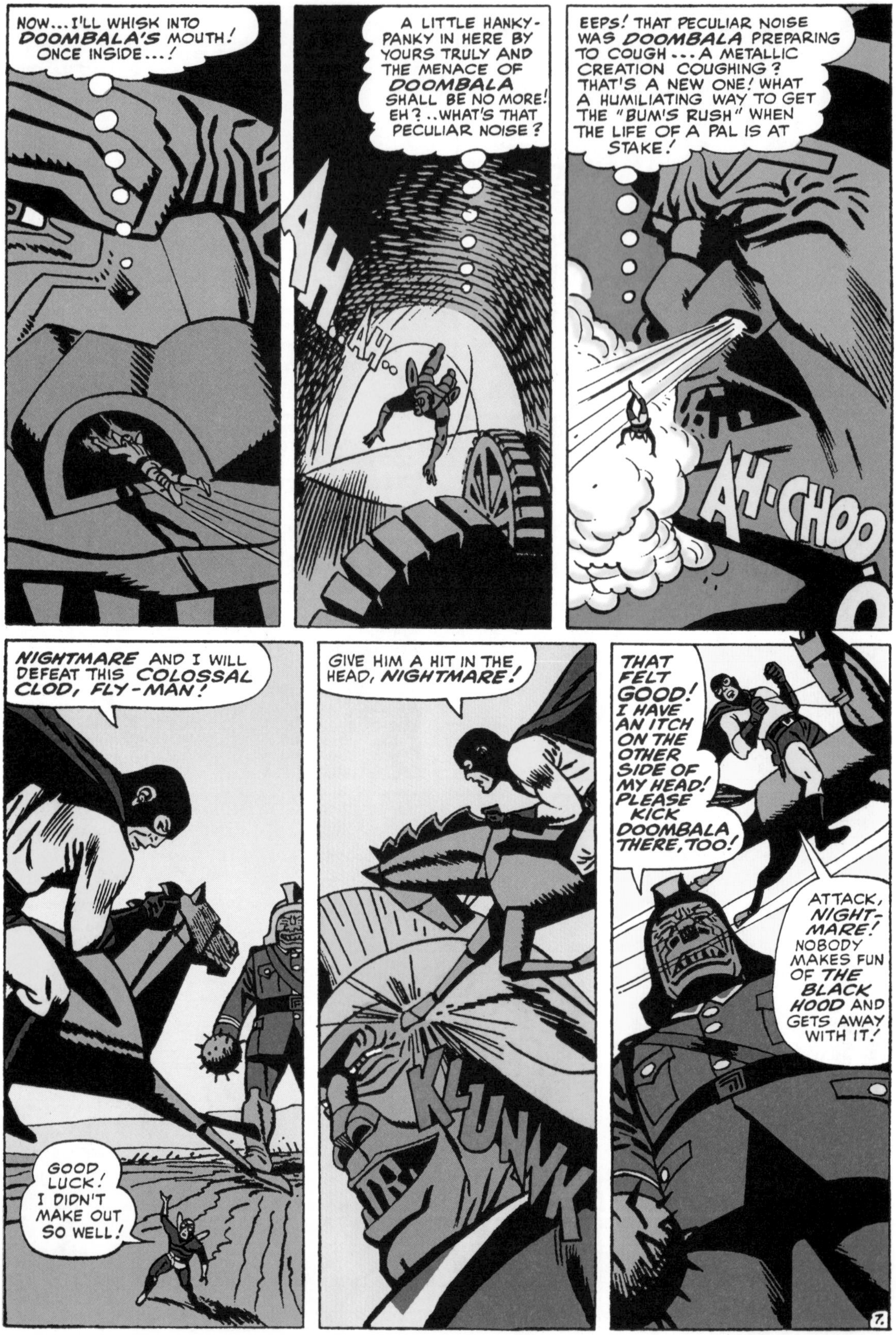
NOW...I'LL WHISK INTO DOOMBALA'S MOUTH! ONCE INSIDE...!
A LITTLE HANKY-PANKY IN HERE BY YOURS TRULY AND THE MENACE OF DOOMBALA SHALL BE NO MORE! EH? ..WHAT'S THAT PECULIAR NOISE?
AH
AH
EEPS! THAT PECULIAR NOISE WAS DOOMBALA PREPARING TO COUGH... A METALLIC CREATION COUGHING? THAT'S A NEW ONE! WHAT A HUMILIATING WAY TO GET THE "BUM'S RUSH" WHEN THE LIFE OF A PAL IS AT STAKE!
AH-CHOO
NIGHTMARE AND I WILL DEFEAT THIS COLOSSAL CLOD, FLY-MAN!
GOOD LUCK! I DIDN'T MAKE OUT SO WELL!
GIVE HIM A HIT IN THE HEAD, NIGHTMARE!
KLUNNK
THAT FELT GOOD! I HAVE AN ITCH ON THE OTHER SIDE OF MY HEAD! PLEASE KICK DOOMBALA THERE, TOO!
ATTACK, NIGHT-MARE! NOBODY MAKES FUN OF THE BLACK HOOD AND GETS AWAY WITH IT!
7.

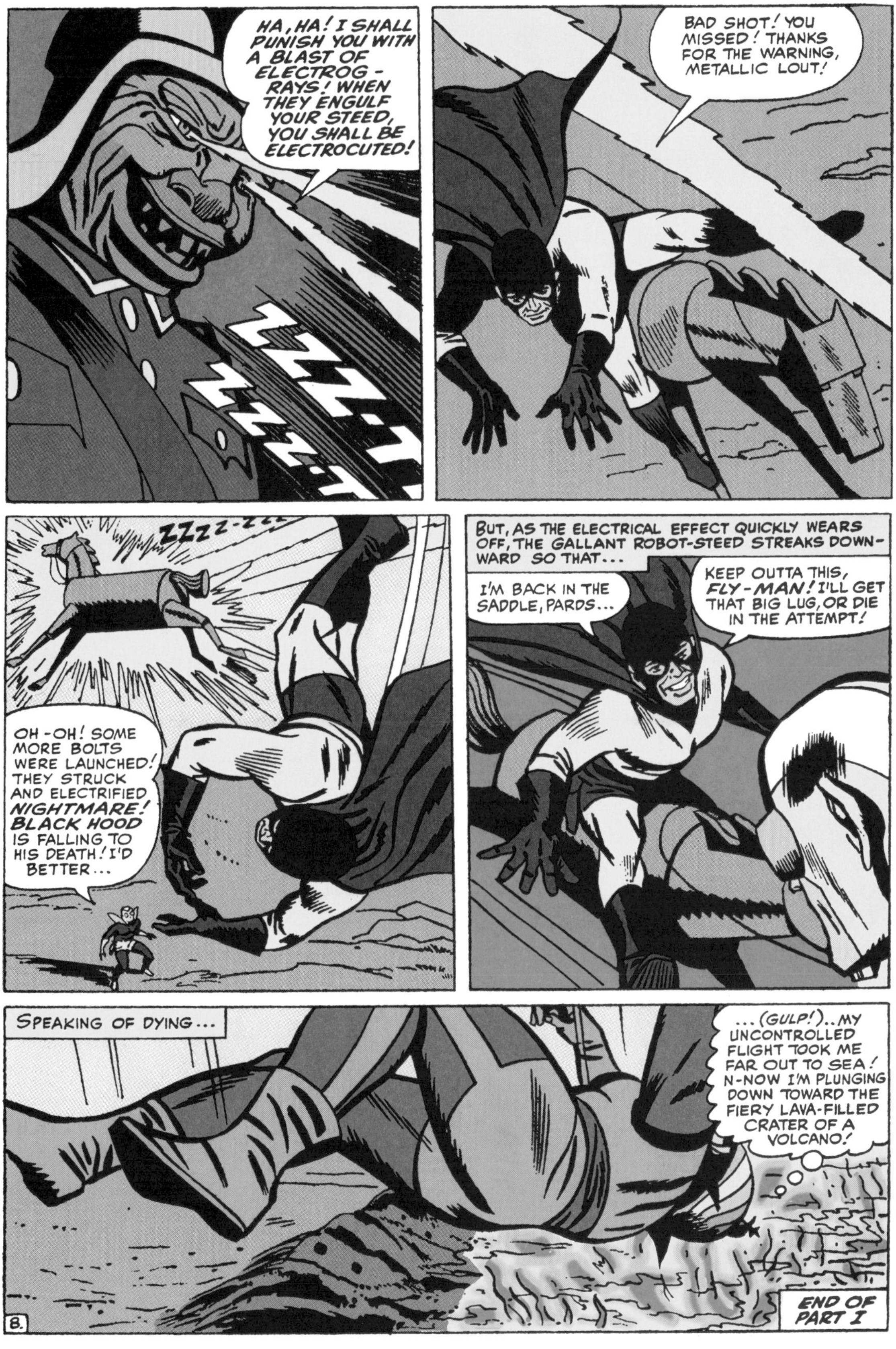
HA, HA! I SHALL PUNISH YOU WITH A BLAST OF ELECTROG-RAYS! WHEN THEY ENGULF YOUR STEED, YOU SHALL BE ELECTROCUTED!
ZZZ-T-T
BAD SHOT! YOU MISSED! THANKS FOR THE WARNING, METALLIC LOUT!
ZZZZ-ZZZ
OH-OH! SOME MORE BOLTS WERE LAUNCHED! THEY STRUCK AND ELECTRIFIED NIGHTMARE! BLACK HOOD IS FALLING TO HIS DEATH! I'D BETTER...
BUT, AS THE ELECTRICAL EFFECT QUICKLY WEARS OFF, THE GALLANT ROBOT-STEED STREAKS DOWNWARD SO THAT...
I'M BACK IN THE SADDLE, PARDS...
KEEP OUTTA THIS, FLY-MAN! I'LL GET THAT BIG LUG, OR DIE IN THE ATTEMPT!
SPEAKING OF DYING...
...(GULP!)..MY UNCONTROLLED FLIGHT TOOK ME FAR OUT TO SEA! N-NOW I'M PLUNGING DOWN TOWARD THE FIERY LAVA-FILLED CRATER OF A VOLCANO!
8.
END OF PART I

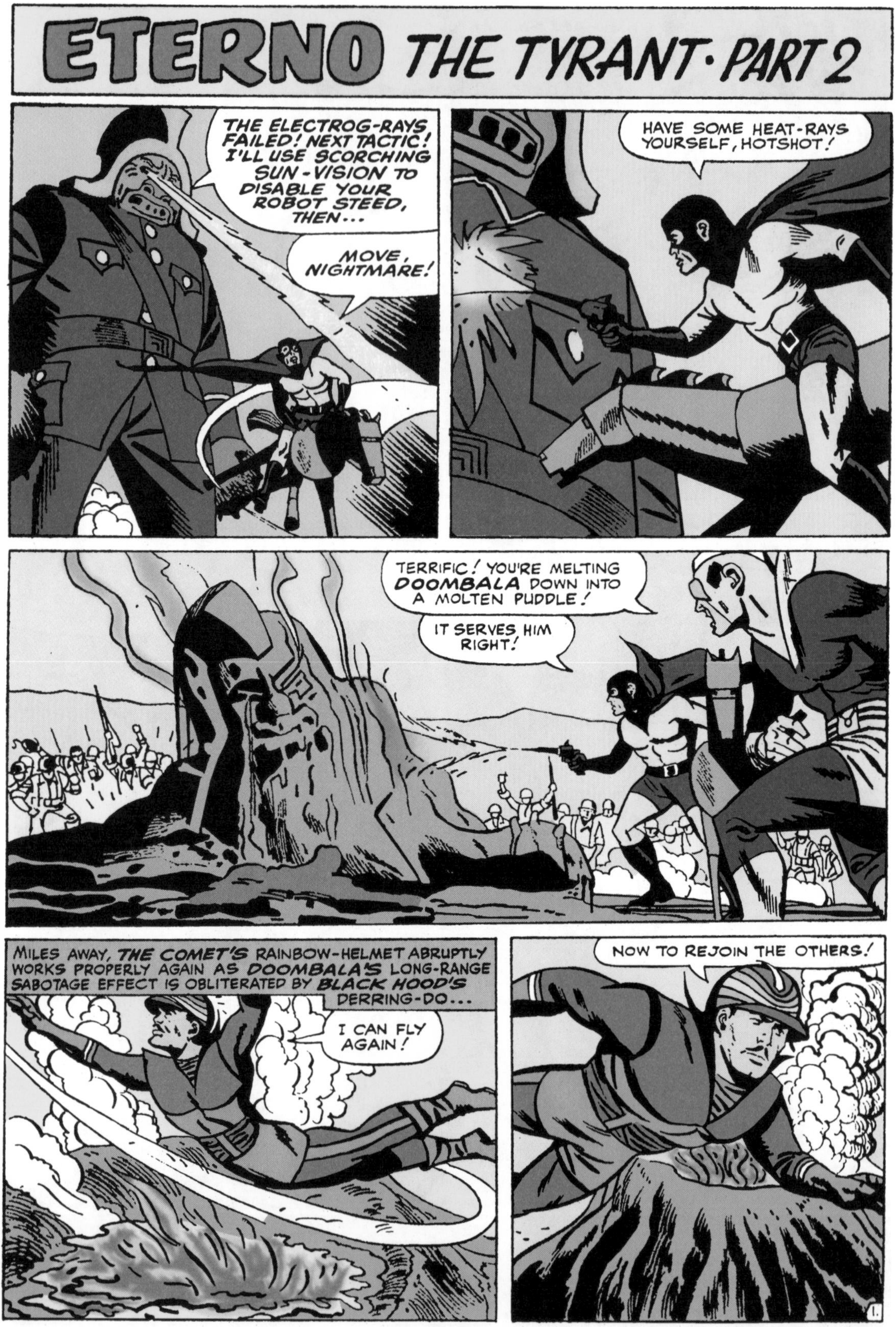
ETERNO THE TYRANT · PART 2
THE ELECTROG-RAYS FAILED! NEXT TACTIC! I'LL USE SCORCHING SUN-VISION TO DISABLE YOUR ROBOT STEED, THEN...
MOVE, NIGHTMARE!
HAVE SOME HEAT-RAYS YOURSELF, HOTSHOT!
TERRIFIC! YOU'RE MELTING DOOMBALA DOWN INTO A MOLTEN PUDDLE!
IT SERVES HIM RIGHT!
MILES AWAY, THE COMET'S RAINBOW-HELMET ABRUPTLY WORKS PROPERLY AGAIN AS DOOMBALA'S LONG-RANGE SABOTAGE EFFECT IS OBLITERATED BY BLACK HOOD'S DERRING-DO...
I CAN FLY AGAIN!
NOW TO REJOIN THE OTHERS!
1.

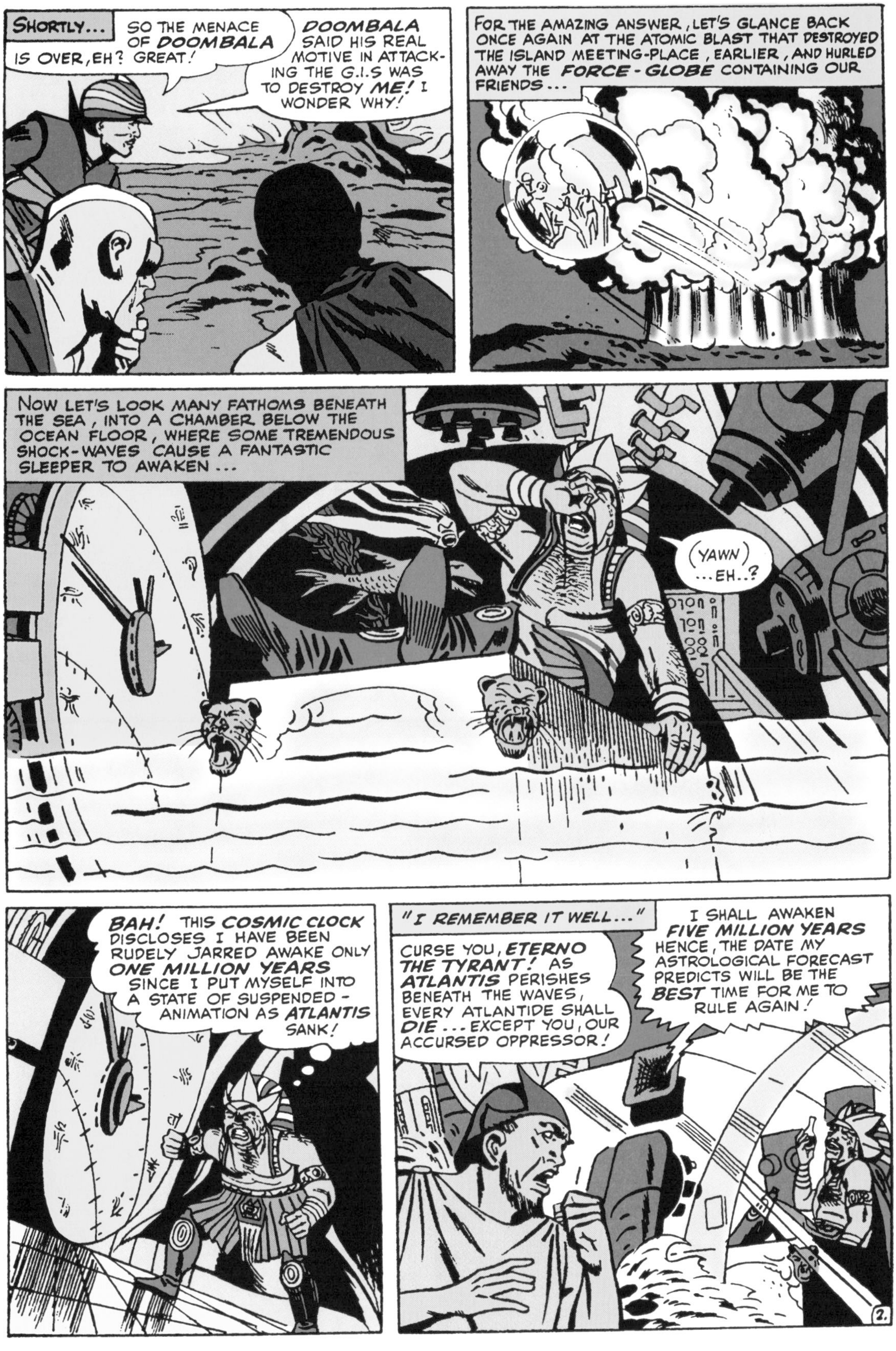
SHORTLY...
SO THE MENACE OF DOOMBALA IS OVER, EH? GREAT!
DOOMBALA SAID HIS REAL MOTIVE IN ATTACKING THE G.I.S WAS TO DESTROY ME! I WONDER WHY!
FOR THE AMAZING ANSWER, LET'S GLANCE BACK ONCE AGAIN AT THE ATOMIC BLAST THAT DESTROYED THE ISLAND MEETING-PLACE, EARLIER, AND HURLED AWAY THE FORCE-GLOBE CONTAINING OUR FRIENDS...
NOW LET'S LOOK MANY FATHOMS BENEATH THE SEA, INTO A CHAMBER BELOW THE OCEAN FLOOR, WHERE SOME TREMENDOUS SHOCK-WAVES CAUSE A FANTASTIC SLEEPER TO AWAKEN...
(YAWN) ...EH..?
BAH! THIS COSMIC CLOCK DISCLOSES I HAVE BEEN RUDELY JARRED AWAKE ONLY ONE MILLION YEARS SINCE I PUT MYSELF INTO A STATE OF SUSPENDED-ANIMATION AS ATLANTIS SANK!
"I REMEMBER IT WELL..."
CURSE YOU, ETERNO THE TYRANT! AS ATLANTIS PERISHES BENEATH THE WAVES, EVERY ATLANTIDE SHALL DIE... EXCEPT YOU, OUR ACCURSED OPPRESSOR!
I SHALL AWAKEN FIVE MILLION YEARS HENCE, THE DATE MY ASTROLOGICAL FORECAST PREDICTS WILL BE THE BEST TIME FOR ME TO RULE AGAIN!
2.

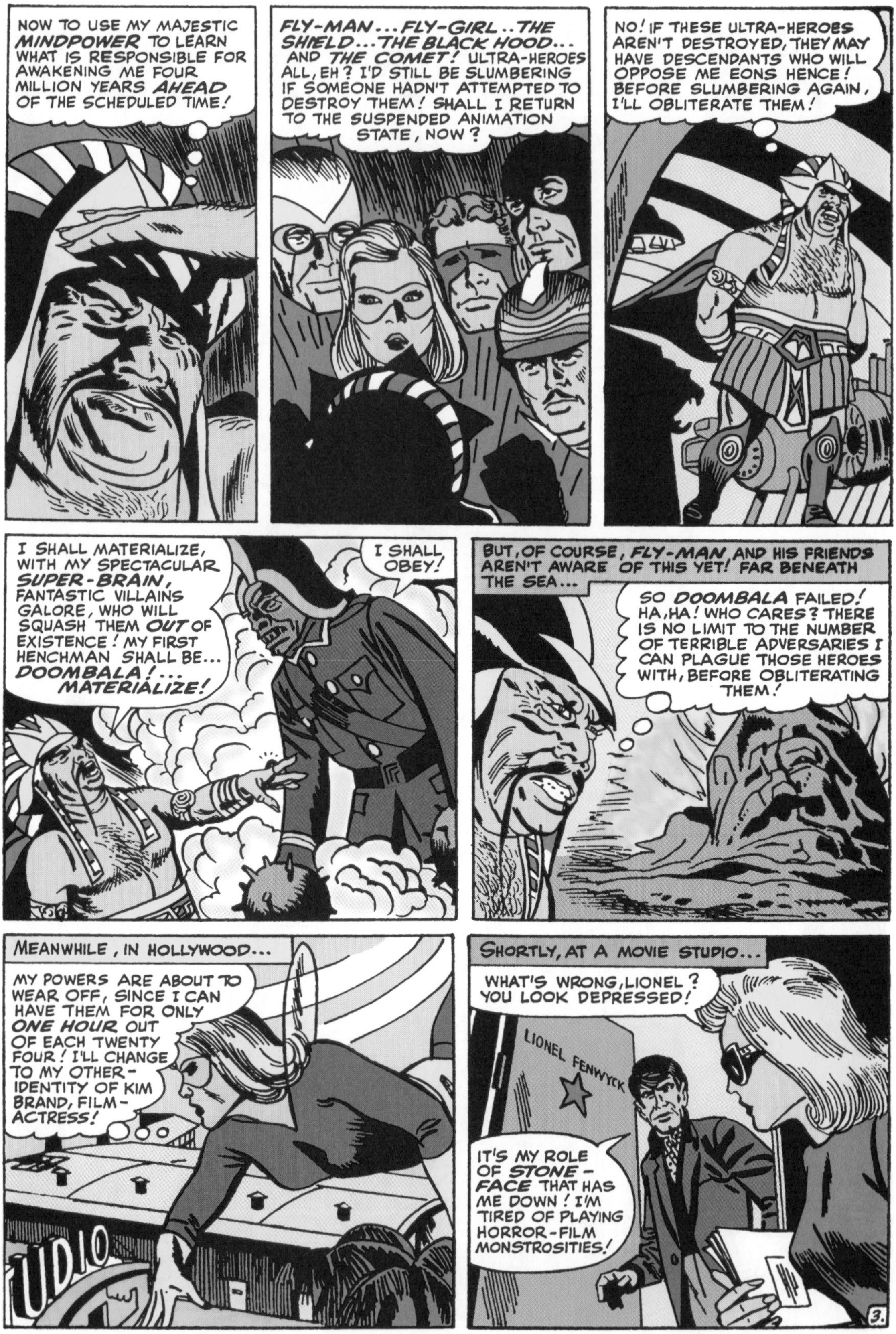
NOW TO USE MY MAJESTIC MINDPOWER TO LEARN WHAT IS RESPONSIBLE FOR AWAKENING ME FOUR MILLION YEARS AHEAD OF THE SCHEDULED TIME!
FLY-MAN...FLY-GIRL..THE SHIELD...THE BLACK HOOD... AND THE COMET! ULTRA-HEROES ALL, EH? I'D STILL BE SLUMBERING IF SOMEONE HADN'T ATTEMPTED TO DESTROY THEM! SHALL I RETURN TO THE SUSPENDED ANIMATION STATE, NOW?
NO! IF THESE ULTRA-HEROES AREN'T DESTROYED, THEY MAY HAVE DESCENDANTS WHO WILL OPPOSE ME EONS HENCE! BEFORE SLUMBERING AGAIN, I'LL OBLITERATE THEM!
I SHALL MATERIALIZE, WITH MY SPECTACULAR SUPER-BRAIN, FANTASTIC VILLAINS GALORE, WHO WILL SQUASH THEM OUT OF EXISTENCE! MY FIRST HENCHMAN SHALL BE... DOOMBALA!... MATERIALIZE!
I SHALL OBEY!
BUT, OF COURSE, FLY-MAN AND HIS FRIENDS AREN'T AWARE OF THIS YET! FAR BENEATH THE SEA...
SO DOOMBALA FAILED! HA, HA! WHO CARES? THERE IS NO LIMIT TO THE NUMBER OF TERRIBLE ADVERSARIES I CAN PLAGUE THOSE HEROES WITH, BEFORE OBLITERATING THEM!
MEANWHILE, IN HOLLYWOOD...
MY POWERS ARE ABOUT TO WEAR OFF, SINCE I CAN HAVE THEM FOR ONLY ONE HOUR OUT OF EACH TWENTY FOUR! I'LL CHANGE TO MY OTHER-IDENTITY OF KIM BRAND, FILM-ACTRESS!
UDIO
SHORTLY, AT A MOVIE STUDIO...
WHAT'S WRONG, LIONEL? YOU LOOK DEPRESSED!
LIONEL FENWYCK
IT'S MY ROLE OF STONE-FACE THAT HAS ME DOWN! I'M TIRED OF PLAYING HORROR-FILM MONSTROSITIES!
3.

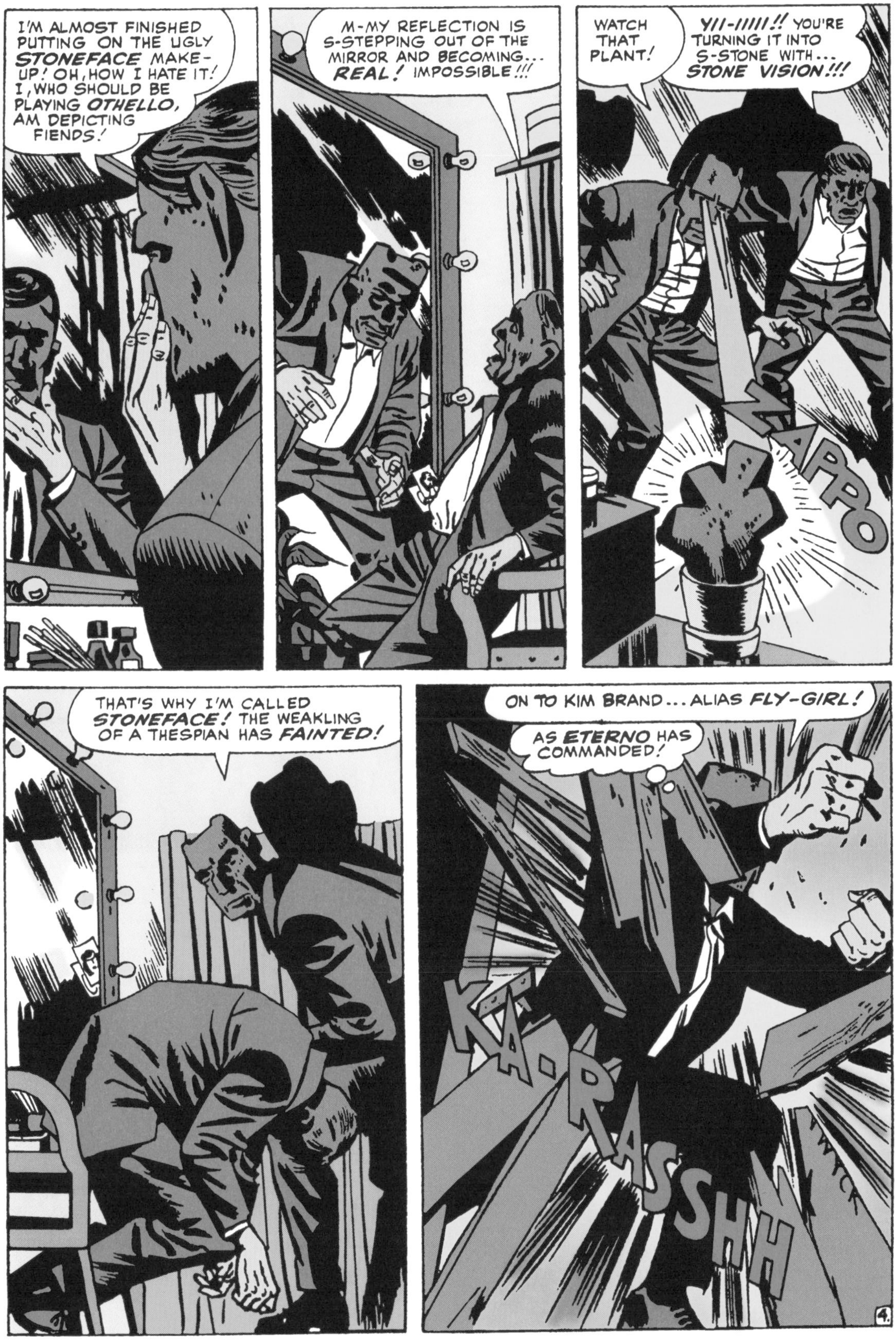
I'M ALMOST FINISHED PUTTING ON THE UGLY STONEFACE MAKE-UP! OH, HOW I HATE IT! I, WHO SHOULD BE PLAYING OTHELLO, AM DEPICTING FIENDS!
M-MY REFLECTION IS S-STEPPING OUT OF THE MIRROR AND BECOMING... REAL! IMPOSSIBLE!!!
WATCH THAT PLANT!
YII-IIIII!! YOU'RE TURNING IT INTO S-STONE WITH... STONE VISION!!!
ZAPPO
THAT'S WHY I'M CALLED STONEFACE! THE WEAKLING OF A THESPIAN HAS FAINTED!
ON TO KIM BRAND... ALIAS FLY-GIRL!
AS ETERNO HAS COMMANDED!
KA-RASSHH
4.

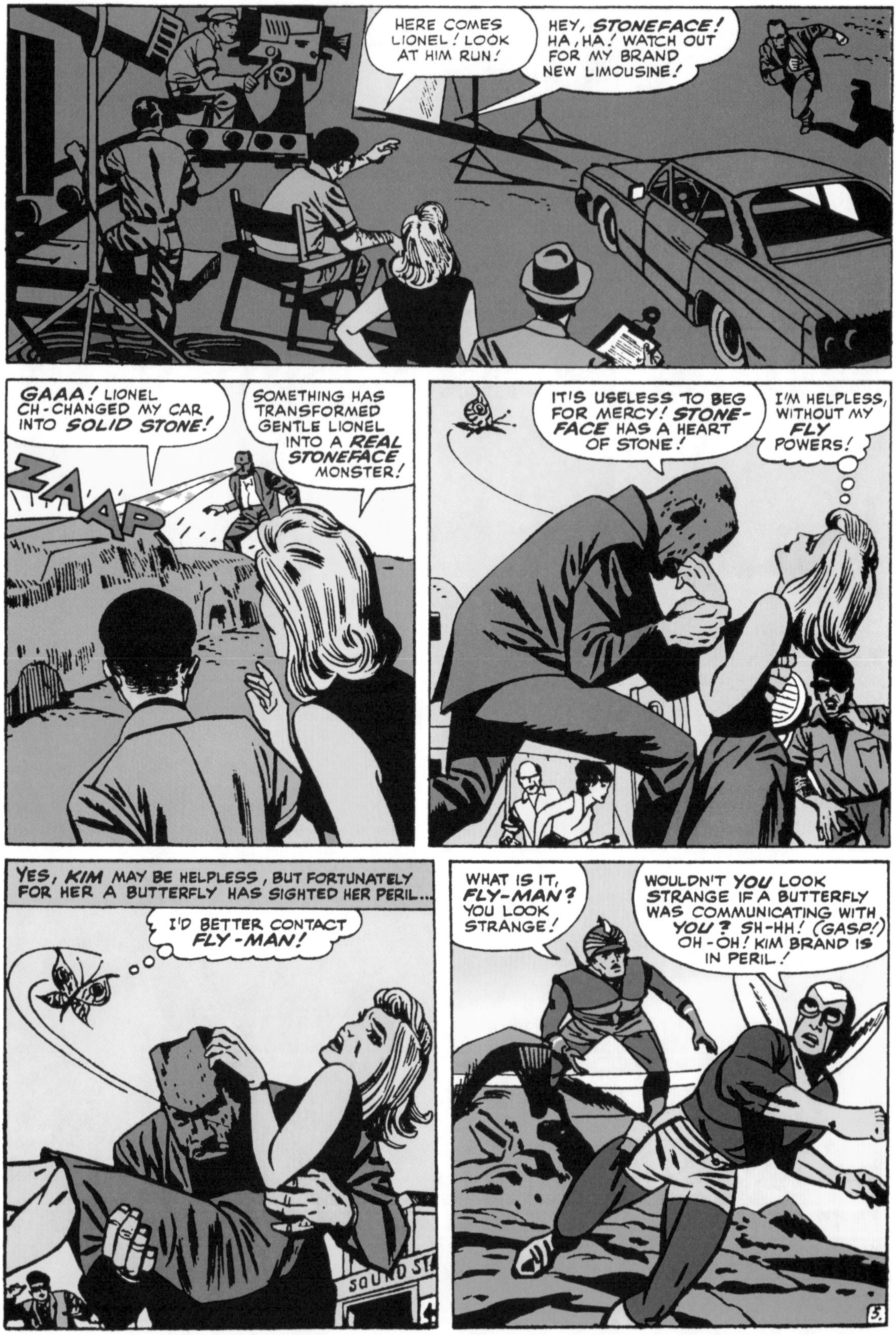
HERE COMES LIONEL! LOOK AT HIM RUN!
HEY, STONEFACE! HA, HA! WATCH OUT FOR MY BRAND NEW LIMOUSINE!
GAAA! LIONEL CH-CHANGED MY CAR INTO SOLID STONE!
SOMETHING HAS TRANSFORMED GENTLE LIONEL INTO A REAL STONEFACE MONSTER!
ZAAP
IT'S USELESS TO BEG FOR MERCY! STONEFACE HAS A HEART OF STONE!
I'M HELPLESS, WITHOUT MY FLY POWERS!
YES, KIM MAY BE HELPLESS, BUT FORTUNATELY FOR HER A BUTTERFLY HAS SIGHTED HER PERIL...
I'D BETTER CONTACT FLY-MAN!
SOUND STA
4.
WHAT IS IT, FLY-MAN? YOU LOOK STRANGE!
WOULDN'T YOU LOOK STRANGE IF A BUTTERFLY WAS COMMUNICATING WITH YOU? SH-HH! (GASP!) OH-OH! KIM BRAND IS IN PERIL!
5.

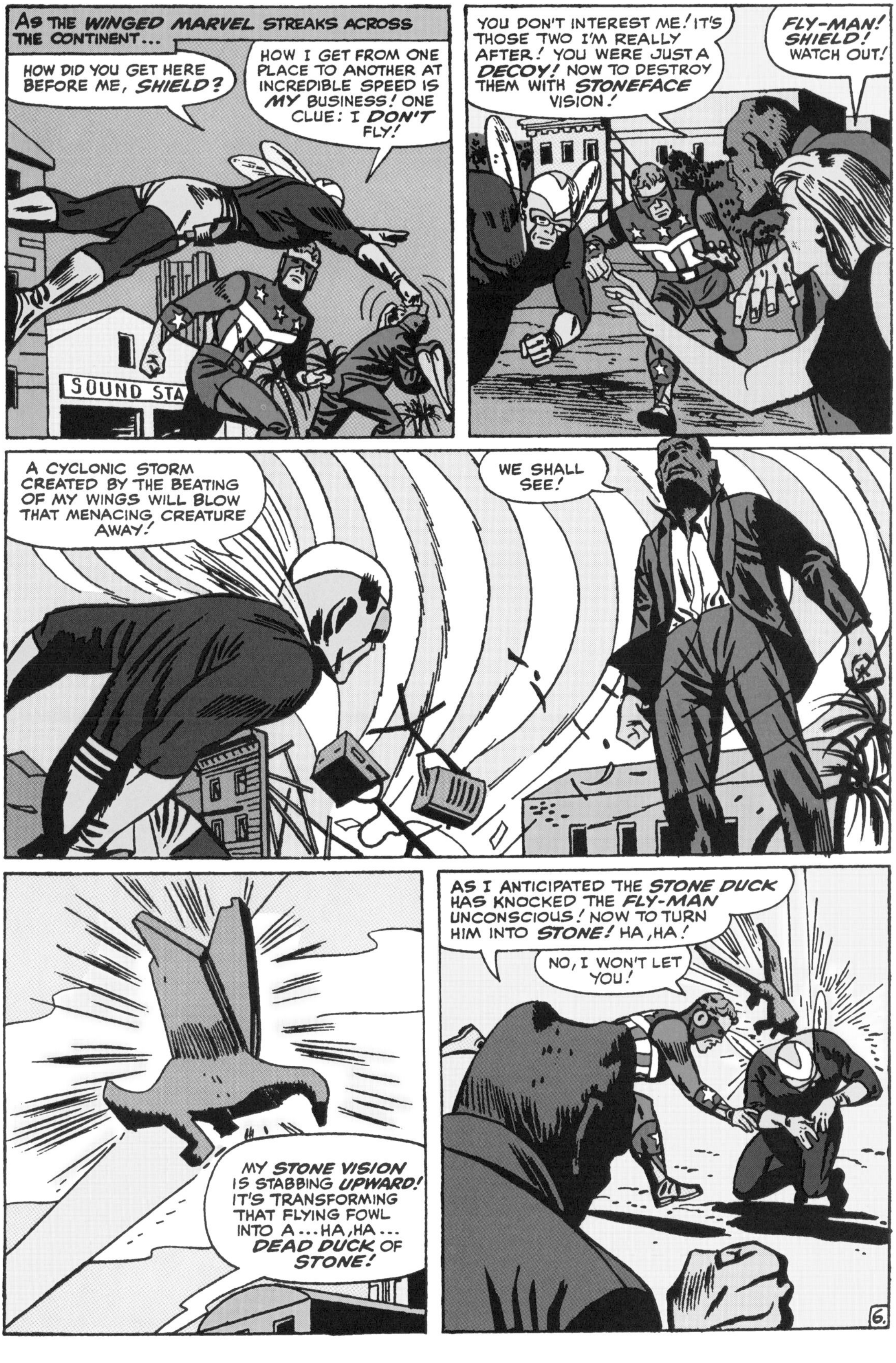
AS THE WINGED MARVEL STREAKS ACROSS THE CONTINENT...
HOW DID YOU GET HERE BEFORE ME, SHIELD?
HOW I GET FROM ONE PLACE TO ANOTHER AT INCREDIBLE SPEED IS MY BUSINESS! ONE CLUE: I DON'T FLY!
SOUND STA
YOU DON'T INTEREST ME! IT'S THOSE TWO I'M REALLY AFTER! YOU WERE JUST A DECOY! NOW TO DESTROY THEM WITH STONEFACE VISION!
FLY-MAN! SHIELD! WATCH OUT!
A CYCLONIC STORM CREATED BY THE BEATING OF MY WINGS WILL BLOW THAT MENACING CREATURE AWAY!
WE SHALL SEE!
MY STONE VISION IS STABBING UPWARD! IT'S TRANSFORMING THAT FLYING FOWL INTO A...HA,HA... DEAD DUCK OF STONE!
AS I ANTICIPATED THE STONE DUCK HAS KNOCKED THE FLY-MAN UNCONSCIOUS! NOW TO TURN HIM INTO STONE! HA,HA!
NO, I WON'T LET YOU!
6.

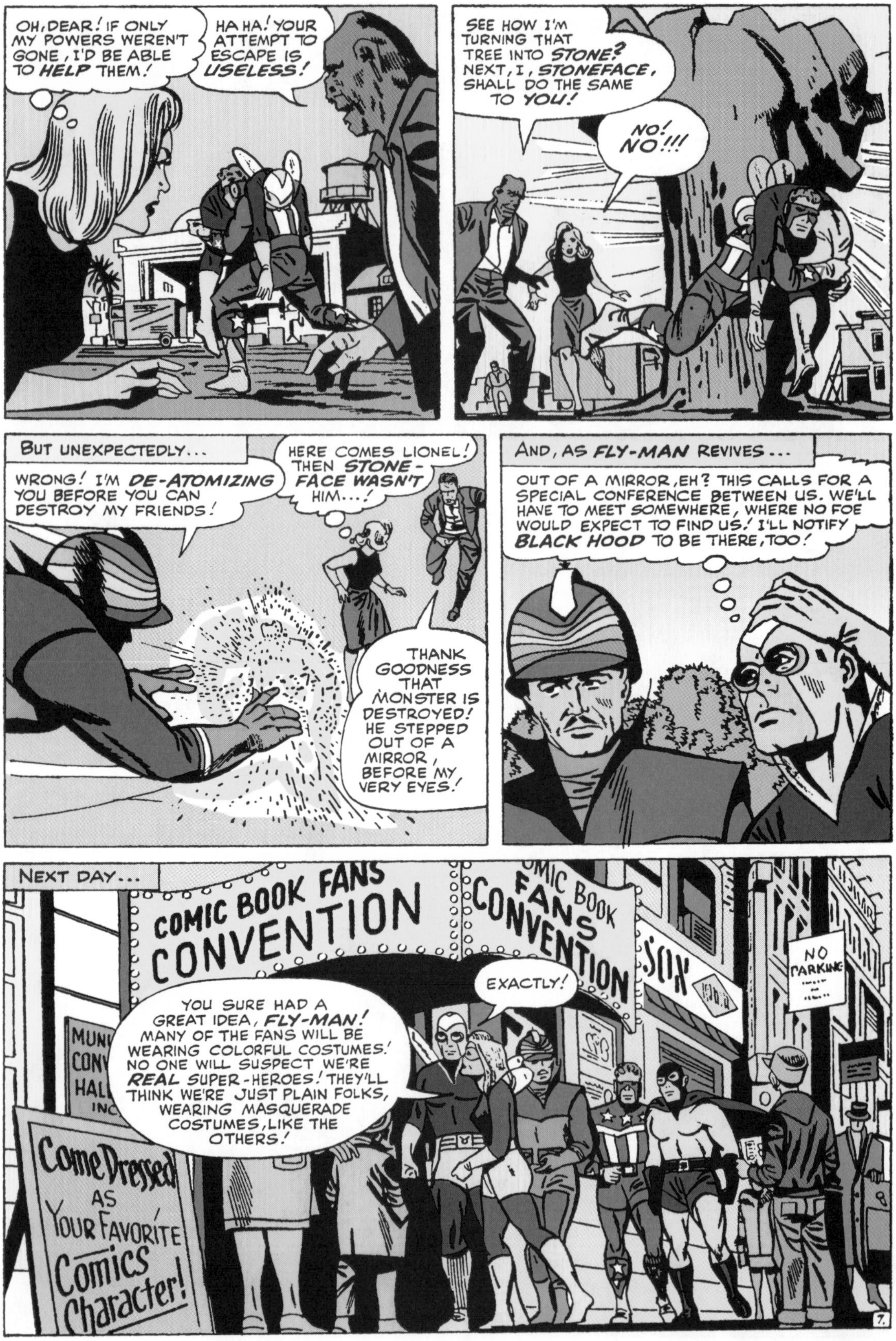
OH, DEAR! IF ONLY MY POWERS WEREN'T GONE, I'D BE ABLE TO HELP THEM!
HA HA! YOUR ATTEMPT TO ESCAPE IS USELESS!
SEE HOW I'M TURNING THAT TREE INTO STONE? NEXT, I, STONEFACE, SHALL DO THE SAME TO YOU!
NO! NO!!!
BUT UNEXPECTEDLY...
WRONG! I'M DE-ATOMIZING YOU BEFORE YOU CAN DESTROY MY FRIENDS!
HERE COMES LIONEL! THEN STONE-FACE WASN'T HIM...!
THANK GOODNESS THAT MONSTER IS DESTROYED! HE STEPPED OUT OF A MIRROR, BEFORE MY VERY EYES!
AND, AS FLY-MAN REVIVES...
OUT OF A MIRROR, EH? THIS CALLS FOR A SPECIAL CONFERENCE BETWEEN US. WE'LL HAVE TO MEET SOMEWHERE, WHERE NO FOE WOULD EXPECT TO FIND US! I'LL NOTIFY BLACK HOOD TO BE THERE, TOO!
NEXT DAY...
COMIC BOOK FANS CONVENTION
COMIC BOOK FANS CONVENTION
NO PARKING
YOU SURE HAD A GREAT IDEA, FLY-MAN! MANY OF THE FANS WILL BE WEARING COLORFUL COSTUMES! NO ONE WILL SUSPECT WE'RE REAL SUPER-HEROES! THEY'LL THINK WE'RE JUST PLAIN FOLKS, WEARING MASQUERADE COSTUMES, LIKE THE OTHERS!
EXACTLY!
Come Dressed AS YOUR FAVORITE Comics Character!
7.

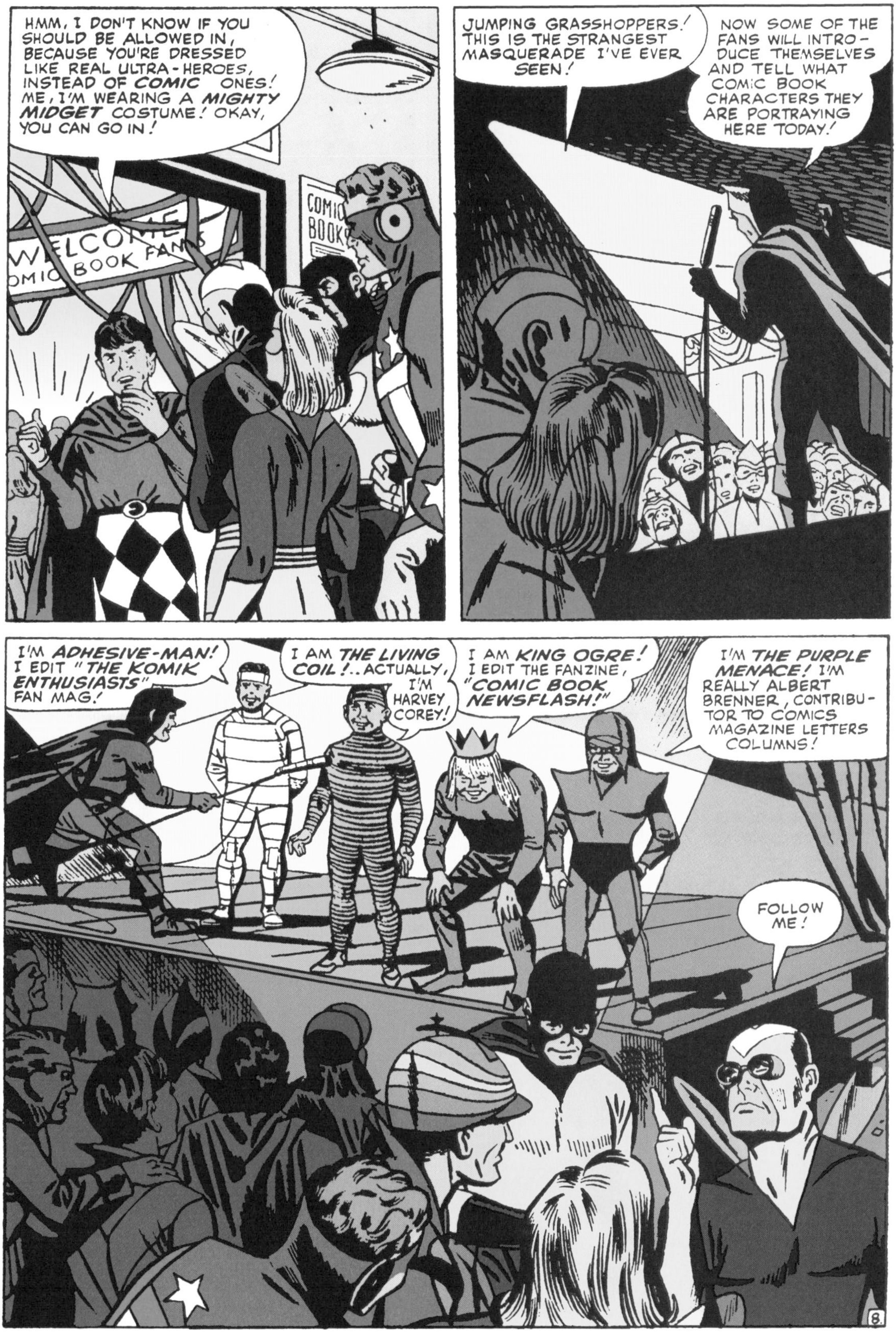
HMM, I DON'T KNOW IF YOU SHOULD BE ALLOWED IN, BECAUSE YOU'RE DRESSED LIKE REAL ULTRA-HEROES, INSTEAD OF **COMIC** ONES! ME, I'M WEARING A **MIGHTY MIDGET** COSTUME! OKAY, YOU CAN GO IN!
WELCOME COMIC BOOK FANS
COMIC BOOK
JUMPING GRASSHOPPERS! THIS IS THE STRANGEST MASQUERADE I'VE EVER SEEN!
NOW SOME OF THE FANS WILL INTRODUCE THEMSELVES AND TELL WHAT COMIC BOOK CHARACTERS THEY ARE PORTRAYING HERE TODAY!
I'M **ADHESIVE-MAN!** I EDIT **"THE KOMIK ENTHUSIASTS"** FAN MAG!
I AM **THE LIVING COIL!**.. ACTUALLY, I'M HARVEY COREY!
I AM **KING OGRE!** I EDIT THE FANZINE, **"COMIC BOOK NEWSFLASH!"**
I'M **THE PURPLE MENACE!** I'M REALLY ALBERT BRENNER, CONTRIBUTOR TO COMICS MAGAZINE LETTERS COLUMNS!
FOLLOW ME!
8.

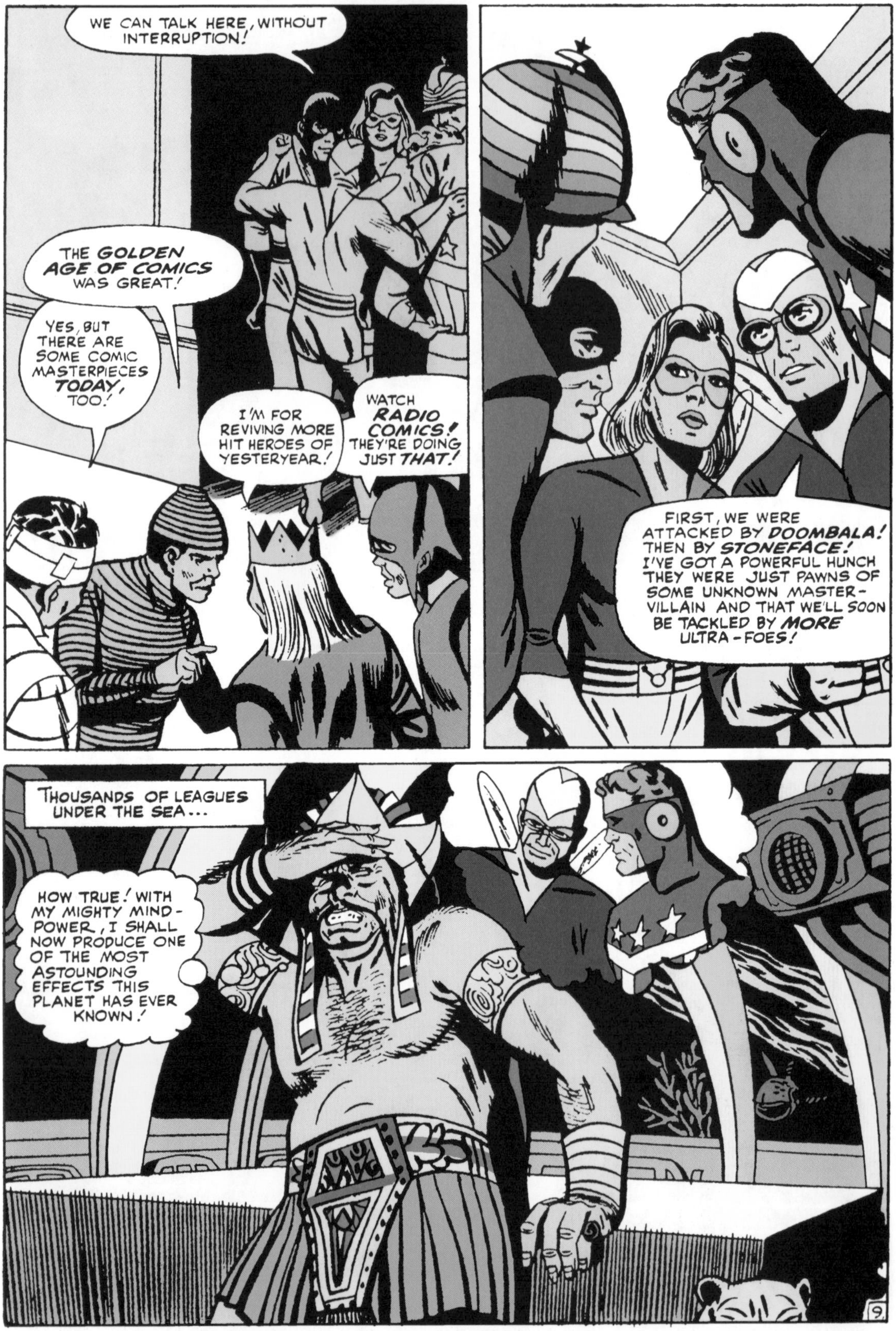
WE CAN TALK HERE, WITHOUT INTERRUPTION!
THE GOLDEN AGE OF COMICS WAS GREAT!
YES, BUT THERE ARE SOME COMIC MASTERPIECES TODAY, TOO!
I'M FOR REVIVING MORE HIT HEROES OF YESTERYEAR!
WATCH RADIO COMICS! THEY'RE DOING JUST THAT!
FIRST, WE WERE ATTACKED BY DOOMBALA! THEN BY STONEFACE! I'VE GOT A POWERFUL HUNCH THEY WERE JUST PAWNS OF SOME UNKNOWN MASTER-VILLAIN AND THAT WE'LL SOON BE TACKLED BY MORE ULTRA-FOES!
THOUSANDS OF LEAGUES UNDER THE SEA...
HOW TRUE! WITH MY MIGHTY MIND-POWER, I SHALL NOW PRODUCE ONE OF THE MOST ASTOUNDING EFFECTS THIS PLANET HAS EVER KNOWN!
9

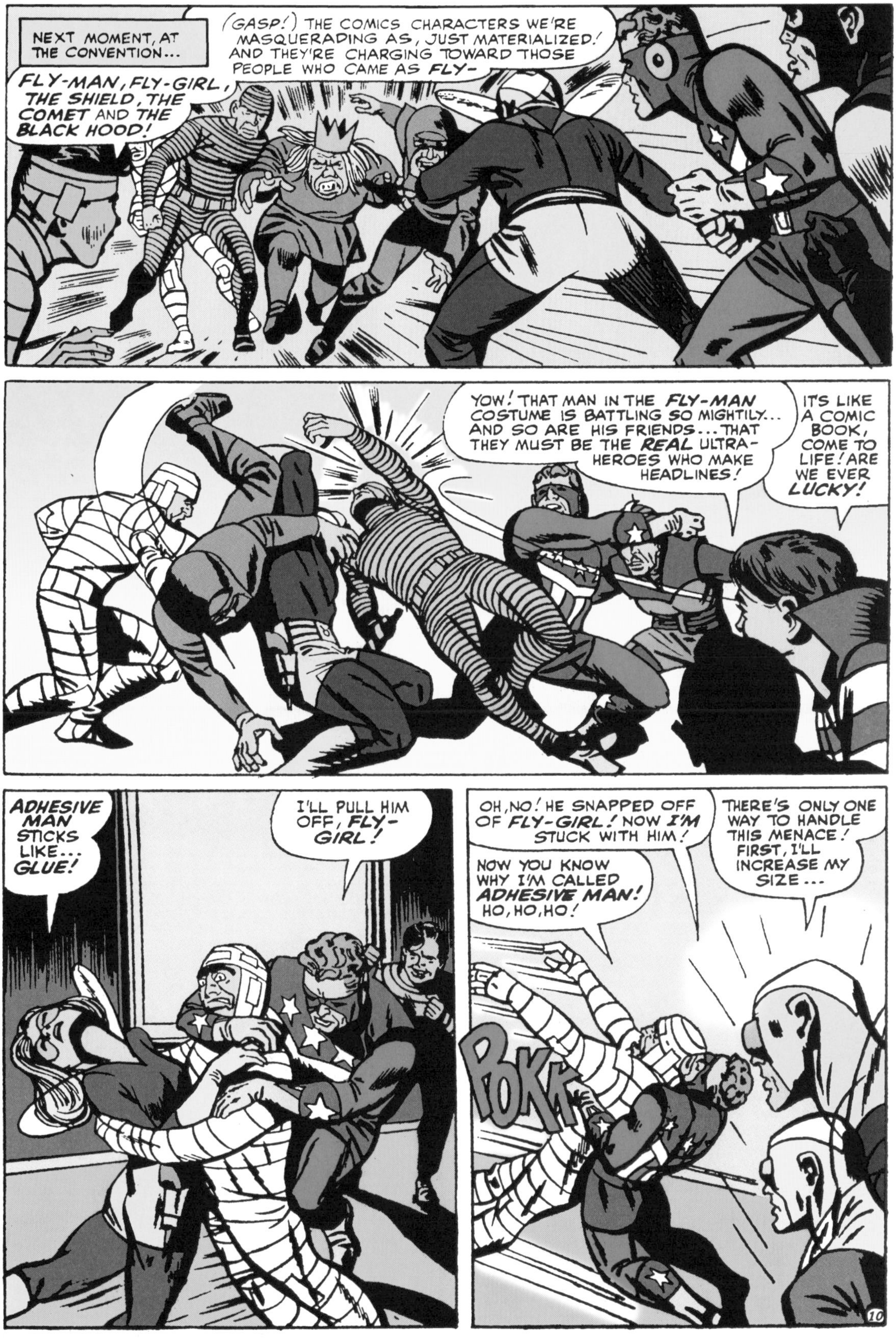
NEXT MOMENT, AT THE CONVENTION...
(GASP!) THE COMICS CHARACTERS WE'RE MASQUERADING AS, JUST MATERIALIZED! AND THEY'RE CHARGING TOWARD THOSE PEOPLE WHO CAME AS FLY-
FLY-MAN, FLY-GIRL, THE SHIELD, THE COMET AND THE BLACK HOOD!
YOW! THAT MAN IN THE FLY-MAN COSTUME IS BATTLING SO MIGHTILY... AND SO ARE HIS FRIENDS... THAT THEY MUST BE THE REAL ULTRA-HEROES WHO MAKE HEADLINES!
IT'S LIKE A COMIC BOOK, COME TO LIFE! ARE WE EVER LUCKY!
ADHESIVE MAN STICKS LIKE... GLUE!
I'LL PULL HIM OFF, FLY-GIRL!
OH, NO! HE SNAPPED OFF OF FLY-GIRL! NOW I'M STUCK WITH HIM!
NOW YOU KNOW WHY I'M CALLED ADHESIVE MAN! HO, HO, HO!
THERE'S ONLY ONE WAY TO HANDLE THIS MENACE! FIRST, I'LL INCREASE MY SIZE...
POKK
10

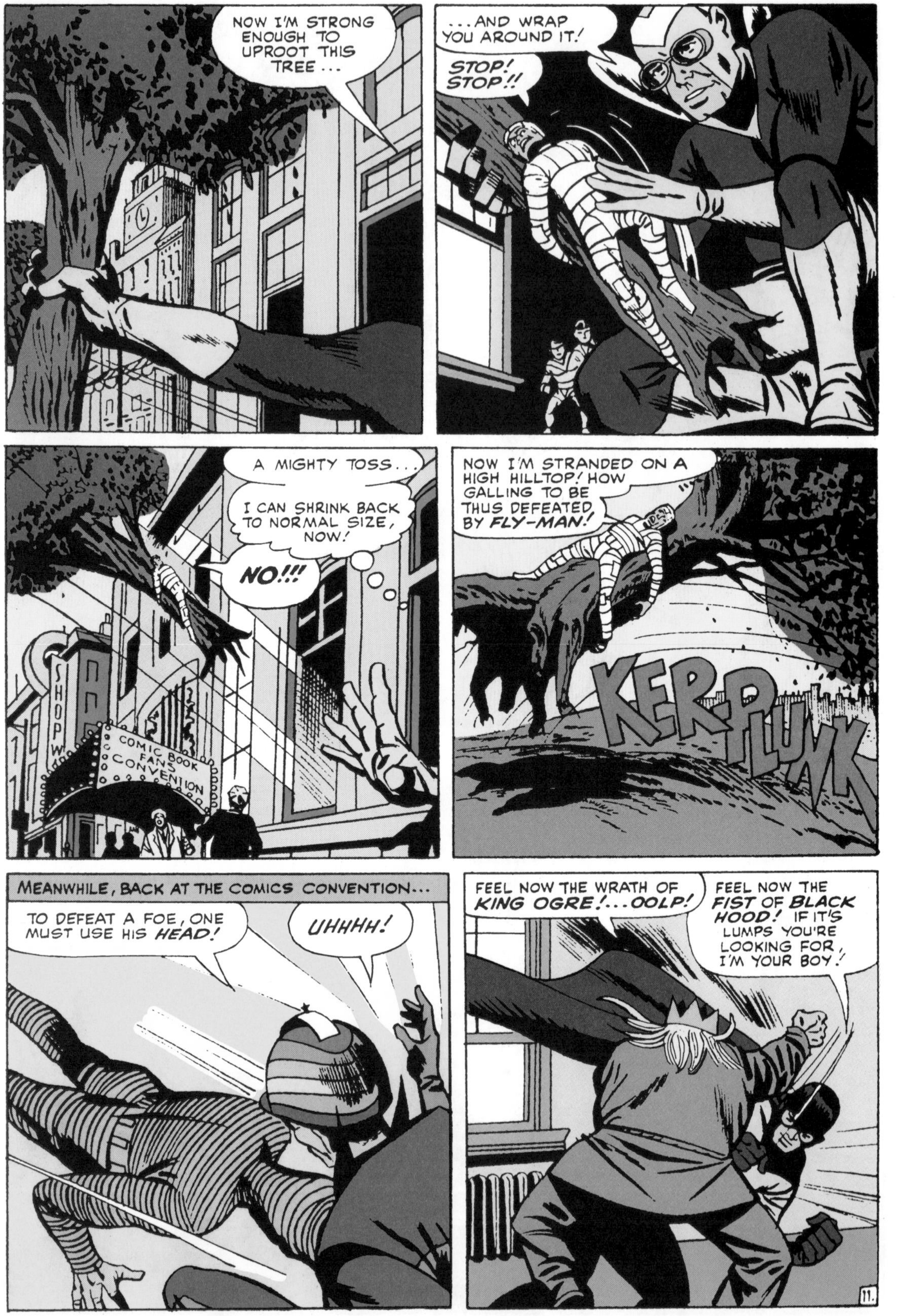
NOW I'M STRONG ENOUGH TO UPROOT THIS TREE ...
...AND WRAP YOU AROUND IT!
STOP! STOP!!
A MIGHTY TOSS...
I CAN SHRINK BACK TO NORMAL SIZE, NOW!
NO!!!
SHOP
COMIC BOOK FANS CONVENTION
NOW I'M STRANDED ON A HIGH HILLTOP! HOW GALLING TO BE THUS DEFEATED BY FLY-MAN!
KER-PLUNK
MEANWHILE, BACK AT THE COMICS CONVENTION...
TO DEFEAT A FOE, ONE MUST USE HIS HEAD!
UHHHH!
FEEL NOW THE WRATH OF KING OGRE!...OOLP!
FEEL NOW THE FIST OF BLACK HOOD! IF IT'S LUMPS YOU'RE LOOKING FOR, I'M YOUR BOY!
11.

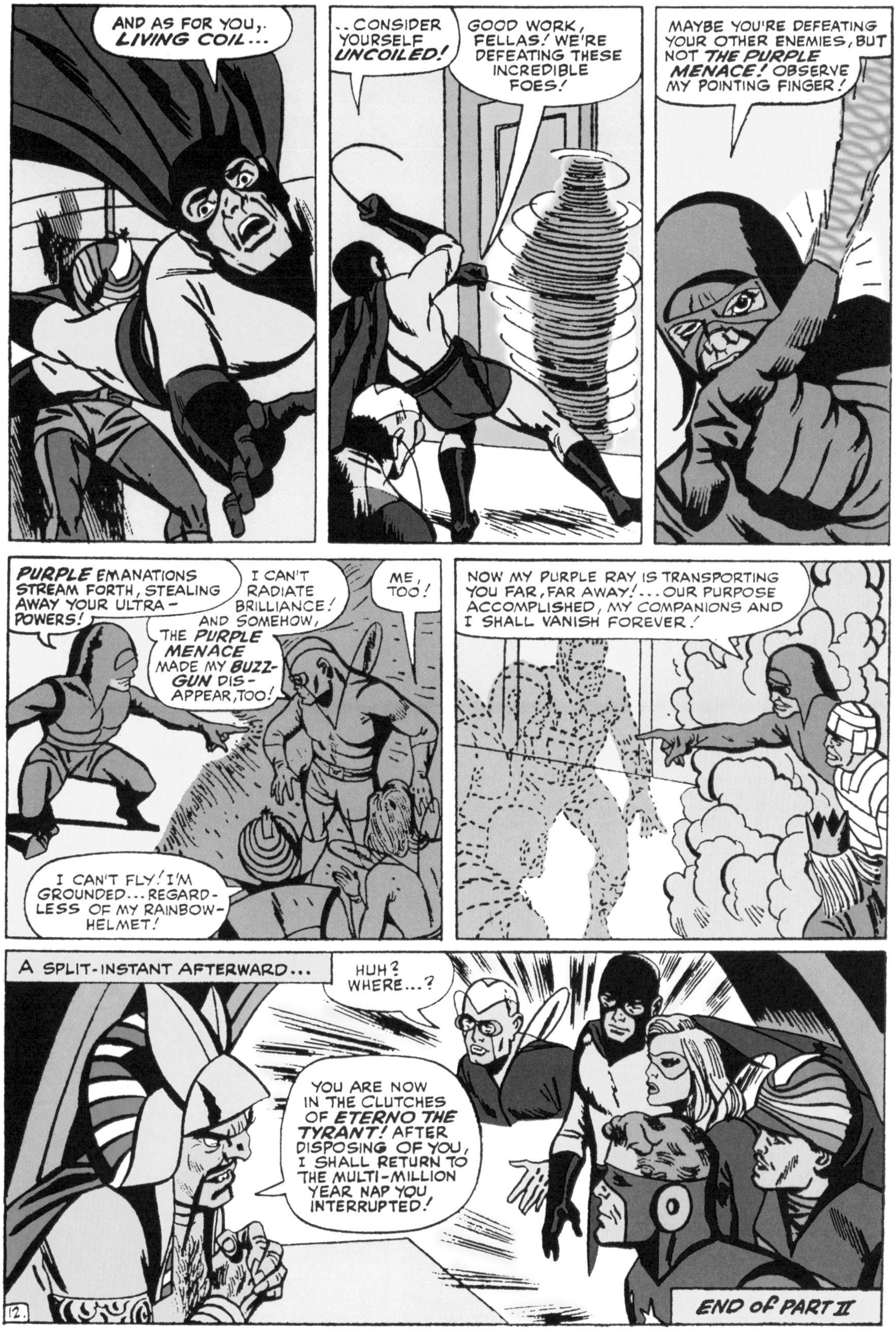
AND AS FOR YOU,. LIVING COIL...
..CONSIDER YOURSELF UNCOILED!
GOOD WORK, FELLAS! WE'RE DEFEATING THESE INCREDIBLE FOES!
MAYBE YOU'RE DEFEATING YOUR OTHER ENEMIES, BUT NOT THE PURPLE MENACE! OBSERVE MY POINTING FINGER!
PURPLE EMANATIONS STREAM FORTH, STEALING AWAY YOUR ULTRA-POWERS!
I CAN'T RADIATE BRILLIANCE! AND SOMEHOW, THE PURPLE MENACE MADE MY BUZZ-GUN DIS-APPEAR, TOO!
ME, TOO!
I CAN'T FLY! I'M GROUNDED... REGARD-LESS OF MY RAINBOW-HELMET!
NOW MY PURPLE RAY IS TRANSPORTING YOU FAR, FAR AWAY!... OUR PURPOSE ACCOMPLISHED, MY COMPANIONS AND I SHALL VANISH FOREVER!
A SPLIT-INSTANT AFTERWARD...
HUH? WHERE...?
YOU ARE NOW IN THE CLUTCHES OF ETERNO THE TYRANT! AFTER DISPOSING OF YOU, I SHALL RETURN TO THE MULTI-MILLION YEAR NAP YOU INTERRUPTED!
12.
END OF PART II

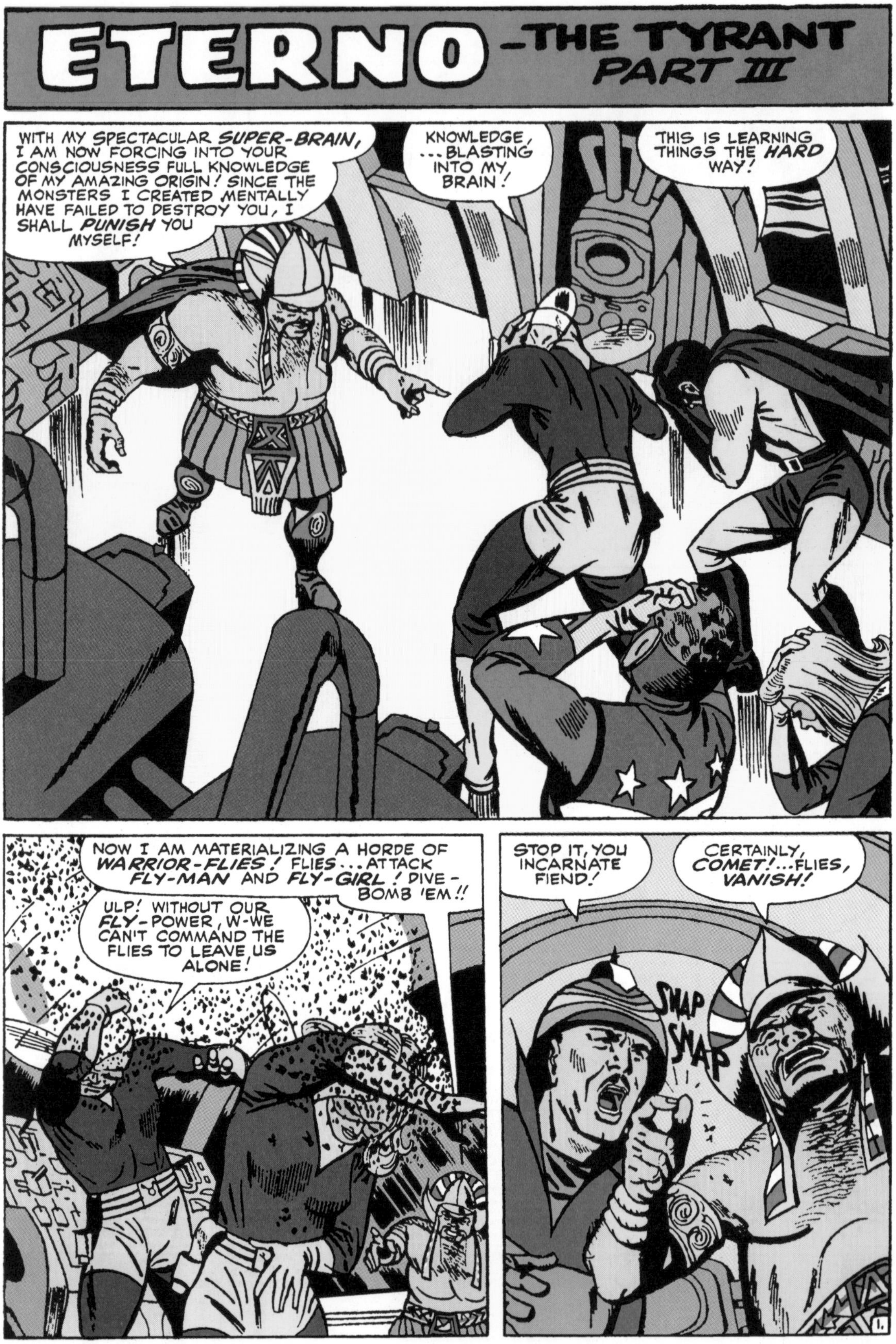
ETERNO -THE TYRANT PART III
WITH MY SPECTACULAR SUPER-BRAIN, I AM NOW FORCING INTO YOUR CONSCIOUSNESS FULL KNOWLEDGE OF MY AMAZING ORIGIN! SINCE THE MONSTERS I CREATED MENTALLY HAVE FAILED TO DESTROY YOU, I SHALL PUNISH YOU MYSELF!
KNOWLEDGE, ...BLASTING INTO MY BRAIN!
THIS IS LEARNING THINGS THE HARD WAY!
NOW I AM MATERIALIZING A HORDE OF WARRIOR-FLIES! FLIES... ATTACK FLY-MAN AND FLY-GIRL! DIVE-BOMB 'EM!!
ULP! WITHOUT OUR FLY-POWER, W-WE CAN'T COMMAND THE FLIES TO LEAVE US ALONE!
STOP IT, YOU INCARNATE FIEND!
CERTAINLY, COMET!... FLIES, VANISH!
SNAP SNAP
1.

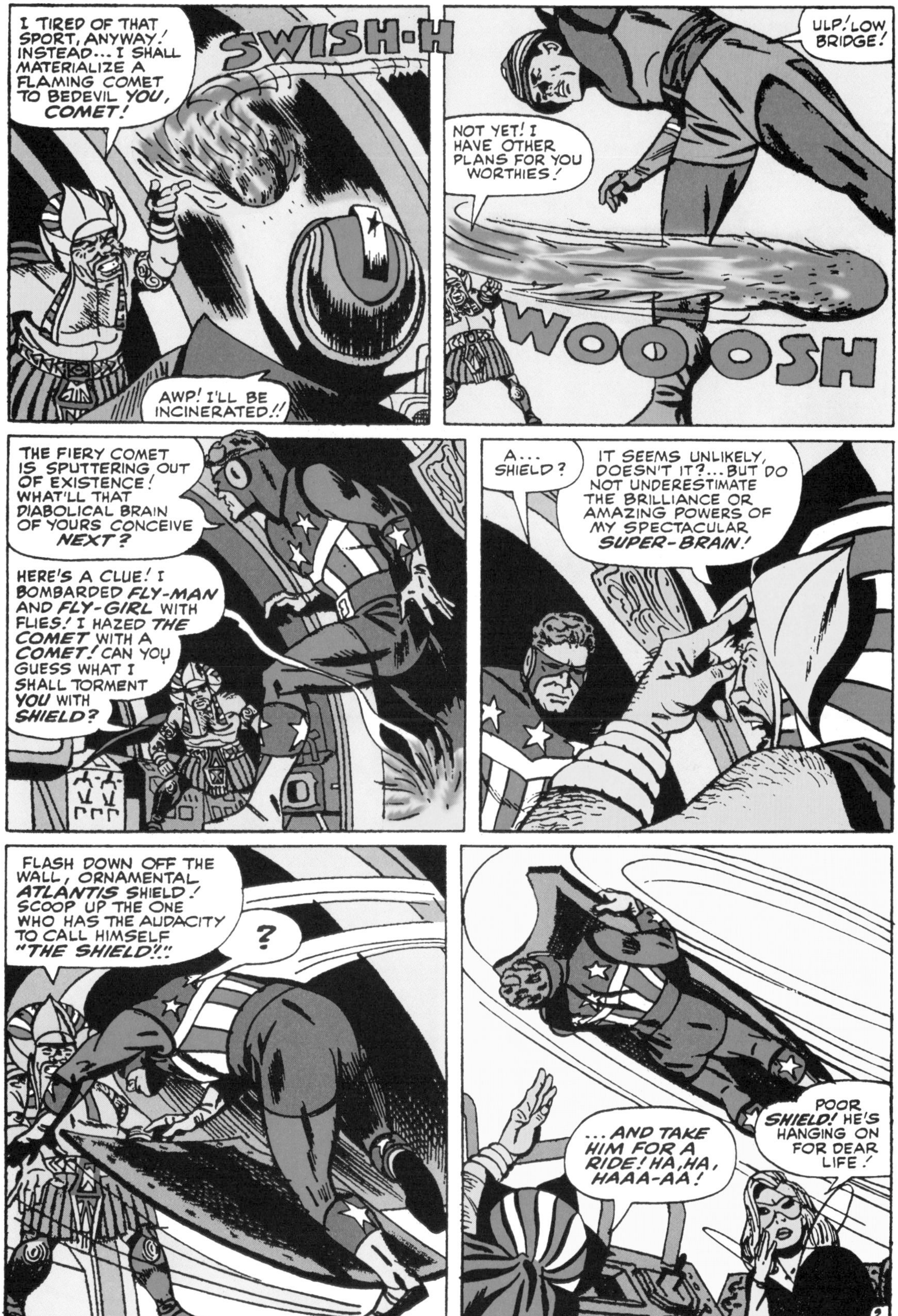
I TIRED OF THAT SPORT, ANYWAY! INSTEAD... I SHALL MATERIALIZE A FLAMING COMET TO BEDEVIL YOU, COMET!
SWISH-H
AWP! I'LL BE INCINERATED!!
ULP! LOW BRIDGE!
NOT YET! I HAVE OTHER PLANS FOR YOU WORTHIES!
WOOOSH
THE FIERY COMET IS SPUTTERING OUT OF EXISTENCE! WHAT'LL THAT DIABOLICAL BRAIN OF YOURS CONCEIVE NEXT?
HERE'S A CLUE! I BOMBARDED FLY-MAN AND FLY-GIRL WITH FLIES! I HAZED THE COMET WITH A COMET! CAN YOU GUESS WHAT I SHALL TORMENT YOU WITH SHIELD?
A... SHIELD?
IT SEEMS UNLIKELY, DOESN'T IT?... BUT DO NOT UNDERESTIMATE THE BRILLIANCE OR AMAZING POWERS OF MY SPECTACULAR SUPER-BRAIN!
FLASH DOWN OFF THE WALL, ORNAMENTAL ATLANTIS SHIELD! SCOOP UP THE ONE WHO HAS THE AUDACITY TO CALL HIMSELF "THE SHIELD!!"
?
...AND TAKE HIM FOR A RIDE! HA, HA, HAAA-AA!
POOR SHIELD! HE'S HANGING ON FOR DEAR LIFE!
2.

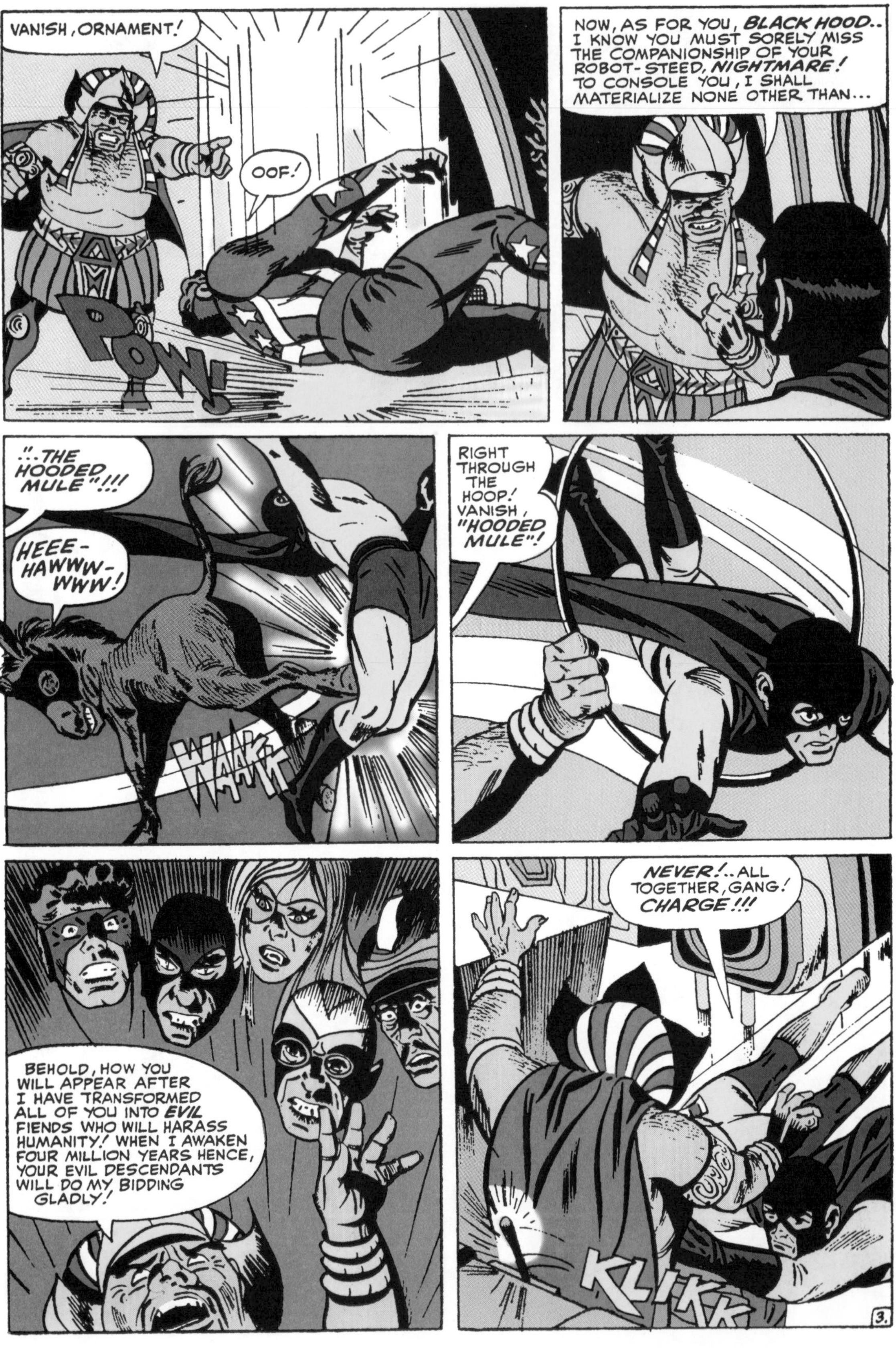
VANISH, ORNAMENT!
OOF!
POW!
NOW, AS FOR YOU, BLACK HOOD.. I KNOW YOU MUST SORELY MISS THE COMPANIONSHIP OF YOUR ROBOT-STEED, NIGHTMARE! TO CONSOLE YOU, I SHALL MATERIALIZE NONE OTHER THAN...
"..THE HOODED MULE"!!!
HEEE-HAWWW-WWW!
WAAKK
RIGHT THROUGH THE HOOP! VANISH, "HOODED MULE"!
BEHOLD, HOW YOU WILL APPEAR AFTER I HAVE TRANSFORMED ALL OF YOU INTO EVIL FIENDS WHO WILL HARASS HUMANITY! WHEN I AWAKEN FOUR MILLION YEARS HENCE, YOUR EVIL DESCENDANTS WILL DO MY BIDDING GLADLY!
NEVER!.. ALL TOGETHER, GANG! CHARGE!!!
KLIKK
3.

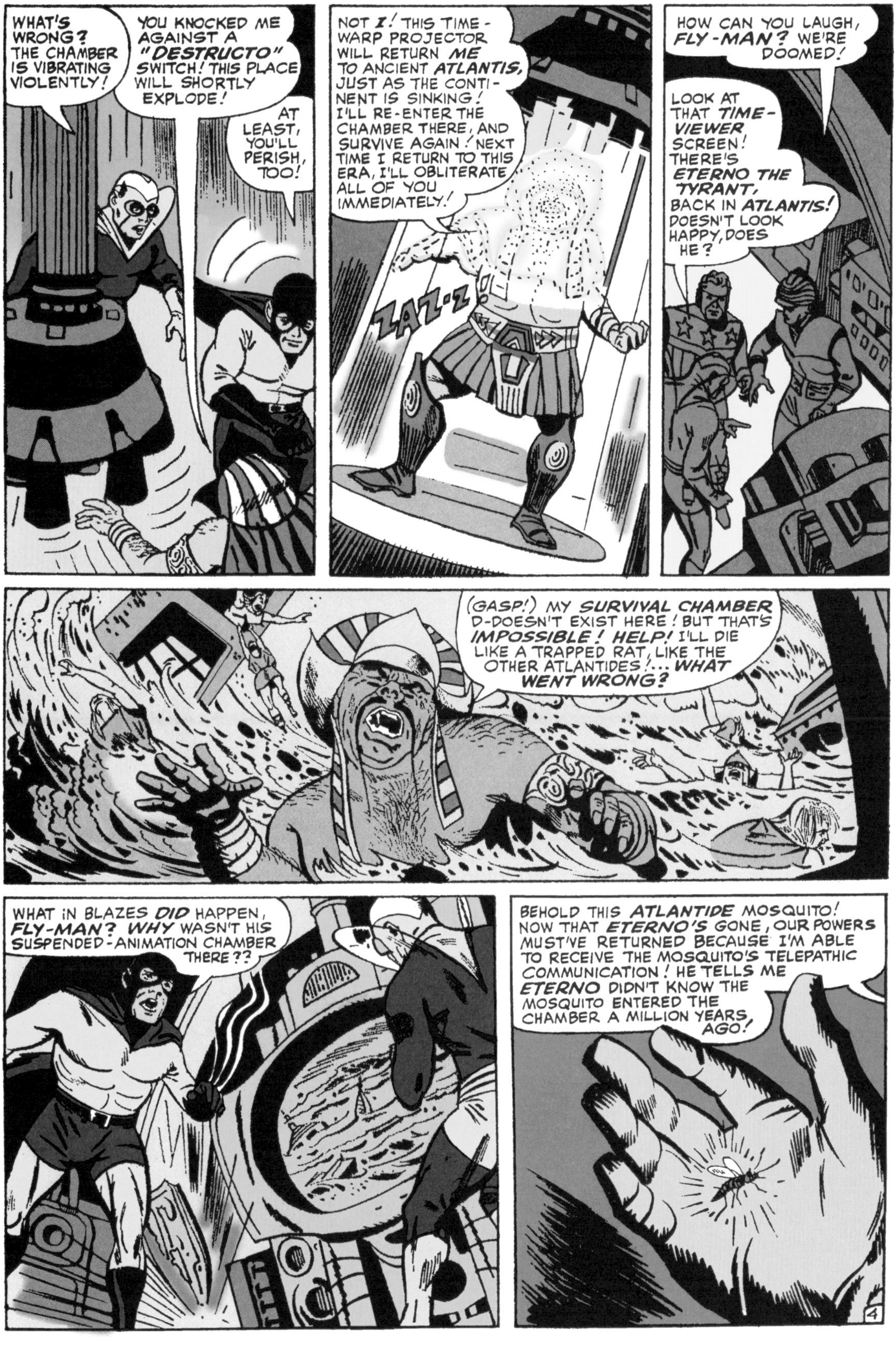
WHAT'S WRONG? THE CHAMBER IS VIBRATING VIOLENTLY!
YOU KNOCKED ME AGAINST A "DESTRUCTO" SWITCH! THIS PLACE WILL SHORTLY EXPLODE!
AT LEAST, YOU'LL PERISH, TOO!
NOT I! THIS TIME-WARP PROJECTOR WILL RETURN ME TO ANCIENT ATLANTIS, JUST AS THE CONTINENT IS SINKING! I'LL RE-ENTER THE CHAMBER THERE, AND SURVIVE AGAIN! NEXT TIME I RETURN TO THIS ERA, I'LL OBLITERATE ALL OF YOU IMMEDIATELY!
ZAZ-Z
HOW CAN YOU LAUGH, FLY-MAN? WE'RE DOOMED!
LOOK AT THAT TIME-VIEWER SCREEN! THERE'S ETERNO THE TYRANT, BACK IN ATLANTIS! DOESN'T LOOK HAPPY, DOES HE?
(GASP!) MY SURVIVAL CHAMBER D-DOESN'T EXIST HERE! BUT THAT'S IMPOSSIBLE! HELP! I'LL DIE LIKE A TRAPPED RAT, LIKE THE OTHER ATLANTIDES!... WHAT WENT WRONG?
WHAT IN BLAZES DID HAPPEN, FLY-MAN? WHY WASN'T HIS SUSPENDED-ANIMATION CHAMBER THERE??
BEHOLD THIS ATLANTIDE MOSQUITO! NOW THAT ETERNO'S GONE, OUR POWERS MUST'VE RETURNED BECAUSE I'M ABLE TO RECEIVE THE MOSQUITO'S TELEPATHIC COMMUNICATION! HE TELLS ME ETERNO DIDN'T KNOW THE MOSQUITO ENTERED THE CHAMBER A MILLION YEARS AGO!
4

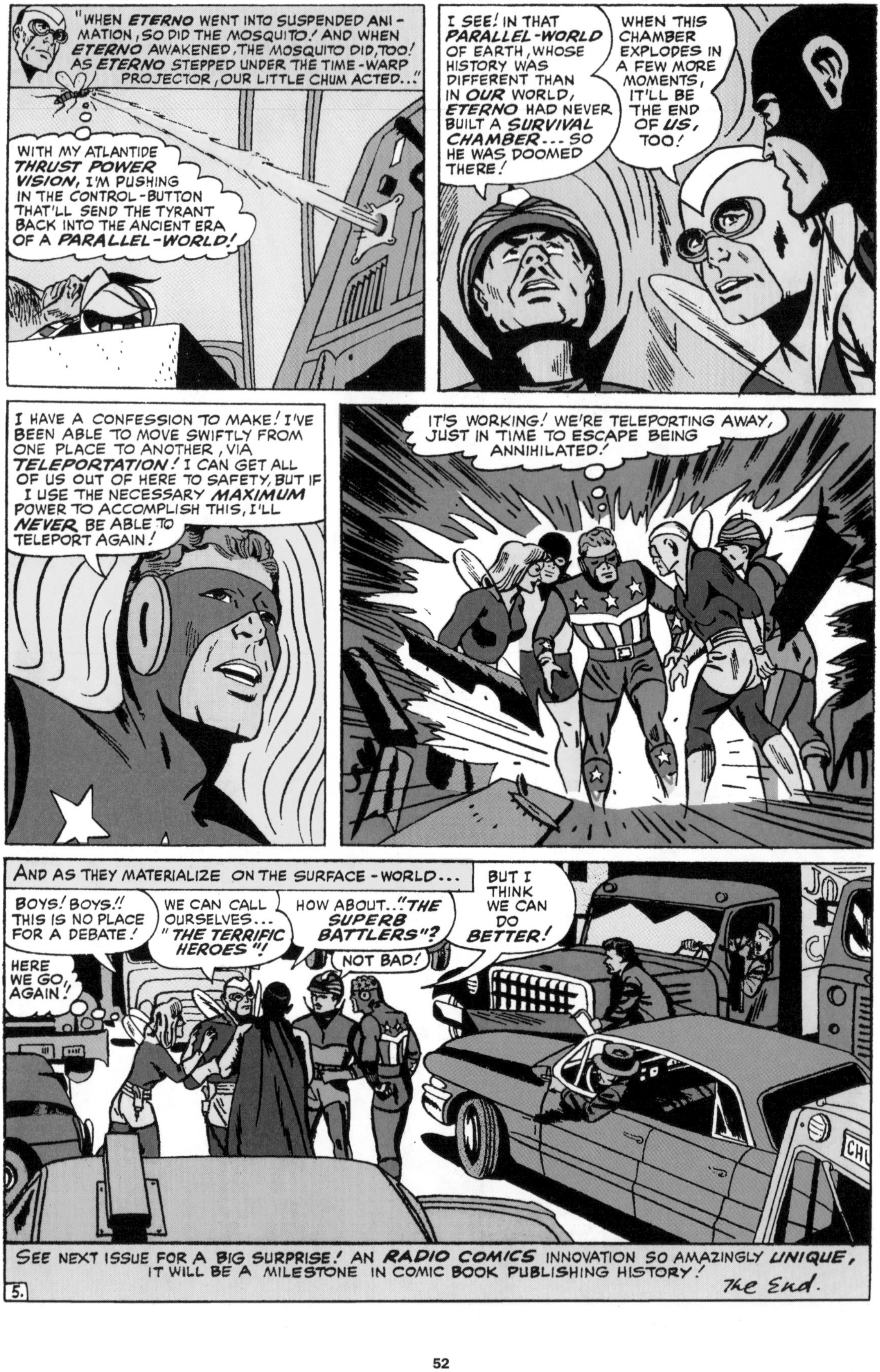
"WHEN ETERNO WENT INTO SUSPENDED ANI-MATION, SO DID THE MOSQUITO! AND WHEN ETERNO AWAKENED, THE MOSQUITO DID, TOO! AS ETERNO STEPPED UNDER THE TIME-WARP PROJECTOR, OUR LITTLE CHUM ACTED..."
WITH MY ATLANTIDE THRUST POWER VISION, I'M PUSHING IN THE CONTROL-BUTTON THAT'LL SEND THE TYRANT BACK INTO THE ANCIENT ERA OF A PARALLEL-WORLD!
I SEE! IN THAT PARALLEL-WORLD OF EARTH, WHOSE HISTORY WAS DIFFERENT THAN IN OUR WORLD, ETERNO HAD NEVER BUILT A SURVIVAL CHAMBER... SO HE WAS DOOMED THERE!
WHEN THIS CHAMBER EXPLODES IN A FEW MORE MOMENTS, IT'LL BE THE END OF US, TOO!
I HAVE A CONFESSION TO MAKE! I'VE BEEN ABLE TO MOVE SWIFTLY FROM ONE PLACE TO ANOTHER, VIA TELEPORTATION! I CAN GET ALL OF US OUT OF HERE TO SAFETY, BUT IF I USE THE NECESSARY MAXIMUM POWER TO ACCOMPLISH THIS, I'LL NEVER BE ABLE TO TELEPORT AGAIN!
IT'S WORKING! WE'RE TELEPORTING AWAY, JUST IN TIME TO ESCAPE BEING ANNIHILATED!
AND AS THEY MATERIALIZE ON THE SURFACE-WORLD...
BOYS! BOYS!! THIS IS NO PLACE FOR A DEBATE!
HERE WE GO, AGAIN!
WE CAN CALL OURSELVES... "THE TERRIFIC HEROES"!
HOW ABOUT..."THE SUPERB BATTLERS"?
NOT BAD!
BUT I THINK WE CAN DO BETTER!
SEE NEXT ISSUE FOR A BIG SURPRISE! AN RADIO COMICS INNOVATION SO AMAZINGLY UNIQUE, IT WILL BE A MILESTONE IN COMIC BOOK PUBLISHING HISTORY!
5.
The End.

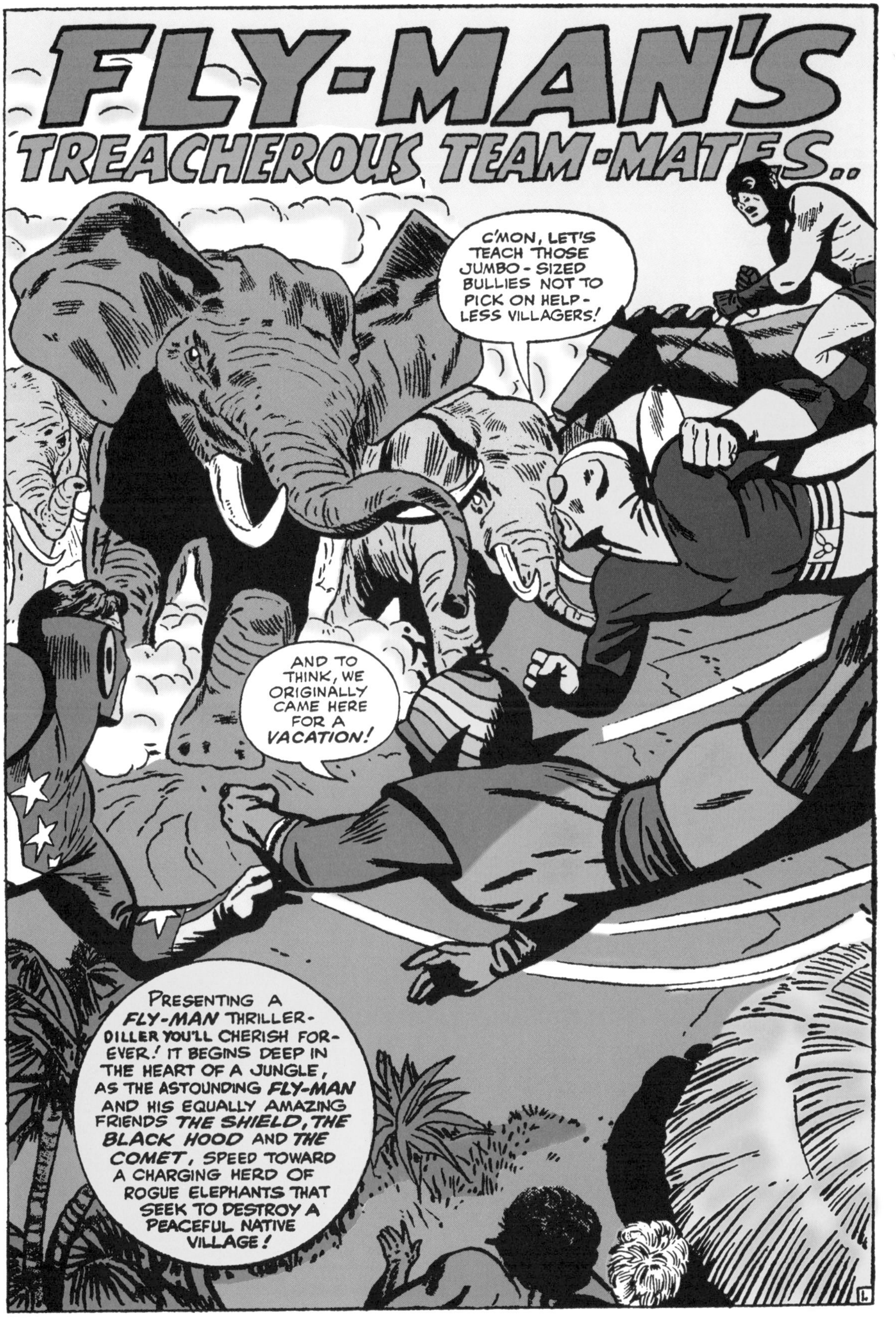
FLY-MAN'S
TREACHEROUS TEAM-MATES..
C'MON, LET'S TEACH THOSE JUMBO-SIZED BULLIES NOT TO PICK ON HELP-LESS VILLAGERS!
AND TO THINK, WE ORIGINALLY CAME HERE FOR A VACATION!
PRESENTING A FLY-MAN THRILLER-DILLER YOU'LL CHERISH FOR-EVER! IT BEGINS DEEP IN THE HEART OF A JUNGLE, AS THE ASTOUNDING FLY-MAN AND HIS EQUALLY AMAZING FRIENDS THE SHIELD, THE BLACK HOOD AND THE COMET, SPEED TOWARD A CHARGING HERD OF ROGUE ELEPHANTS THAT SEEK TO DESTROY A PEACEFUL NATIVE VILLAGE!
1

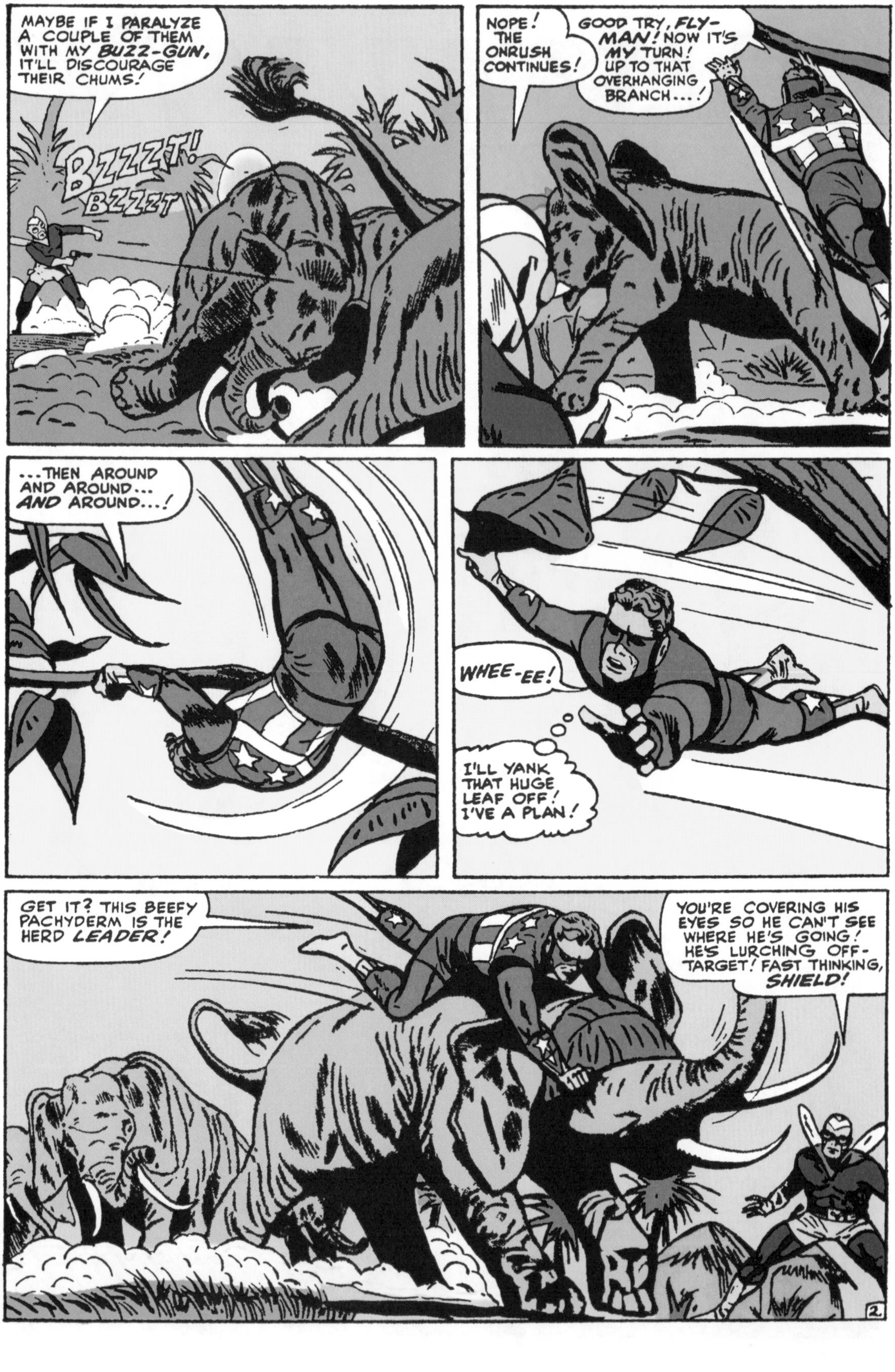
MAYBE IF I PARALYZE A COUPLE OF THEM WITH MY BUZZ-GUN, IT'LL DISCOURAGE THEIR CHUMS!
BZZZT! BZZZT
NOPE! THE ONRUSH CONTINUES!
GOOD TRY, FLY-MAN! NOW IT'S MY TURN! UP TO THAT OVERHANGING BRANCH...!
...THEN AROUND AND AROUND... AND AROUND...!
WHEE-EE!
I'LL YANK THAT HUGE LEAF OFF! I'VE A PLAN!
GET IT? THIS BEEFY PACHYDERM IS THE HERD LEADER!
YOU'RE COVERING HIS EYES SO HE CAN'T SEE WHERE HE'S GOING! HE'S LURCHING OFF-TARGET! FAST THINKING, SHIELD!
2

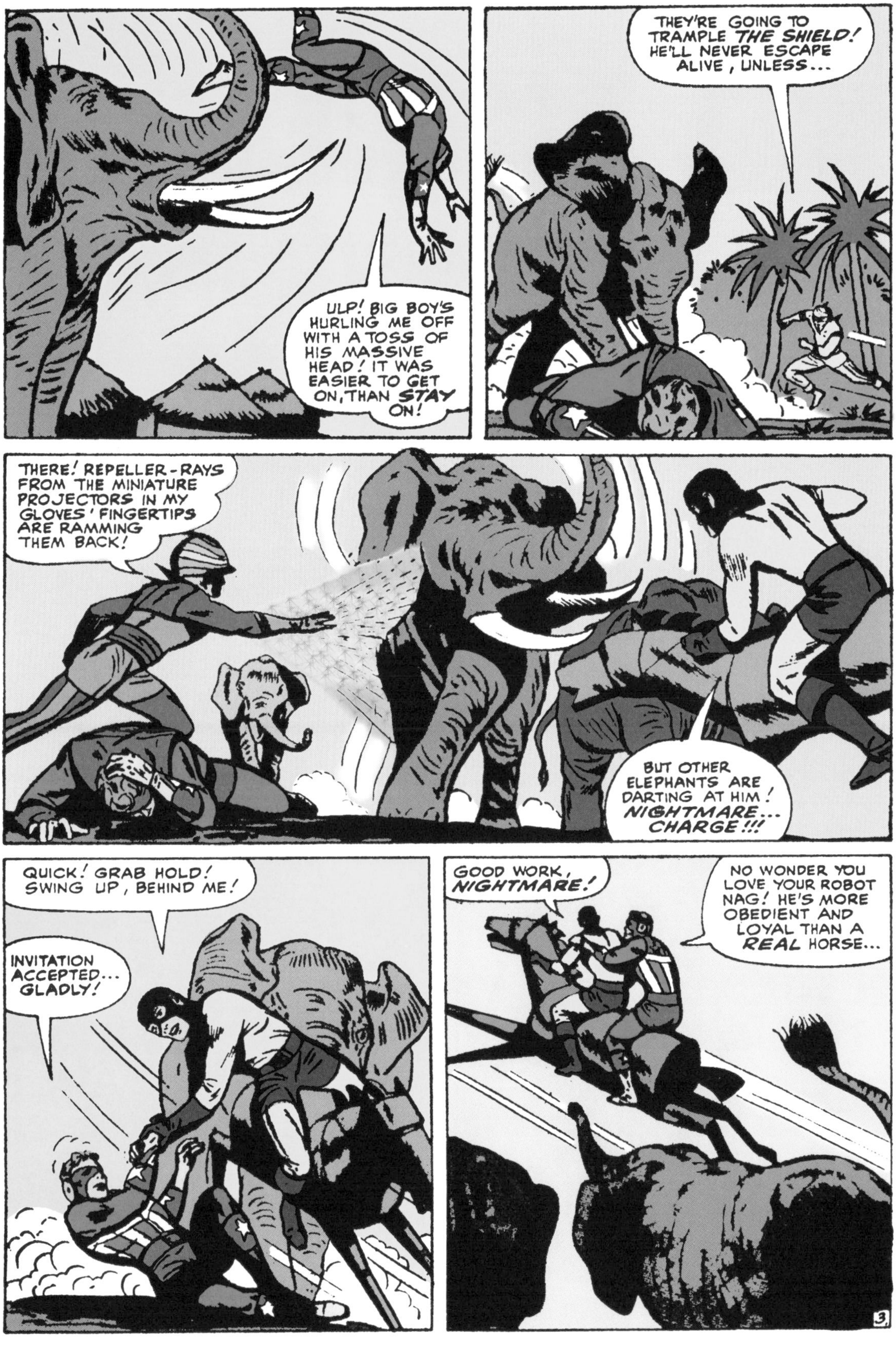
ULP! BIG BOY'S HURLING ME OFF WITH A TOSS OF HIS MASSIVE HEAD! IT WAS EASIER TO GET ON, THAN STAY ON!
THEY'RE GOING TO TRAMPLE THE SHIELD! HE'LL NEVER ESCAPE ALIVE, UNLESS...
THERE! REPELLER-RAYS FROM THE MINIATURE PROJECTORS IN MY GLOVES' FINGERTIPS ARE RAMMING THEM BACK!
BUT OTHER ELEPHANTS ARE DARTING AT HIM! NIGHTMARE... CHARGE!!!
QUICK! GRAB HOLD! SWING UP, BEHIND ME!
INVITATION ACCEPTED... GLADLY!
GOOD WORK, NIGHTMARE!
NO WONDER YOU LOVE YOUR ROBOT NAG! HE'S MORE OBEDIENT AND LOYAL THAN A REAL HORSE...
3

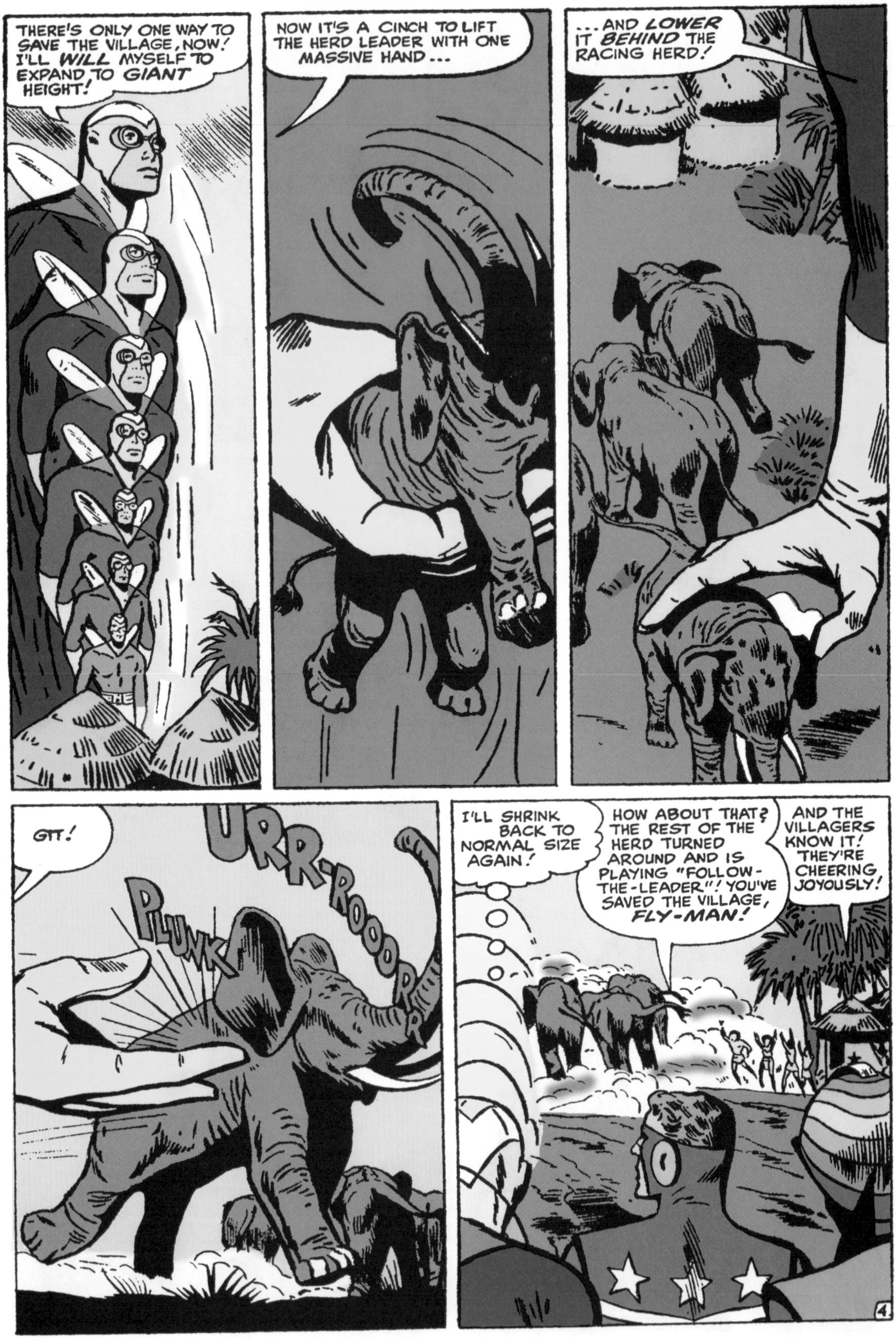
THERE'S ONLY ONE WAY TO SAVE THE VILLAGE, NOW! I'LL WILL MYSELF TO EXPAND TO GIANT HEIGHT!
NOW IT'S A CINCH TO LIFT THE HERD LEADER WITH ONE MASSIVE HAND...
...AND LOWER IT BEHIND THE RACING HERD!
GTT!
URR-ROOOR-R
PLUNK!
I'LL SHRINK BACK TO NORMAL SIZE AGAIN!
HOW ABOUT THAT? THE REST OF THE HERD TURNED AROUND AND IS PLAYING "FOLLOW-THE-LEADER"! YOU'VE SAVED THE VILLAGE, FLY-MAN!
AND THE VILLAGERS KNOW IT! THEY'RE CHEERING JOYOUSLY!
4

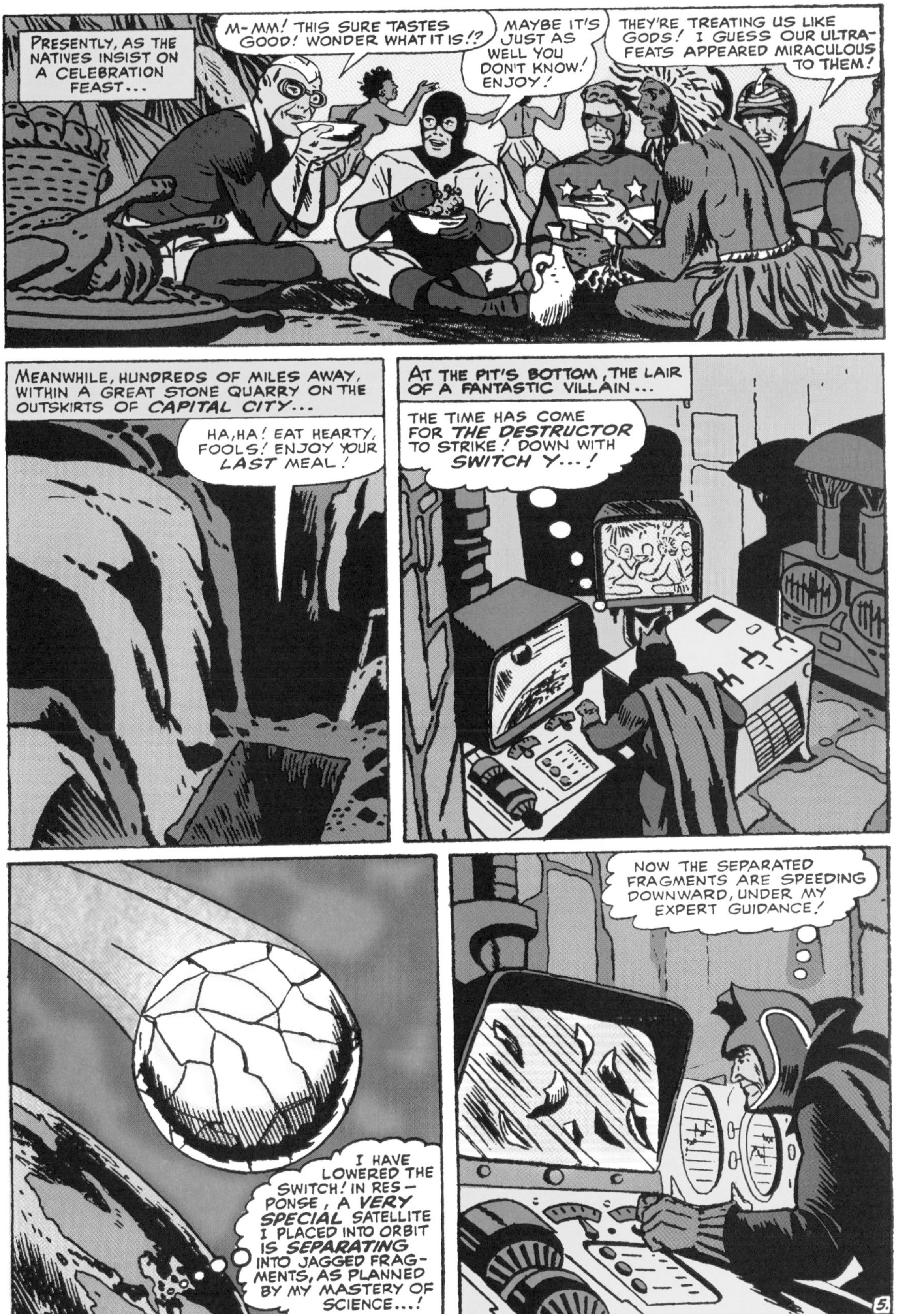
PRESENTLY, AS THE NATIVES INSIST ON A CELEBRATION FEAST...
M-MM! THIS SURE TASTES GOOD! WONDER WHAT IT IS!?
MAYBE IT'S JUST AS WELL YOU DON'T KNOW! ENJOY!
THEY'RE TREATING US LIKE GODS! I GUESS OUR ULTRA-FEATS APPEARED MIRACULOUS TO THEM!
MEANWHILE, HUNDREDS OF MILES AWAY, WITHIN A GREAT STONE QUARRY ON THE OUTSKIRTS OF CAPITAL CITY...
HA, HA! EAT HEARTY, FOOLS! ENJOY YOUR LAST MEAL!
AT THE PIT'S BOTTOM, THE LAIR OF A FANTASTIC VILLAIN...
THE TIME HAS COME FOR THE DESTRUCTOR TO STRIKE! DOWN WITH SWITCH Y...!
I HAVE LOWERED THE SWITCH! IN RES-PONSE, A VERY SPECIAL SATELLITE I PLACED INTO ORBIT IS SEPARATING INTO JAGGED FRAG-MENTS, AS PLANNED BY MY MASTERY OF SCIENCE...!
NOW THE SEPARATED FRAGMENTS ARE SPEEDING DOWNWARD, UNDER MY EXPERT GUIDANCE!
5.

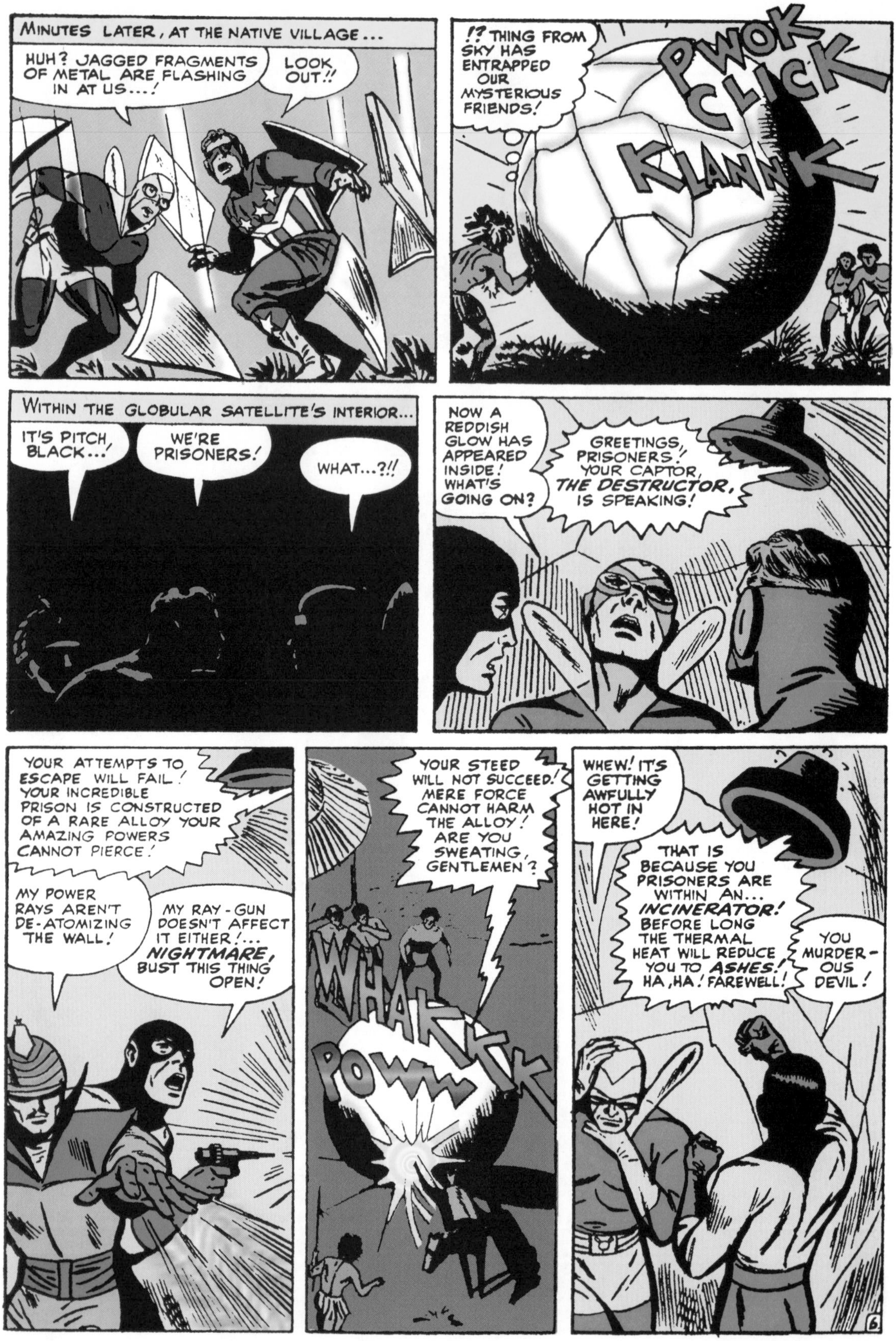

MINUTES LATER, AT THE NATIVE VILLAGE...
HUH? JAGGED FRAGMENTS OF METAL ARE FLASHING IN AT US...!
LOOK OUT!!
!? THING FROM SKY HAS ENTRAPPED OUR MYSTERIOUS FRIENDS!
PWOK
CLICK
KLANNK
WITHIN THE GLOBULAR SATELLITE'S INTERIOR...
IT'S PITCH BLACK...!
WE'RE PRISONERS!
WHAT...?!!
NOW A REDDISH GLOW HAS APPEARED INSIDE! WHAT'S GOING ON?
GREETINGS, PRISONERS! YOUR CAPTOR, THE DESTRUCTOR, IS SPEAKING!
YOUR ATTEMPTS TO ESCAPE WILL FAIL! YOUR INCREDIBLE PRISON IS CONSTRUCTED OF A RARE ALLOY YOUR AMAZING POWERS CANNOT PIERCE!
MY POWER RAYS AREN'T DE-ATOMIZING THE WALL!
MY RAY-GUN DOESN'T AFFECT IT EITHER!... NIGHTMARE, BUST THIS THING OPEN!
YOUR STEED WILL NOT SUCCEED! MERE FORCE CANNOT HARM THE ALLOY! ARE YOU SWEATING, GENTLEMEN?
WHAKKK
POWW
WHEW! IT'S GETTING AWFULLY HOT IN HERE!
THAT IS BECAUSE YOU PRISONERS ARE WITHIN AN... INCINERATOR! BEFORE LONG THE THERMAL HEAT WILL REDUCE YOU TO ASHES! HA, HA! FAREWELL!
YOU MURDER-OUS DEVIL!
6

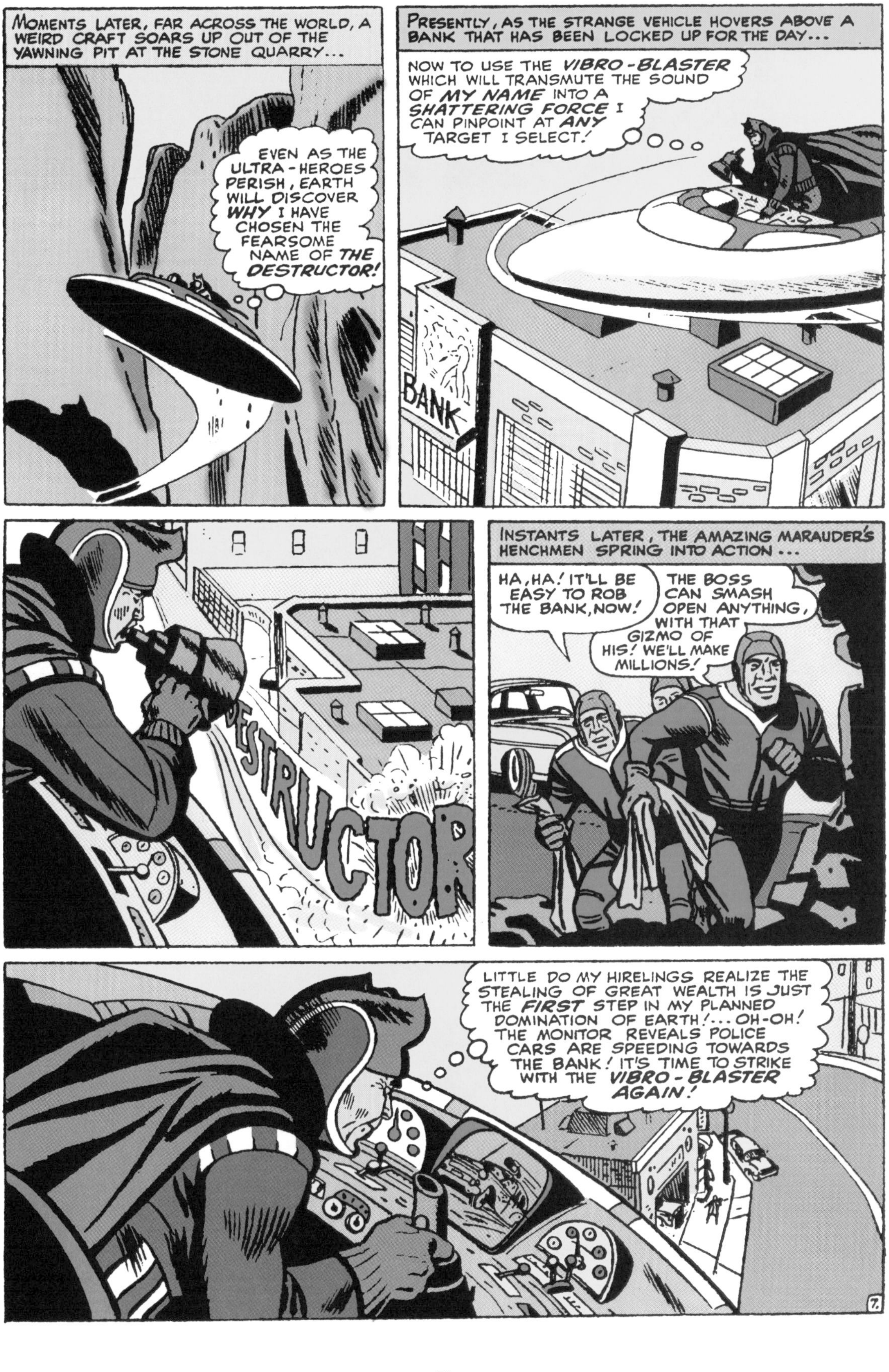
MOMENTS LATER, FAR ACROSS THE WORLD, A WEIRD CRAFT SOARS UP OUT OF THE YAWNING PIT AT THE STONE QUARRY...
EVEN AS THE ULTRA-HEROES PERISH, EARTH WILL DISCOVER WHY I HAVE CHOSEN THE FEARSOME NAME OF THE DESTRUCTOR!
PRESENTLY, AS THE STRANGE VEHICLE HOVERS ABOVE A BANK THAT HAS BEEN LOCKED UP FOR THE DAY...
NOW TO USE THE VIBRO-BLASTER WHICH WILL TRANSMUTE THE SOUND OF MY NAME INTO A SHATTERING FORCE I CAN PINPOINT AT ANY TARGET I SELECT!
BANK
DESTRUCTOR
INSTANTS LATER, THE AMAZING MARAUDER'S HENCHMEN SPRING INTO ACTION...
HA, HA! IT'LL BE EASY TO ROB THE BANK, NOW!
THE BOSS CAN SMASH OPEN ANYTHING, WITH THAT GIZMO OF HIS! WE'LL MAKE MILLIONS!
LITTLE DO MY HIRELINGS REALIZE THE STEALING OF GREAT WEALTH IS JUST THE FIRST STEP IN MY PLANNED DOMINATION OF EARTH!... OH-OH! THE MONITOR REVEALS POLICE CARS ARE SPEEDING TOWARDS THE BANK! IT'S TIME TO STRIKE WITH THE VIBRO-BLASTER AGAIN!
7.

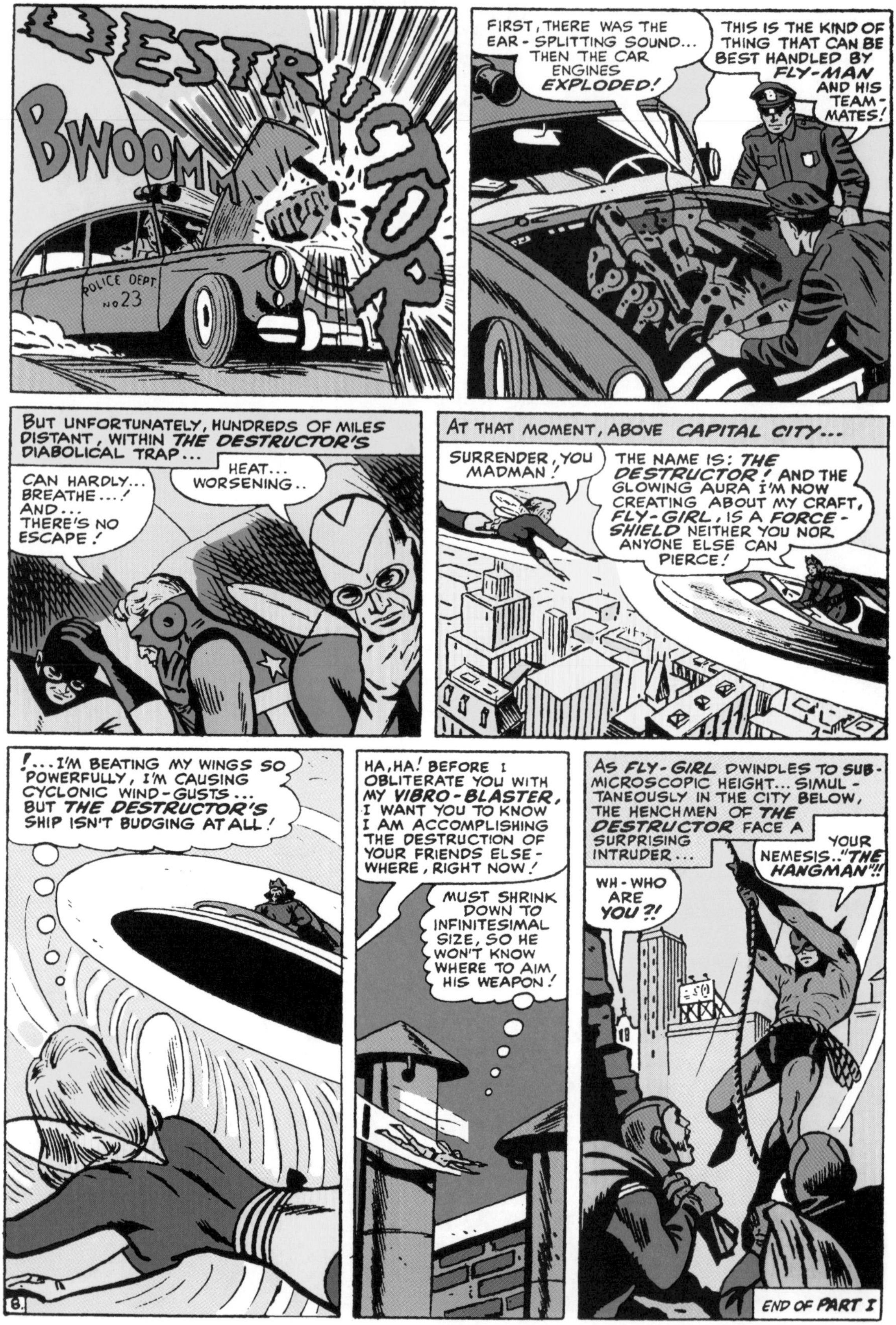
DESTRUCTOR
BWOOMM
FIRST, THERE WAS THE EAR-SPLITTING SOUND... THEN THE CAR ENGINES EXPLODED!
THIS IS THE KIND OF THING THAT CAN BE BEST HANDLED BY FLY-MAN AND HIS TEAM-MATES!
POLICE DEPT. NO 23
BUT UNFORTUNATELY, HUNDREDS OF MILES DISTANT, WITHIN THE DESTRUCTOR'S DIABOLICAL TRAP...
CAN HARDLY... BREATHE...! AND... THERE'S NO ESCAPE!
HEAT... WORSENING..
AT THAT MOMENT, ABOVE CAPITAL CITY...
SURRENDER, YOU MADMAN!
THE NAME IS: THE DESTRUCTOR! AND THE GLOWING AURA I'M NOW CREATING ABOUT MY CRAFT, FLY-GIRL, IS A FORCE-SHIELD NEITHER YOU NOR ANYONE ELSE CAN PIERCE!
!... I'M BEATING MY WINGS SO POWERFULLY, I'M CAUSING CYCLONIC WIND-GUSTS... BUT THE DESTRUCTOR'S SHIP ISN'T BUDGING AT ALL!
8.
HA, HA! BEFORE I OBLITERATE YOU WITH MY VIBRO-BLASTER, I WANT YOU TO KNOW I AM ACCOMPLISHING THE DESTRUCTION OF YOUR FRIENDS ELSE-WHERE, RIGHT NOW!
MUST SHRINK DOWN TO INFINITESIMAL SIZE, SO HE WON'T KNOW WHERE TO AIM HIS WEAPON!
AS FLY-GIRL DWINDLES TO SUB-MICROSCOPIC HEIGHT... SIMUL-TANEOUSLY IN THE CITY BELOW, THE HENCHMEN OF THE DESTRUCTOR FACE A SURPRISING INTRUDER...
YOUR NEMESIS.."THE HANGMAN"!!
WH-WHO ARE YOU?!
END OF PART I

FLY-MAN'S TREACHEROUS TEAM-MATES PART TWO

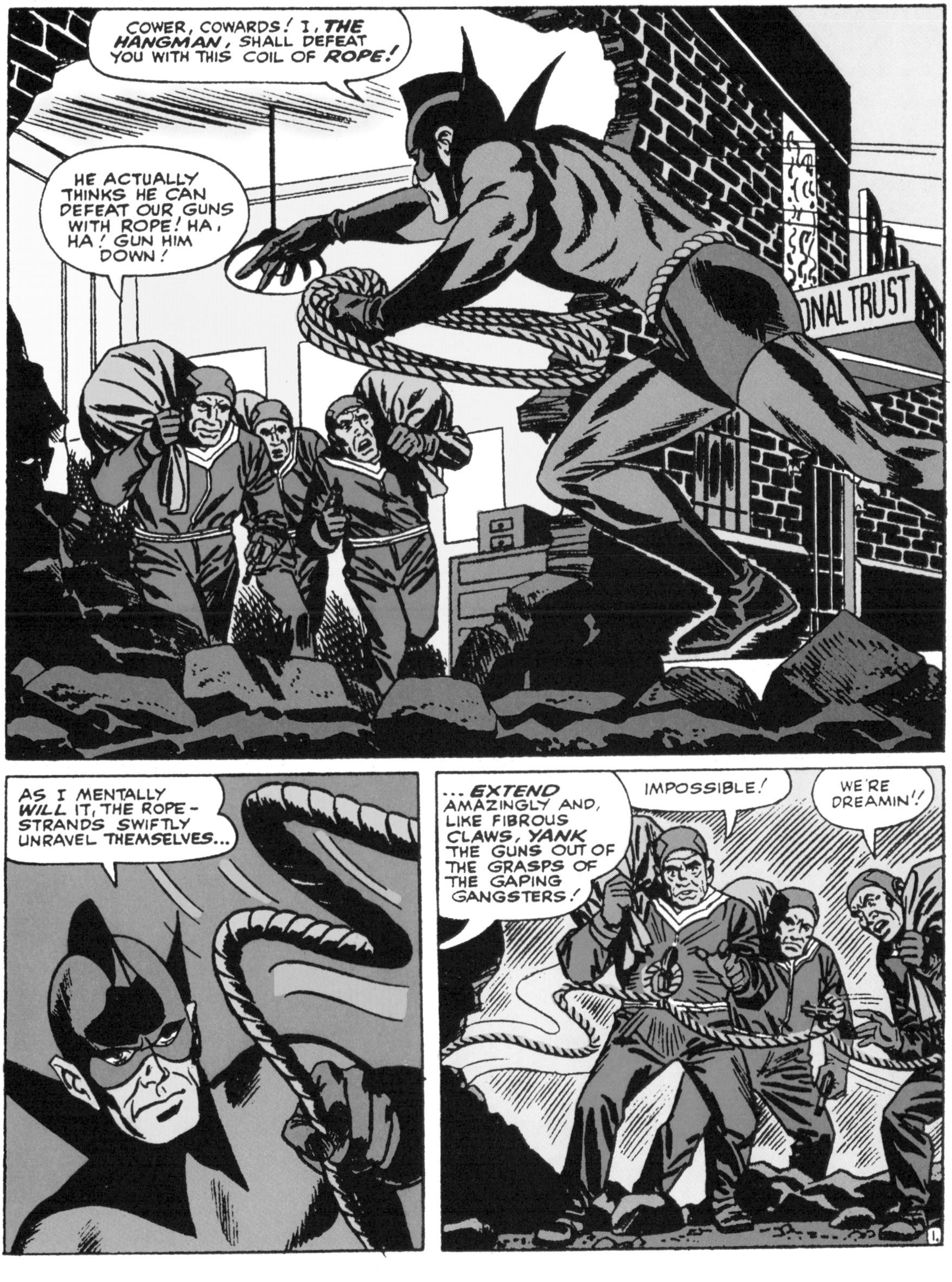
COWER, COWARDS! I, THE HANGMAN, SHALL DEFEAT YOU WITH THIS COIL OF ROPE!
HE ACTUALLY THINKS HE CAN DEFEAT OUR GUNS WITH ROPE! HA, HA! GUN HIM DOWN!
AS I MENTALLY WILL IT, THE ROPE-STRANDS SWIFTLY UNRAVEL THEMSELVES...
...EXTEND AMAZINGLY AND, LIKE FIBROUS CLAWS, YANK THE GUNS OUT OF THE GRASPS OF THE GAPING GANGSTERS!
IMPOSSIBLE!
WE'RE DREAMIN'!

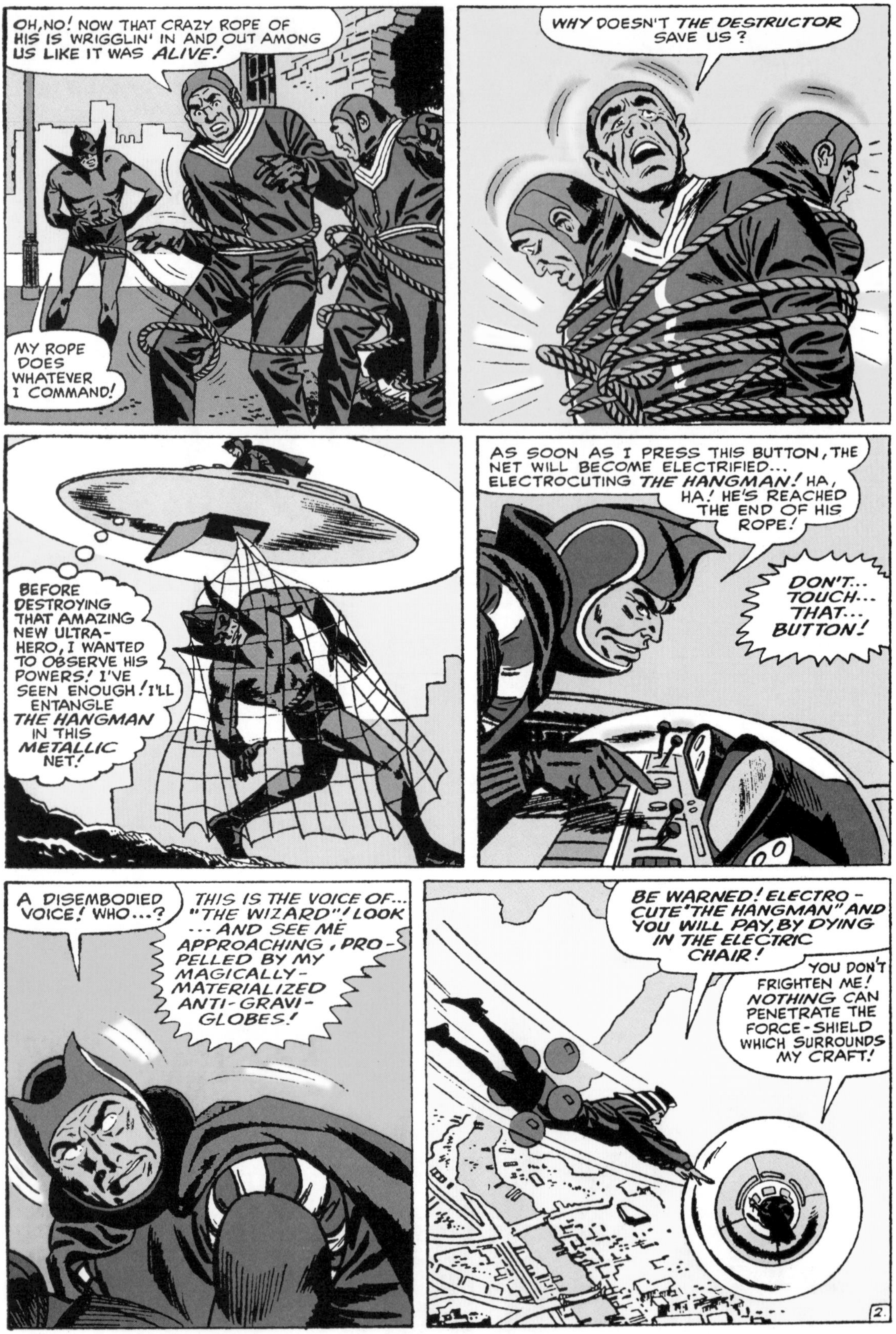
OH, NO! NOW THAT CRAZY ROPE OF HIS IS WRIGGLIN' IN AND OUT AMONG US LIKE IT WAS ALIVE!
MY ROPE DOES WHATEVER I COMMAND!
WHY DOESN'T THE DESTRUCTOR SAVE US?
BEFORE DESTROYING THAT AMAZING NEW ULTRA-HERO, I WANTED TO OBSERVE HIS POWERS! I'VE SEEN ENOUGH! I'LL ENTANGLE THE HANGMAN IN THIS METALLIC NET!
AS SOON AS I PRESS THIS BUTTON, THE NET WILL BECOME ELECTRIFIED... ELECTROCUTING THE HANGMAN! HA, HA! HE'S REACHED THE END OF HIS ROPE!
DON'T... TOUCH... THAT... BUTTON!
A DISEMBODIED VOICE! WHO...?
THIS IS THE VOICE OF... "THE WIZARD"! LOOK ... AND SEE ME APPROACHING, PRO-PELLED BY MY MAGICALLY-MATERIALIZED ANTI-GRAVI-GLOBES!
BE WARNED! ELECTRO-CUTE "THE HANGMAN" AND YOU WILL PAY, BY DYING IN THE ELECTRIC CHAIR!
YOU DON'T FRIGHTEN ME! NOTHING CAN PENETRATE THE FORCE-SHIELD WHICH SURROUNDS MY CRAFT!
2.

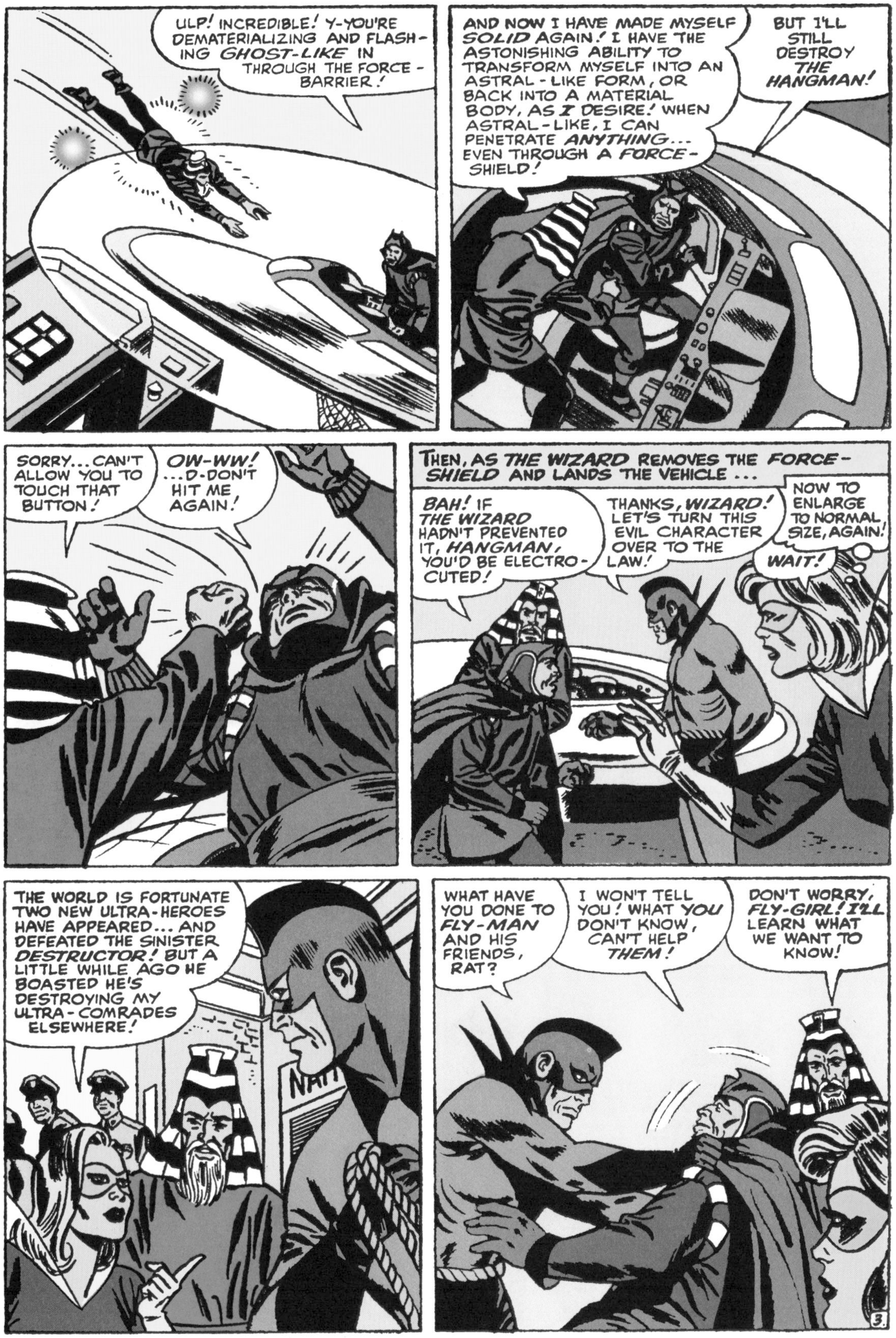

ULP! INCREDIBLE! Y-YOU'RE DEMATERIALIZING AND FLASHING GHOST-LIKE IN THROUGH THE FORCE-BARRIER!
AND NOW I HAVE MADE MYSELF SOLID AGAIN! I HAVE THE ASTONISHING ABILITY TO TRANSFORM MYSELF INTO AN ASTRAL-LIKE FORM, OR BACK INTO A MATERIAL BODY, AS I DESIRE! WHEN ASTRAL-LIKE, I CAN PENETRATE ANYTHING... EVEN THROUGH A FORCE-SHIELD!
BUT I'LL STILL DESTROY THE HANGMAN!
SORRY... CAN'T ALLOW YOU TO TOUCH THAT BUTTON!
OW-WW! ...D-DON'T HIT ME AGAIN!
THEN, AS THE WIZARD REMOVES THE FORCE-SHIELD AND LANDS THE VEHICLE...
BAH! IF THE WIZARD HADN'T PREVENTED IT, HANGMAN, YOU'D BE ELECTROCUTED!
THANKS, WIZARD! LET'S TURN THIS EVIL CHARACTER OVER TO THE LAW!
NOW TO ENLARGE TO NORMAL SIZE, AGAIN!
WAIT!
THE WORLD IS FORTUNATE TWO NEW ULTRA-HEROES HAVE APPEARED... AND DEFEATED THE SINISTER DESTRUCTOR! BUT A LITTLE WHILE AGO HE BOASTED HE'S DESTROYING MY ULTRA-COMRADES ELSEWHERE!
WHAT HAVE YOU DONE TO FLY-MAN AND HIS FRIENDS, RAT?
I WON'T TELL YOU! WHAT YOU DON'T KNOW, CAN'T HELP THEM!
DON'T WORRY, FLY-GIRL! I'LL LEARN WHAT WE WANT TO KNOW!
3.

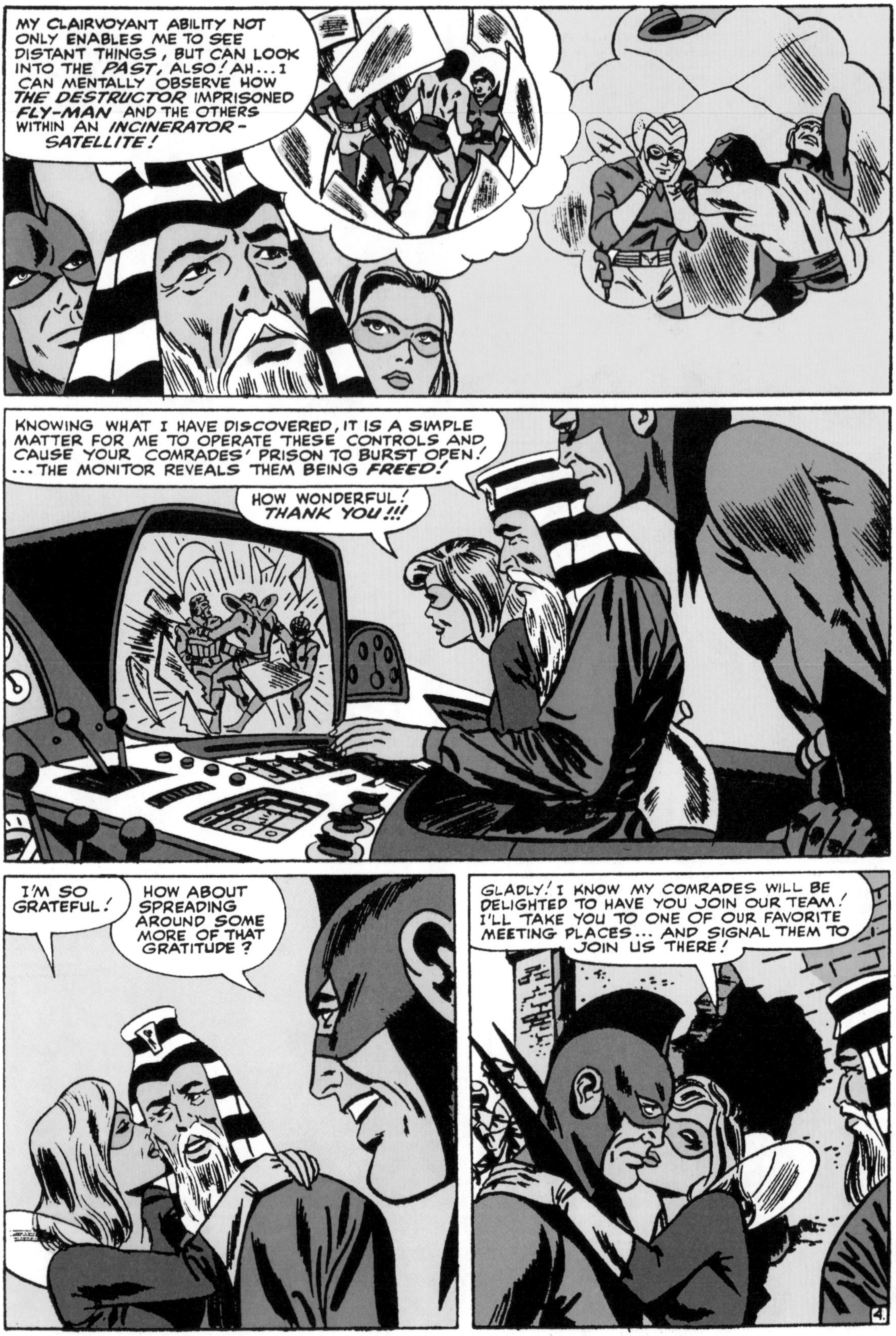
MY CLAIRVOYANT ABILITY NOT ONLY ENABLES ME TO SEE DISTANT THINGS, BUT CAN LOOK INTO THE PAST, ALSO! AH... I CAN MENTALLY OBSERVE HOW THE DESTRUCTOR IMPRISONED FLY-MAN AND THE OTHERS WITHIN AN INCINERATOR-SATELLITE!
KNOWING WHAT I HAVE DISCOVERED, IT IS A SIMPLE MATTER FOR ME TO OPERATE THESE CONTROLS AND CAUSE YOUR COMRADES' PRISON TO BURST OPEN! ...THE MONITOR REVEALS THEM BEING FREED!
HOW WONDERFUL! THANK YOU!!!
I'M SO GRATEFUL!
HOW ABOUT SPREADING AROUND SOME MORE OF THAT GRATITUDE?
GLADLY! I KNOW MY COMRADES WILL BE DELIGHTED TO HAVE YOU JOIN OUR TEAM! I'LL TAKE YOU TO ONE OF OUR FAVORITE MEETING PLACES... AND SIGNAL THEM TO JOIN US THERE!
4.

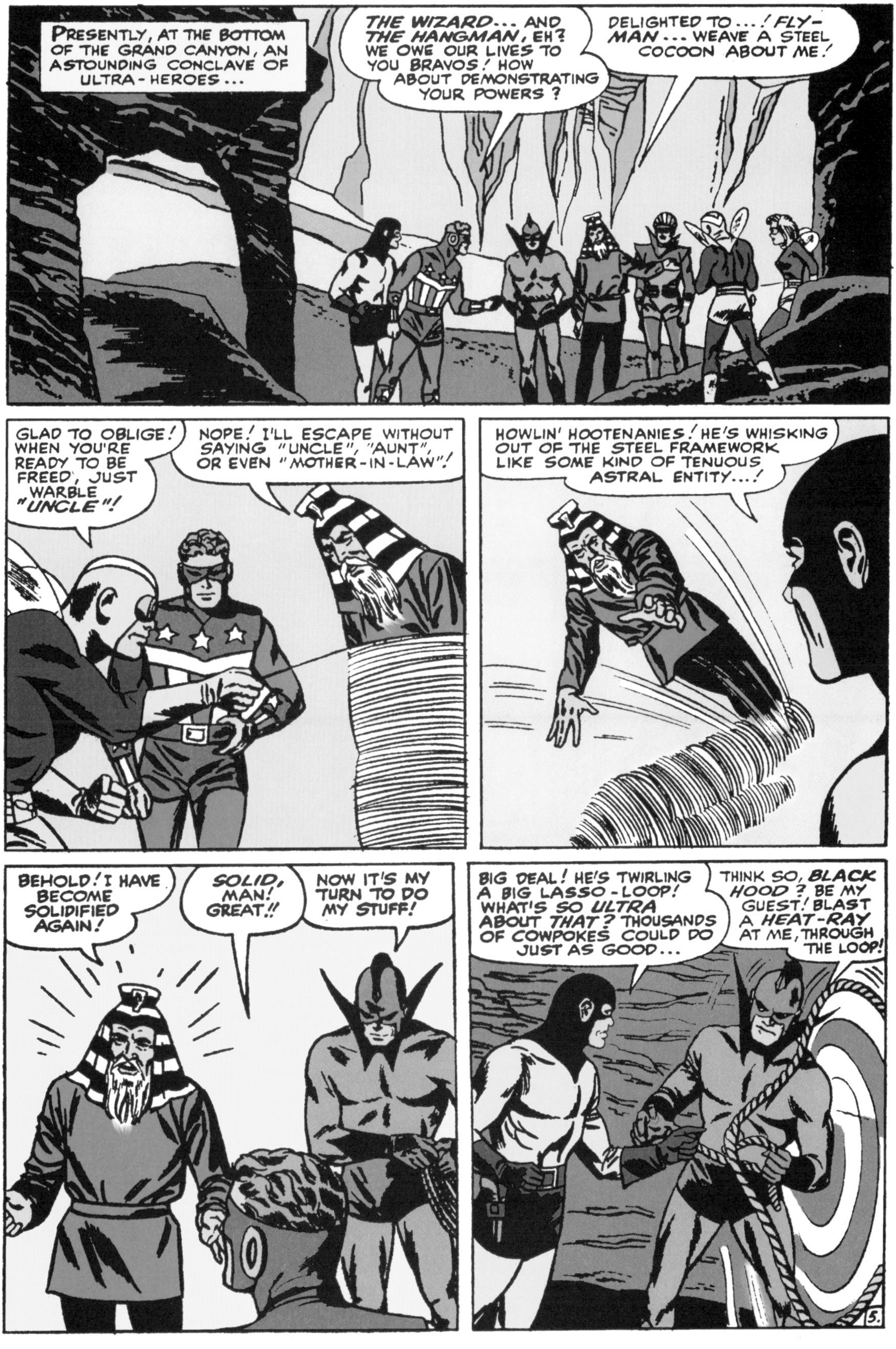
PRESENTLY, AT THE BOTTOM OF THE GRAND CANYON, AN ASTOUNDING CONCLAVE OF ULTRA-HEROES...
THE WIZARD... AND THE HANGMAN, EH? WE OWE OUR LIVES TO YOU BRAVOS! HOW ABOUT DEMONSTRATING YOUR POWERS?
DELIGHTED TO...! FLY-MAN... WEAVE A STEEL COCOON ABOUT ME!
GLAD TO OBLIGE! WHEN YOU'RE READY TO BE FREED, JUST WARBLE "UNCLE"!
NOPE! I'LL ESCAPE WITHOUT SAYING "UNCLE", "AUNT", OR EVEN "MOTHER-IN-LAW"!
HOWLIN' HOOTENANIES! HE'S WHISKING OUT OF THE STEEL FRAMEWORK LIKE SOME KIND OF TENUOUS ASTRAL ENTITY...!
BEHOLD! I HAVE BECOME SOLIDIFIED AGAIN!
SOLID, MAN! GREAT!!
NOW IT'S MY TURN TO DO MY STUFF!
BIG DEAL! HE'S TWIRLING A BIG LASSO-LOOP! WHAT'S SO ULTRA ABOUT THAT? THOUSANDS OF COWPOKES COULD DO JUST AS GOOD...
THINK SO, BLACK HOOD? BE MY GUEST! BLAST A HEAT-RAY AT ME, THROUGH THE LOOP!
5.

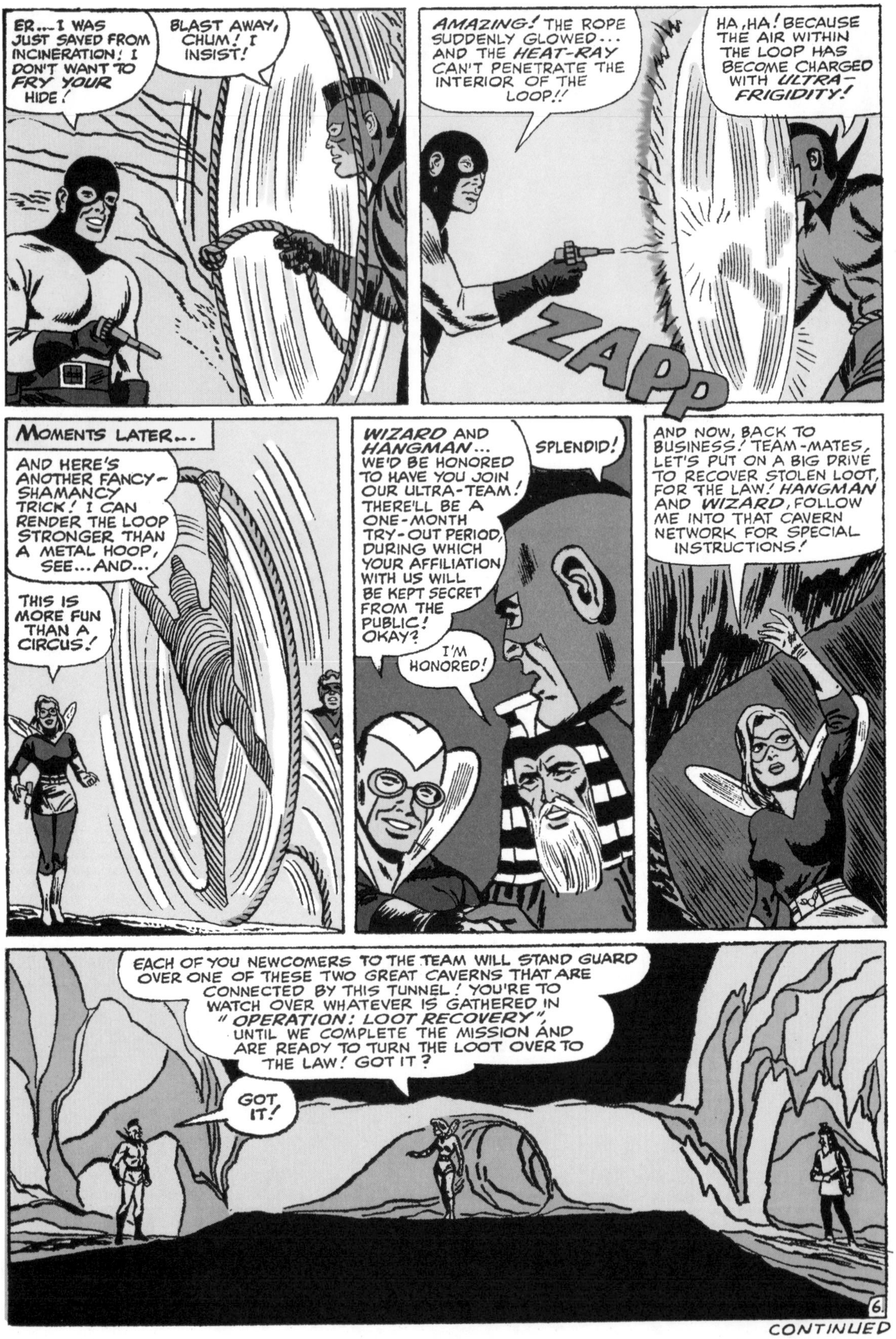
ER...I WAS JUST SAVED FROM INCINERATION! I DON'T WANT TO FRY YOUR HIDE!
BLAST AWAY, CHUM! I INSIST!
AMAZING! THE ROPE SUDDENLY GLOWED... AND THE HEAT-RAY CAN'T PENETRATE THE INTERIOR OF THE LOOP!!
HA, HA! BECAUSE THE AIR WITHIN THE LOOP HAS BECOME CHARGED WITH ULTRA-FRIGIDITY!
ZAPP
MOMENTS LATER...
AND HERE'S ANOTHER FANCY-SHAMANCY TRICK! I CAN RENDER THE LOOP STRONGER THAN A METAL HOOP, SEE...AND...
THIS IS MORE FUN THAN A CIRCUS!
WIZARD AND HANGMAN... WE'D BE HONORED TO HAVE YOU JOIN OUR ULTRA-TEAM! THERE'LL BE A ONE-MONTH TRY-OUT PERIOD, DURING WHICH YOUR AFFILIATION WITH US WILL BE KEPT SECRET FROM THE PUBLIC! OKAY?
SPLENDID!
I'M HONORED!
AND NOW, BACK TO BUSINESS! TEAM-MATES, LET'S PUT ON A BIG DRIVE TO RECOVER STOLEN LOOT FOR THE LAW! HANGMAN AND WIZARD, FOLLOW ME INTO THAT CAVERN NETWORK FOR SPECIAL INSTRUCTIONS!
EACH OF YOU NEWCOMERS TO THE TEAM WILL STAND GUARD OVER ONE OF THESE TWO GREAT CAVERNS THAT ARE CONNECTED BY THIS TUNNEL! YOU'RE TO WATCH OVER WHATEVER IS GATHERED IN "OPERATION: LOOT RECOVERY", UNTIL WE COMPLETE THE MISSION AND ARE READY TO TURN THE LOOT OVER TO THE LAW! GOT IT?
GOT IT!
6.
CONTINUED

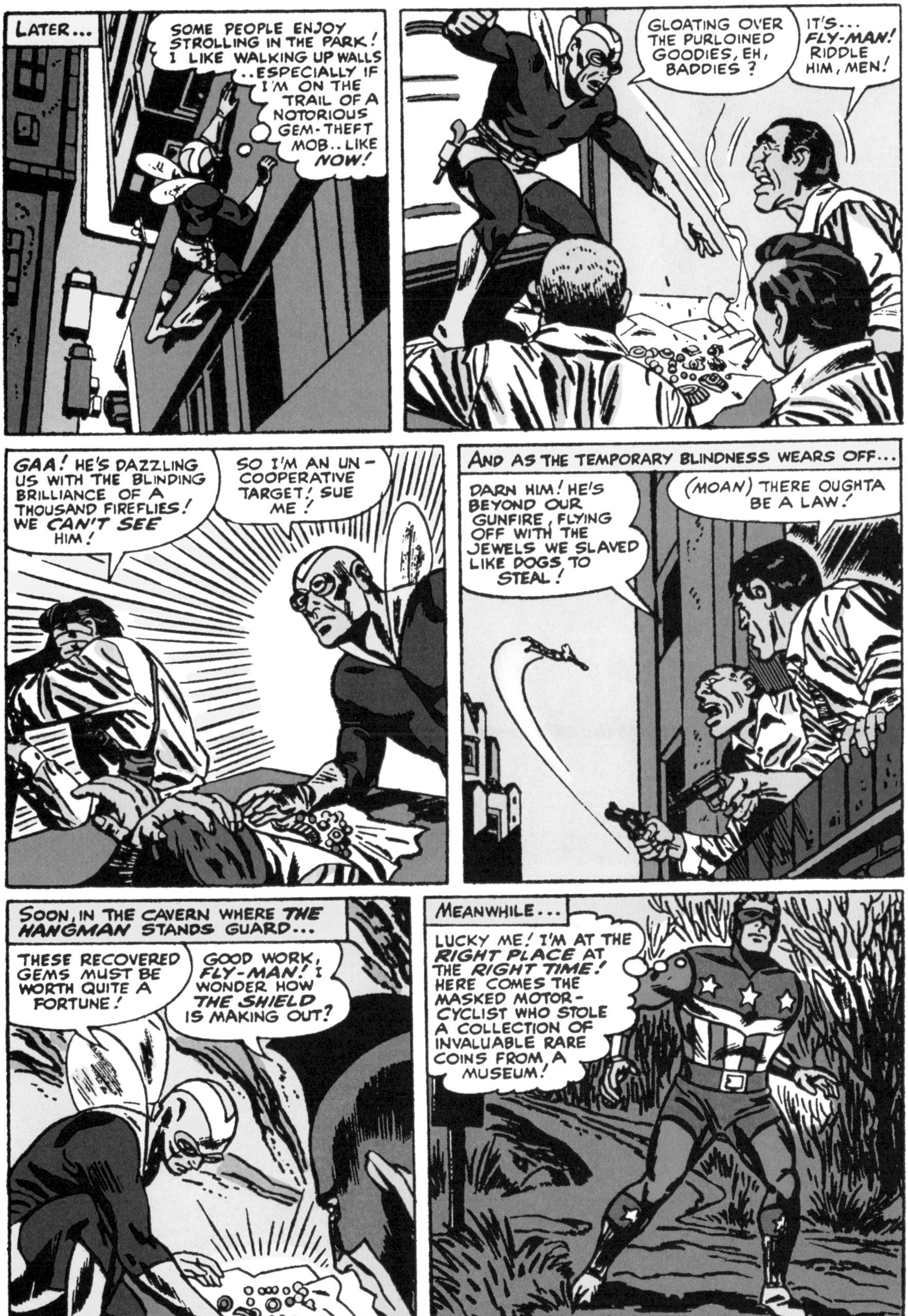
LATER...
SOME PEOPLE ENJOY STROLLING IN THE PARK! I LIKE WALKING UP WALLS ..ESPECIALLY IF I'M ON THE TRAIL OF A NOTORIOUS GEM-THEFT MOB.. LIKE NOW!
GLOATING OVER THE PURLOINED GOODIES, EH, BADDIES?
IT'S... FLY-MAN! RIDDLE HIM, MEN!
GAA! HE'S DAZZLING US WITH THE BLINDING BRILLIANCE OF A THOUSAND FIREFLIES! WE CAN'T SEE HIM!
SO I'M AN UN-COOPERATIVE TARGET! SUE ME!
AND AS THE TEMPORARY BLINDNESS WEARS OFF...
DARN HIM! HE'S BEYOND OUR GUNFIRE, FLYING OFF WITH THE JEWELS WE SLAVED LIKE DOGS TO STEAL!
(MOAN) THERE OUGHTA BE A LAW!
SOON, IN THE CAVERN WHERE THE HANGMAN STANDS GUARD...
THESE RECOVERED GEMS MUST BE WORTH QUITE A FORTUNE!
GOOD WORK, FLY-MAN! I WONDER HOW THE SHIELD IS MAKING OUT?
MEANWHILE...
LUCKY ME! I'M AT THE RIGHT PLACE AT THE RIGHT TIME! HERE COMES THE MASKED MOTOR-CYCLIST WHO STOLE A COLLECTION OF INVALUABLE RARE COINS FROM A MUSEUM!
7.

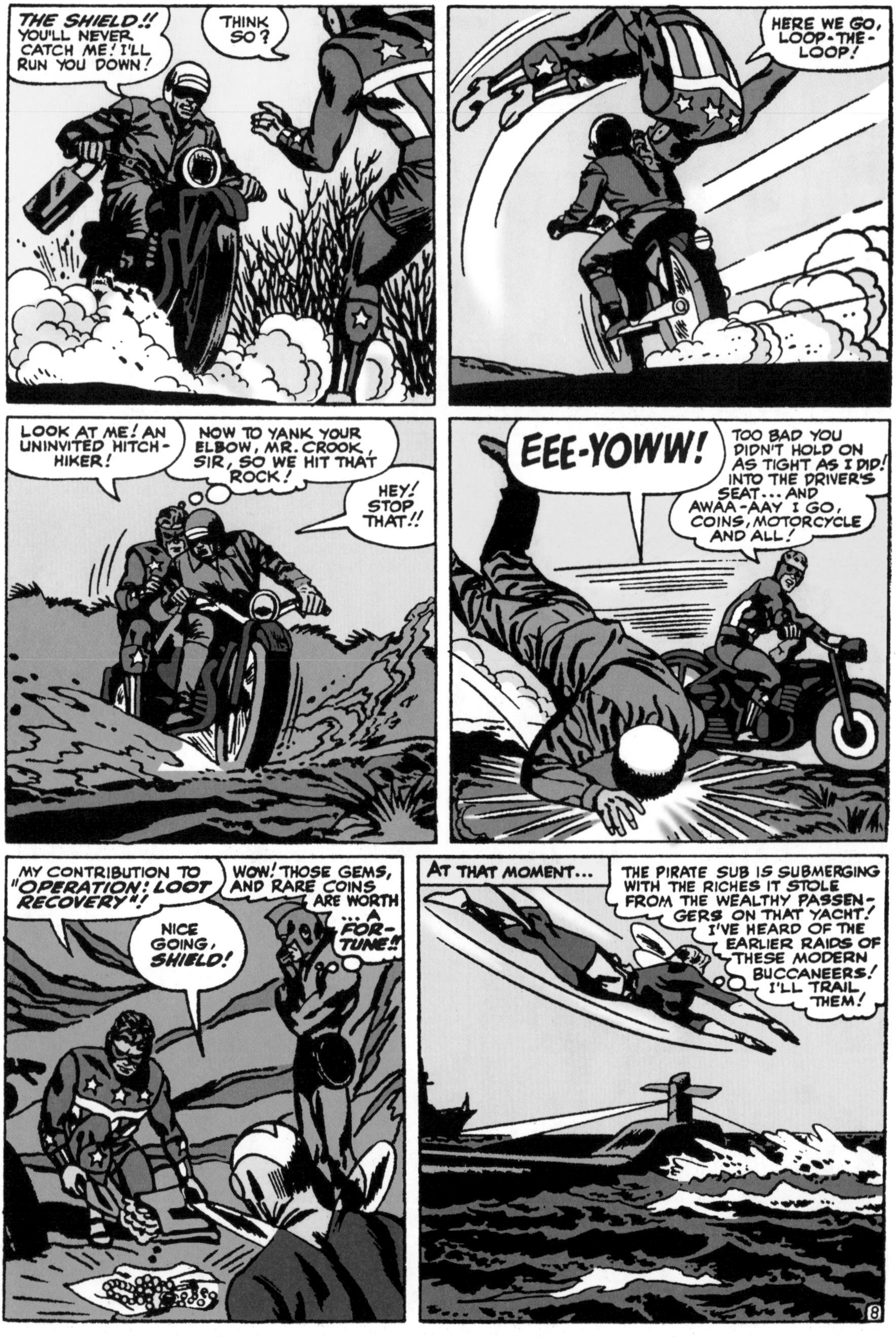
THE SHIELD!! YOU'LL NEVER CATCH ME! I'LL RUN YOU DOWN!
THINK SO?
HERE WE GO, LOOP-THE-LOOP!
LOOK AT ME! AN UNINVITED HITCH-HIKER!
NOW TO YANK YOUR ELBOW, MR. CROOK, SIR, SO WE HIT THAT ROCK!
HEY! STOP THAT!!
EEE-YOWW!
TOO BAD YOU DIDN'T HOLD ON AS TIGHT AS I DID! INTO THE DRIVER'S SEAT... AND AWAA-AAY I GO, COINS, MOTORCYCLE AND ALL!
MY CONTRIBUTION TO "OPERATION: LOOT RECOVERY"!
NICE GOING, SHIELD!
WOW! THOSE GEMS, AND RARE COINS ARE WORTH ... A FOR-TUNE!!
AT THAT MOMENT...
THE PIRATE SUB IS SUBMERGING WITH THE RICHES IT STOLE FROM THE WEALTHY PASSEN-GERS ON THAT YACHT! I'VE HEARD OF THE EARLIER RAIDS OF THESE MODERN BUCCANEERS! I'LL TRAIL THEM!
8

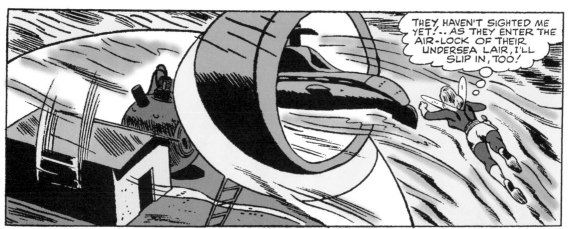

THEY HAVEN'T SIGHTED ME YET! .. AS THEY ENTER THE AIR-LOCK OF THEIR UNDERSEA LAIR, I'LL SLIP IN, TOO!

SOON...

A GREAT TREASURE-TROVE FROM ALL THEIR RAIDS! NOW TO EXPAND TO *GIANT* SIZE AND SPOIL THE GLEE OF THOSE GLOATING PIRATES!

ALL THIS BOOTY IS GOING BACK TO ITS RIGHTFUL OWNERS, BUCCANEERS!

YOU CAN'T DO THIS TO US, FLY-GIRL!

SHE *IS* DOING IT, DUMMY! AIM FOR HER HEART!

SHE BROKE RIGHT OUT THROUGH THE SIDE OF THE LAIR-WALL! QUICK! INTO THE EMERGENCY BATHYSCAPH, SO WE WON'T DROWN!!

KRASHH!

9.

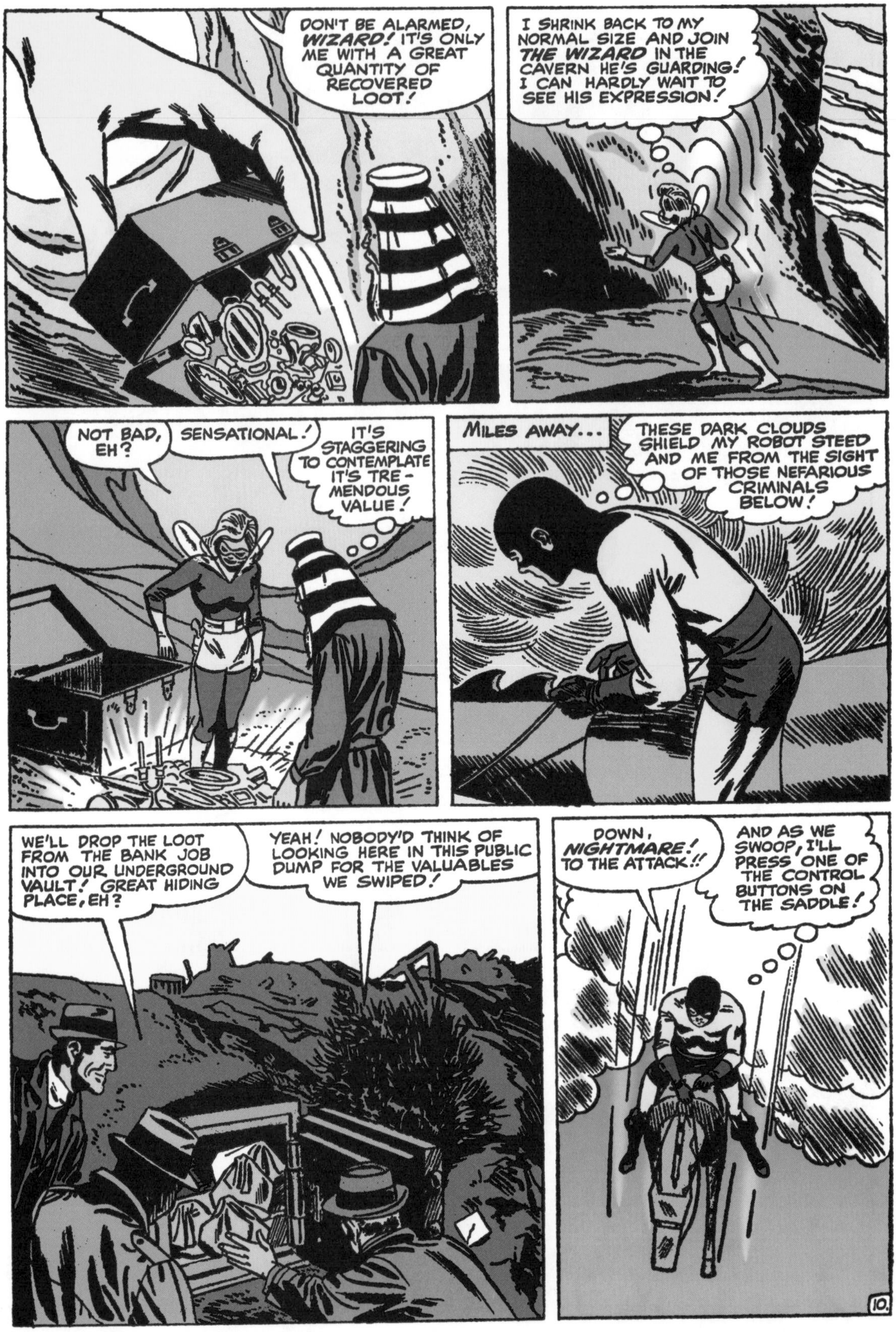
DON'T BE ALARMED, WIZARD! IT'S ONLY ME WITH A GREAT QUANTITY OF RECOVERED LOOT!
I SHRINK BACK TO MY NORMAL SIZE AND JOIN THE WIZARD IN THE CAVERN HE'S GUARDING! I CAN HARDLY WAIT TO SEE HIS EXPRESSION!
NOT BAD, EH?
SENSATIONAL!
IT'S STAGGERING TO CONTEMPLATE IT'S TRE-MENDOUS VALUE!
MILES AWAY...
THESE DARK CLOUDS SHIELD MY ROBOT STEED AND ME FROM THE SIGHT OF THOSE NEFARIOUS CRIMINALS BELOW!
WE'LL DROP THE LOOT FROM THE BANK JOB INTO OUR UNDERGROUND VAULT! GREAT HIDING PLACE, EH?
YEAH! NOBODY'D THINK OF LOOKING HERE IN THIS PUBLIC DUMP FOR THE VALUABLES WE SWIPED!
DOWN, NIGHTMARE! TO THE ATTACK!!
AND AS WE SWOOP, I'LL PRESS ONE OF THE CONTROL BUTTONS ON THE SADDLE!
10.

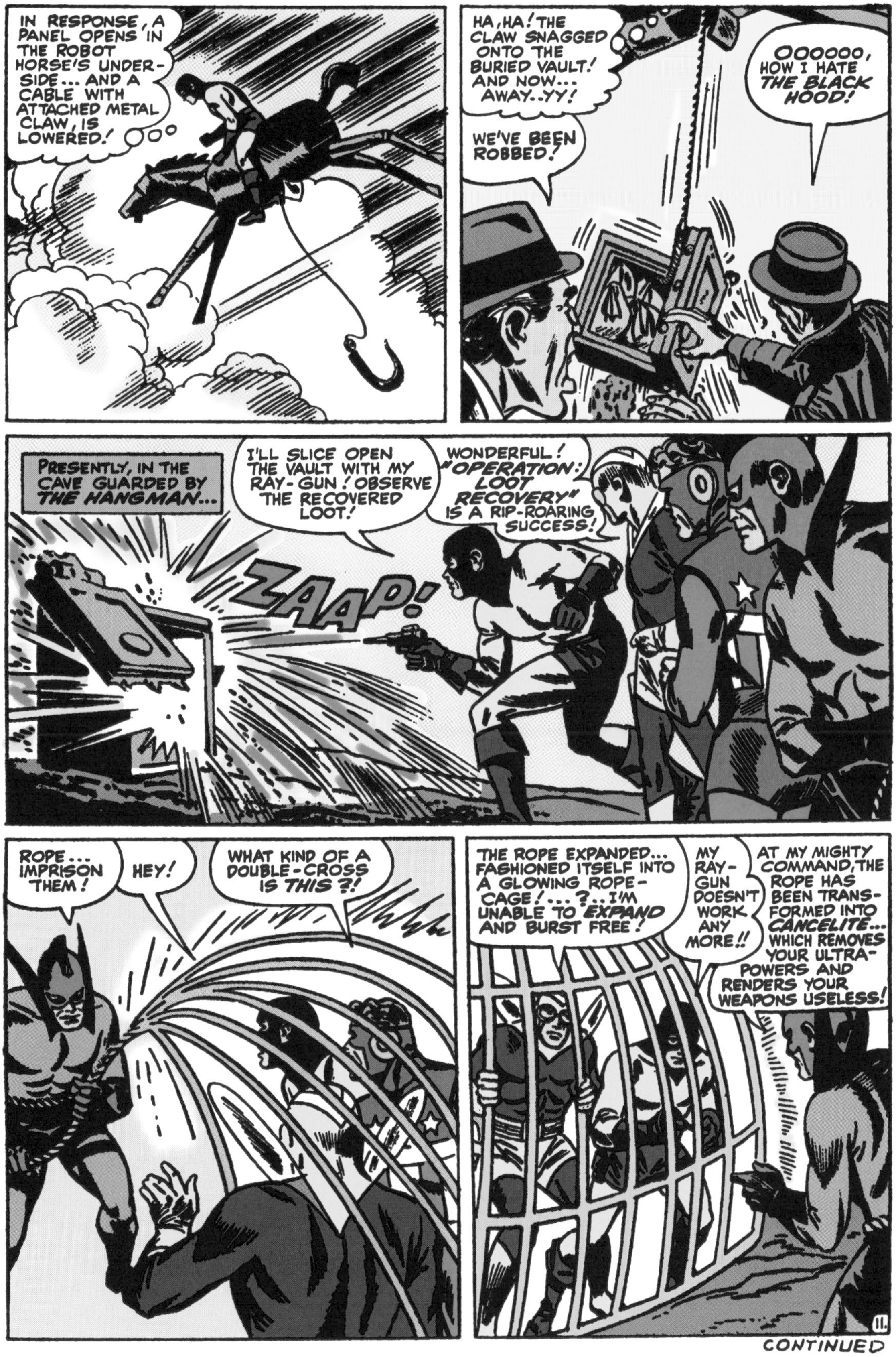

IN RESPONSE, A PANEL OPENS IN THE ROBOT HORSE'S UNDER-SIDE... AND A CABLE WITH ATTACHED METAL CLAW, IS LOWERED!
HA, HA! THE CLAW SNAGGED ONTO THE BURIED VAULT! AND NOW... AWAY..YY!
WE'VE BEEN ROBBED!
OOOOOO, HOW I HATE THE BLACK HOOD!
PRESENTLY, IN THE CAVE GUARDED BY THE HANGMAN...
I'LL SLICE OPEN THE VAULT WITH MY RAY-GUN! OBSERVE THE RECOVERED LOOT!
WONDERFUL! "OPERATION: LOOT RECOVERY" IS A RIP-ROARING SUCCESS!
ZAAP!
ROPE... IMPRISON THEM!
HEY!
WHAT KIND OF A DOUBLE-CROSS IS THIS ?!
THE ROPE EXPANDED... FASHIONED ITSELF INTO A GLOWING ROPE-CAGE! ... ?.. I'M UNABLE TO EXPAND AND BURST FREE!
MY RAY-GUN DOESN'T WORK ANY MORE!!
AT MY MIGHTY COMMAND, THE ROPE HAS BEEN TRANS-FORMED INTO CANCELITE... WHICH REMOVES YOUR ULTRA-POWERS AND RENDERS YOUR WEAPONS USELESS!
11.

CONTINUED

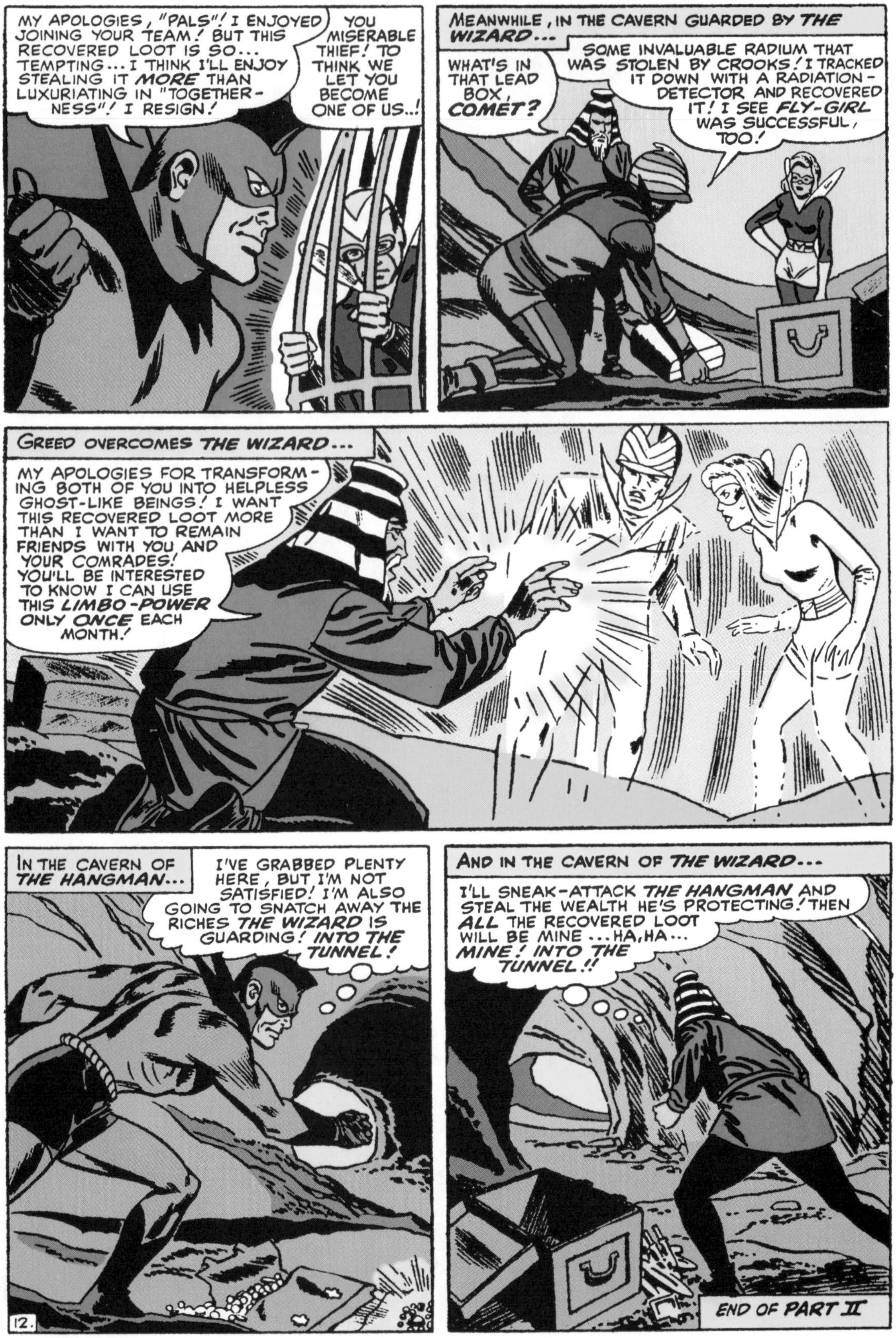
MY APOLOGIES, "PALS"! I ENJOYED JOINING YOUR TEAM! BUT THIS RECOVERED LOOT IS SO... TEMPTING... I THINK I'LL ENJOY STEALING IT MORE THAN LUXURIATING IN "TOGETHER-NESS"! I RESIGN!
YOU MISERABLE THIEF! TO THINK WE LET YOU BECOME ONE OF US..!
MEANWHILE, IN THE CAVERN GUARDED BY THE WIZARD...
WHAT'S IN THAT LEAD BOX, COMET?
SOME INVALUABLE RADIUM THAT WAS STOLEN BY CROOKS! I TRACKED IT DOWN WITH A RADIATION-DETECTOR AND RECOVERED IT! I SEE FLY-GIRL WAS SUCCESSFUL, TOO!
GREED OVERCOMES THE WIZARD...
MY APOLOGIES FOR TRANSFORMING BOTH OF YOU INTO HELPLESS GHOST-LIKE BEINGS! I WANT THIS RECOVERED LOOT MORE THAN I WANT TO REMAIN FRIENDS WITH YOU AND YOUR COMRADES! YOU'LL BE INTERESTED TO KNOW I CAN USE THIS LIMBO-POWER ONLY ONCE EACH MONTH!
IN THE CAVERN OF THE HANGMAN...
I'VE GRABBED PLENTY HERE, BUT I'M NOT SATISFIED! I'M ALSO GOING TO SNATCH AWAY THE RICHES THE WIZARD IS GUARDING! INTO THE TUNNEL!
12.
AND IN THE CAVERN OF THE WIZARD...
I'LL SNEAK-ATTACK THE HANGMAN AND STEAL THE WEALTH HE'S PROTECTING! THEN ALL THE RECOVERED LOOT WILL BE MINE ...HA,HA... MINE! INTO THE TUNNEL!!
END OF PART II

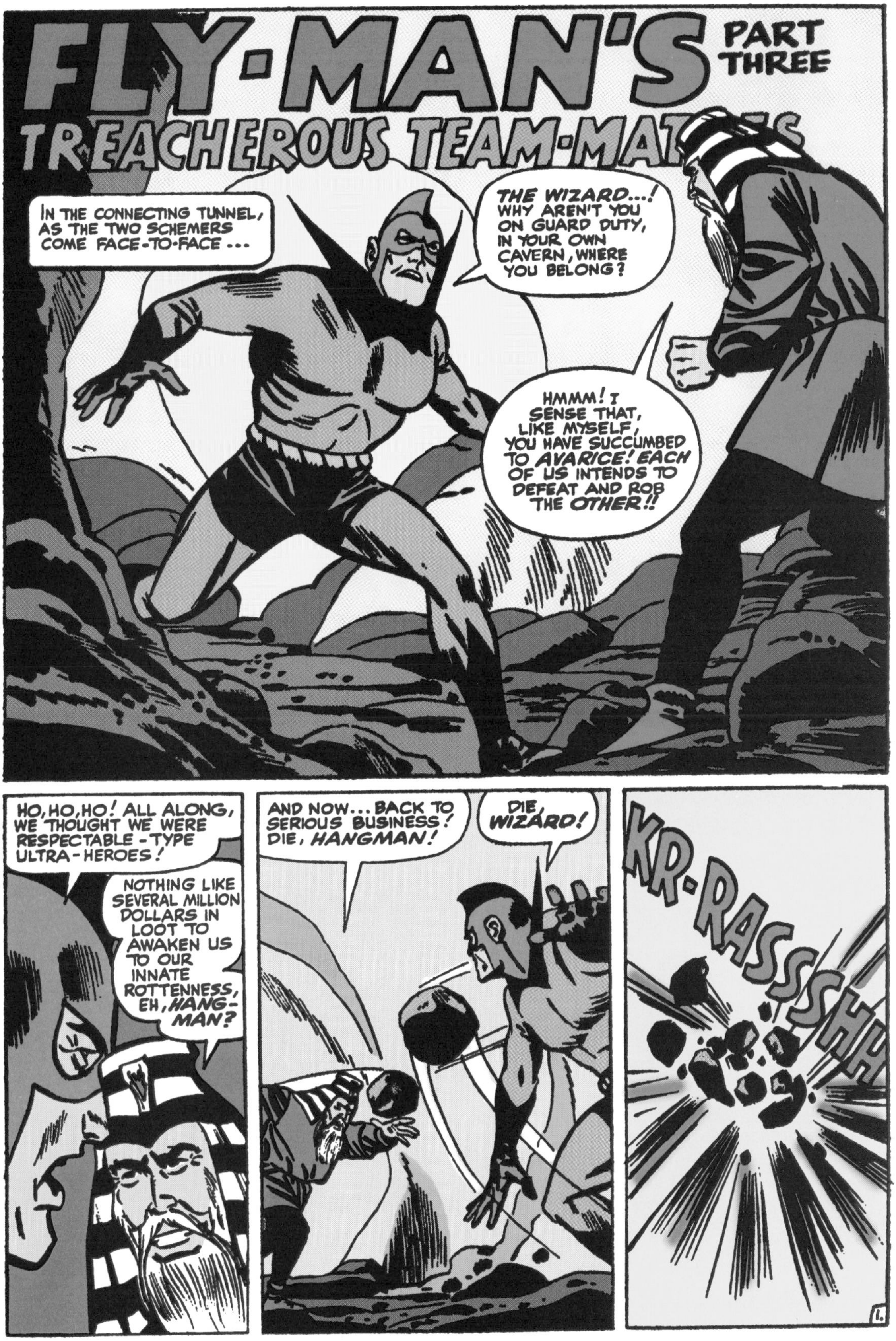
FLY-MAN'S
PART THREE
TREACHEROUS TEAM-MAT
IN THE CONNECTING TUNNEL, AS THE TWO SCHEMERS COME FACE-TO-FACE ...
THE WIZARD...! WHY AREN'T YOU ON GUARD DUTY, IN YOUR OWN CAVERN, WHERE YOU BELONG?
HMMM! I SENSE THAT, LIKE MYSELF, YOU HAVE SUCCUMBED TO AVARICE! EACH OF US INTENDS TO DEFEAT AND ROB THE OTHER!!
HO, HO, HO! ALL ALONG, WE THOUGHT WE WERE RESPECTABLE-TYPE ULTRA-HEROES!
NOTHING LIKE SEVERAL MILLION DOLLARS IN LOOT TO AWAKEN US TO OUR INNATE ROTTENNESS, EH, HANGMAN?
AND NOW... BACK TO SERIOUS BUSINESS! DIE, HANGMAN!
DIE, WIZARD!
KR-RASSSHH
1.

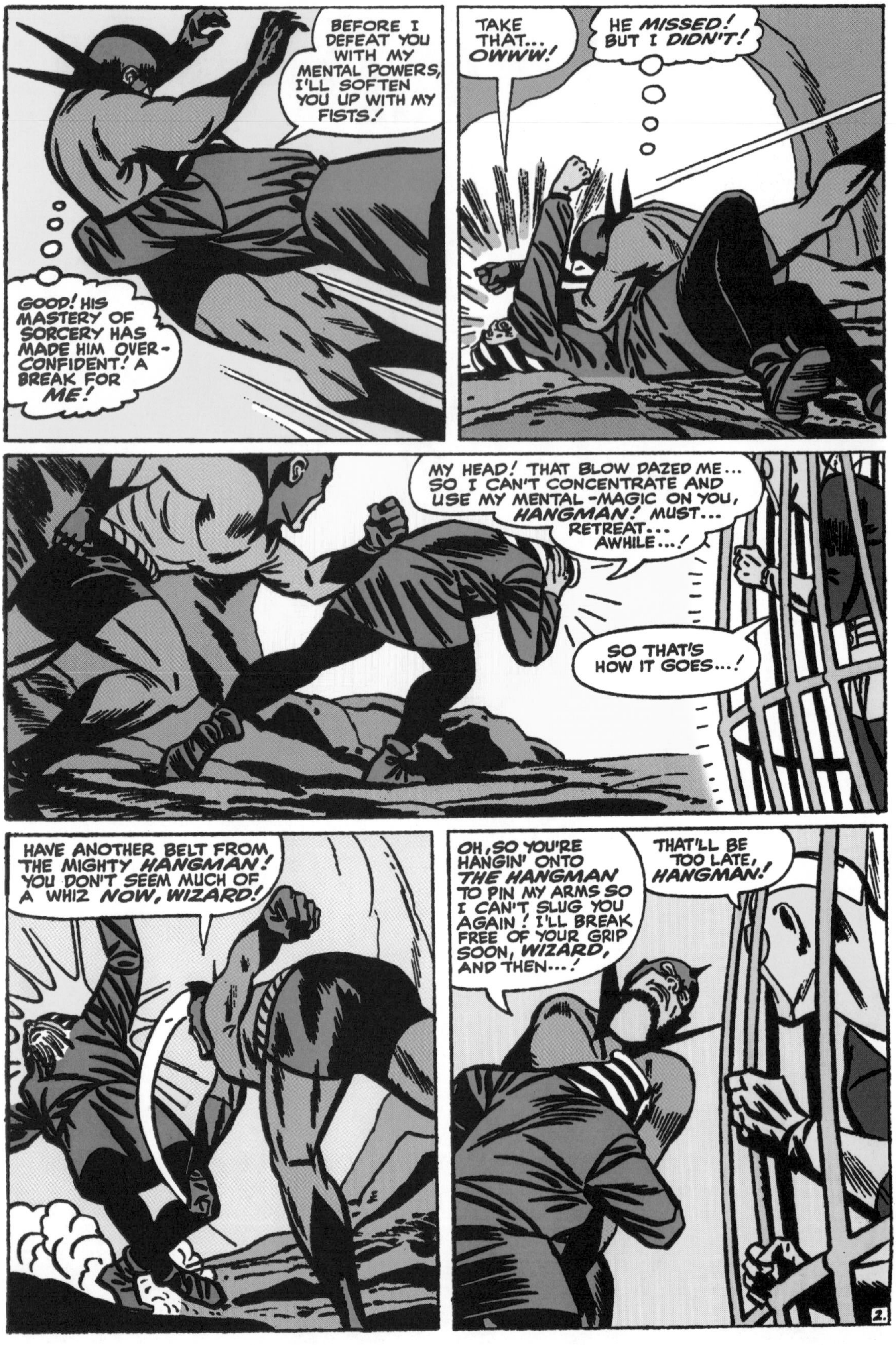
BEFORE I DEFEAT YOU WITH MY MENTAL POWERS, I'LL SOFTEN YOU UP WITH MY FISTS!
GOOD! HIS MASTERY OF SORCERY HAS MADE HIM OVER-CONFIDENT! A BREAK FOR ME!
TAKE THAT... OWWW!
HE MISSED! BUT I DIDN'T!
MY HEAD! THAT BLOW DAZED ME... SO I CAN'T CONCENTRATE AND USE MY MENTAL-MAGIC ON YOU, HANGMAN! MUST... RETREAT... AWHILE...!
SO THAT'S HOW IT GOES...!
HAVE ANOTHER BELT FROM THE MIGHTY HANGMAN! YOU DON'T SEEM MUCH OF A WHIZ NOW, WIZARD!
OH, SO YOU'RE HANGIN' ONTO THE HANGMAN TO PIN MY ARMS SO I CAN'T SLUG YOU AGAIN! I'LL BREAK FREE OF YOUR GRIP SOON, WIZARD, AND THEN...!
THAT'LL BE TOO LATE, HANGMAN!
2.

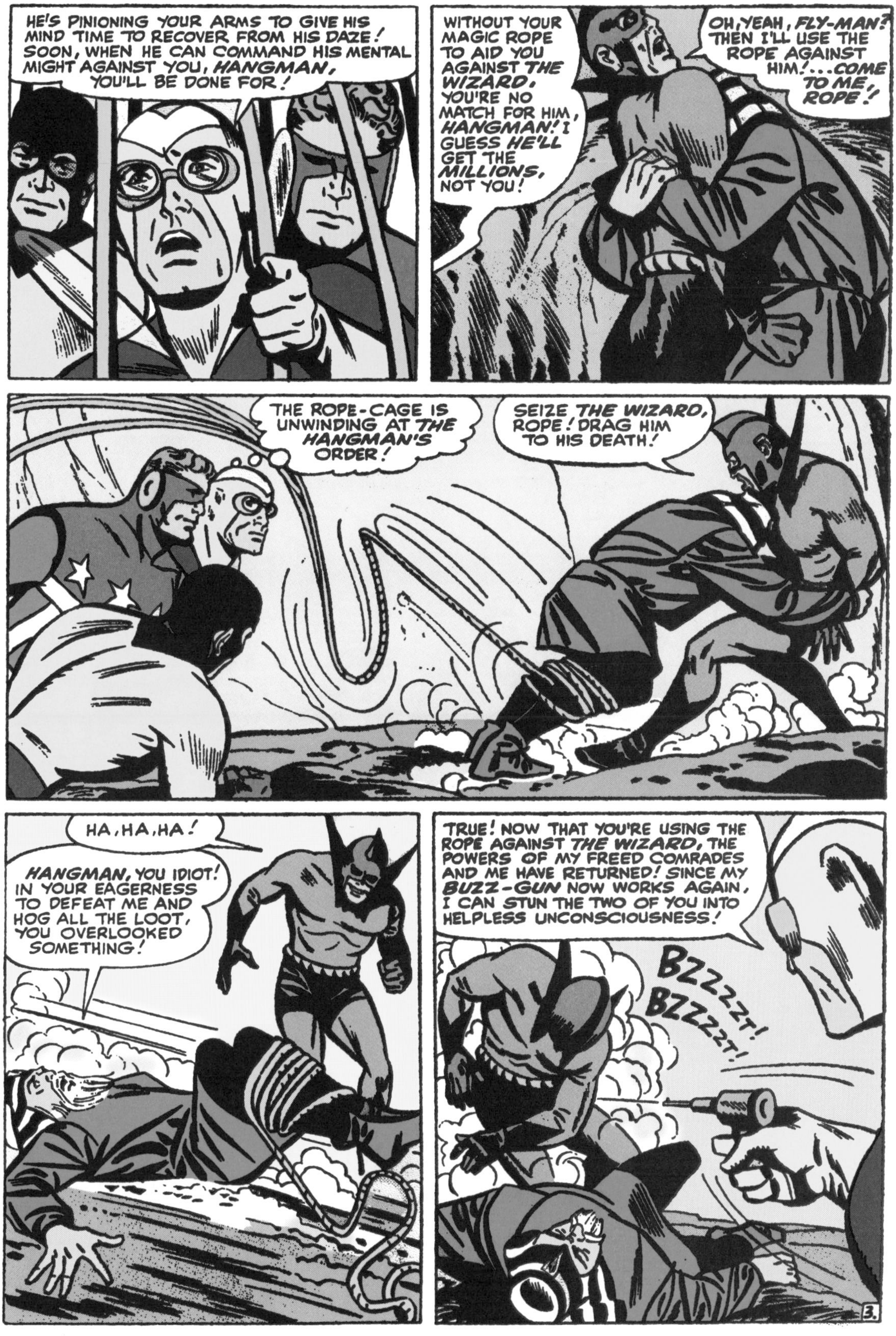
HE'S PINIONING YOUR ARMS TO GIVE HIS MIND TIME TO RECOVER FROM HIS DAZE! SOON, WHEN HE CAN COMMAND HIS MENTAL MIGHT AGAINST YOU, HANGMAN, YOU'LL BE DONE FOR!
WITHOUT YOUR MAGIC ROPE TO AID YOU AGAINST THE WIZARD, YOU'RE NO MATCH FOR HIM, HANGMAN! I GUESS HE'LL GET THE MILLIONS, NOT YOU!
OH, YEAH, FLY-MAN? THEN I'LL USE THE ROPE AGAINST HIM!...COME TO ME, ROPE!
THE ROPE-CAGE IS UNWINDING AT THE HANGMAN'S ORDER!
SEIZE THE WIZARD, ROPE! DRAG HIM TO HIS DEATH!
HA, HA, HA!
HANGMAN, YOU IDIOT! IN YOUR EAGERNESS TO DEFEAT ME AND HOG ALL THE LOOT, YOU OVERLOOKED SOMETHING!
TRUE! NOW THAT YOU'RE USING THE ROPE AGAINST THE WIZARD, THE POWERS OF MY FREED COMRADES AND ME HAVE RETURNED! SINCE MY BUZZ-GUN NOW WORKS AGAIN, I CAN STUN THE TWO OF YOU INTO HELPLESS UNCONSCIOUSNESS!
BZZZZZT! BZZZZZT!
3.

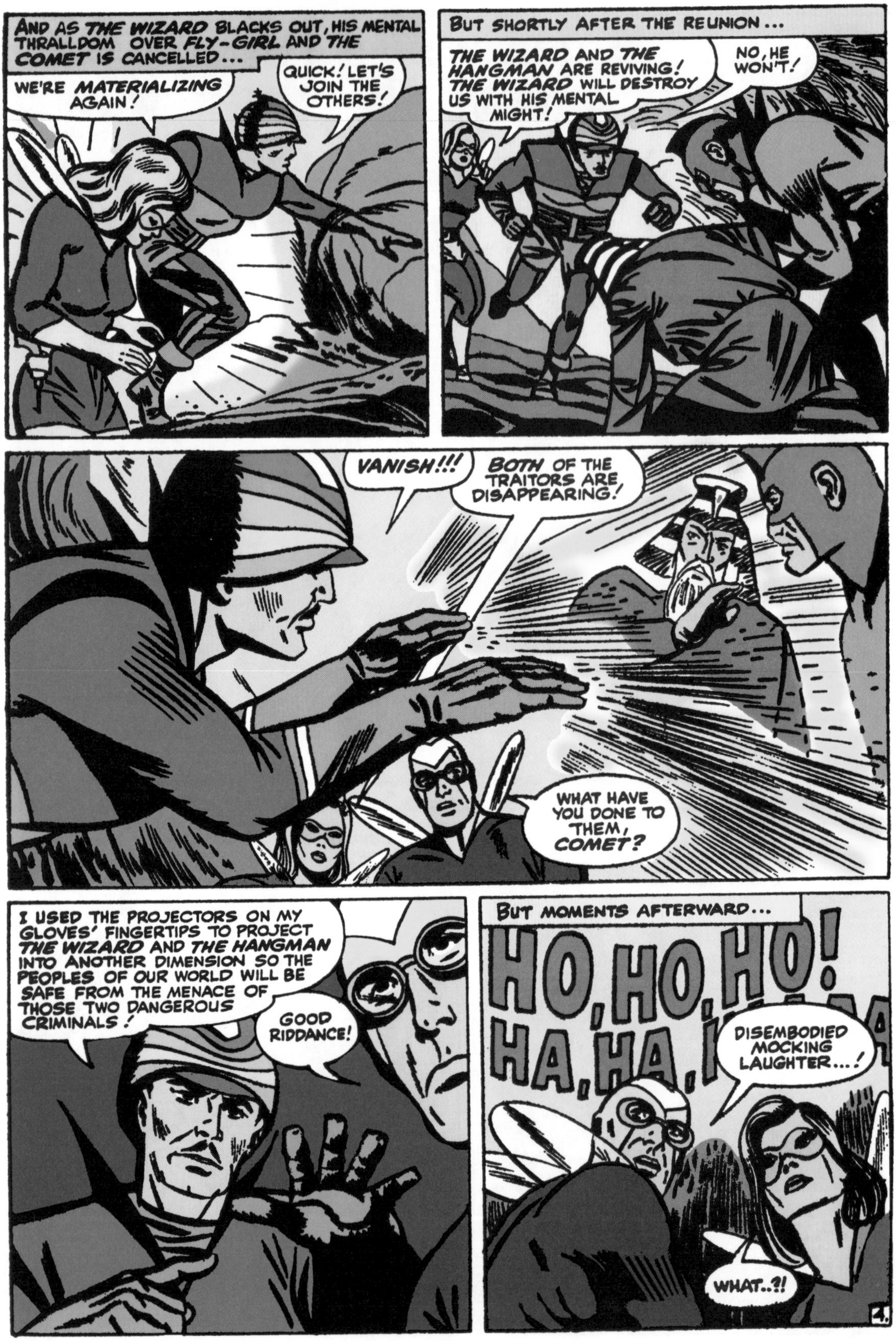
AND AS THE WIZARD BLACKS OUT, HIS MENTAL THRALLDOM OVER FLY-GIRL AND THE COMET IS CANCELLED...
WE'RE MATERIALIZING AGAIN!
QUICK! LET'S JOIN THE OTHERS!
BUT SHORTLY AFTER THE REUNION...
THE WIZARD AND THE HANGMAN ARE REVIVING! THE WIZARD WILL DESTROY US WITH HIS MENTAL MIGHT!
NO, HE WON'T!
VANISH!!!
BOTH OF THE TRAITORS ARE DISAPPEARING!
WHAT HAVE YOU DONE TO THEM, COMET?
I USED THE PROJECTORS ON MY GLOVES' FINGERTIPS TO PROJECT THE WIZARD AND THE HANGMAN INTO ANOTHER DIMENSION SO THE PEOPLES OF OUR WORLD WILL BE SAFE FROM THE MENACE OF THOSE TWO DANGEROUS CRIMINALS!
GOOD RIDDANCE!
BUT MOMENTS AFTERWARD...
HO, HO, HO!
HA, HA,
DISEMBODIED MOCKING LAUGHTER...!
WHAT..?!
4.

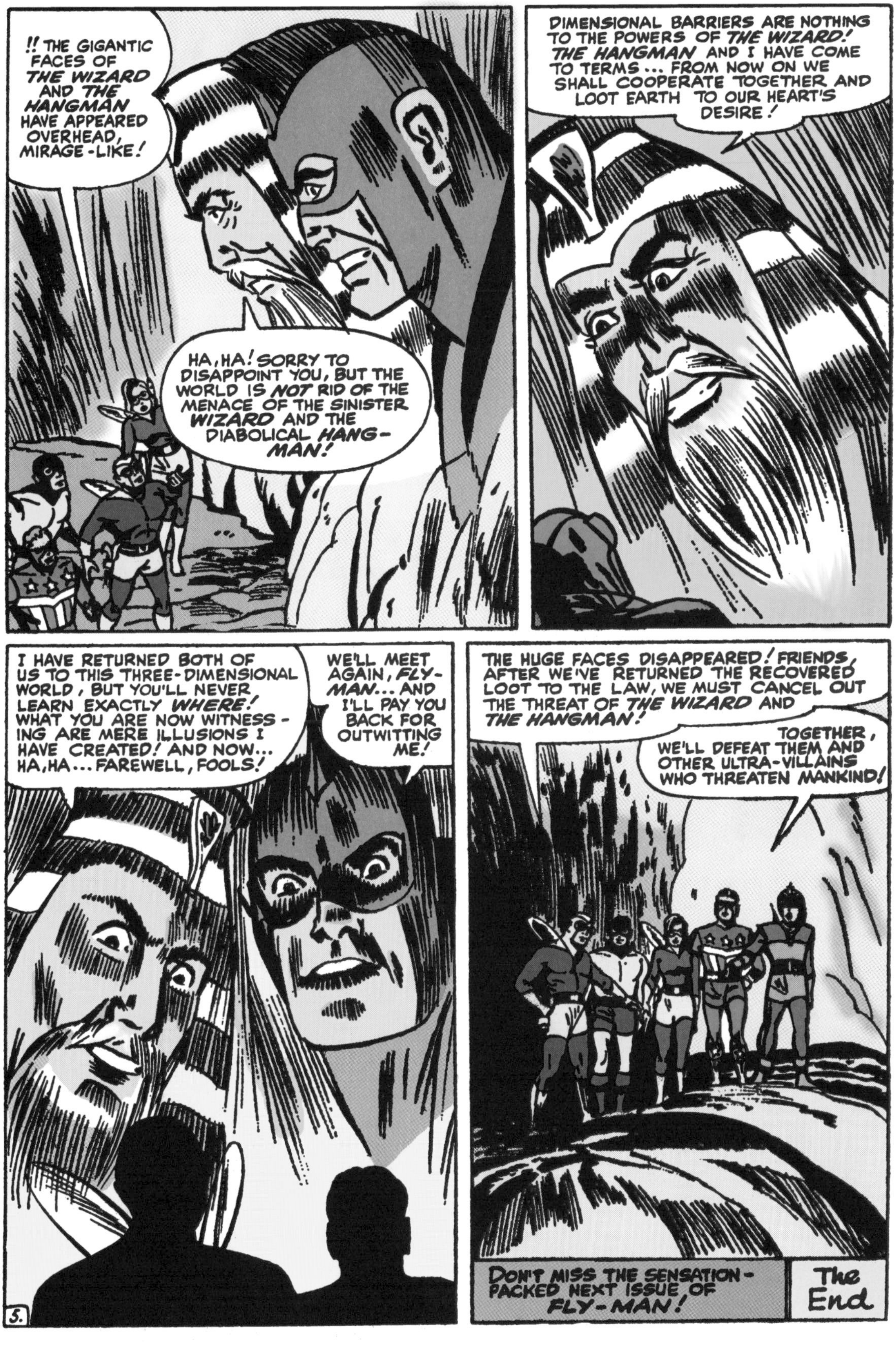
!! THE GIGANTIC FACES OF THE WIZARD AND THE HANGMAN HAVE APPEARED OVERHEAD, MIRAGE-LIKE!
HA, HA! SORRY TO DISAPPOINT YOU, BUT THE WORLD IS NOT RID OF THE MENACE OF THE SINISTER WIZARD AND THE DIABOLICAL HANG-MAN!
DIMENSIONAL BARRIERS ARE NOTHING TO THE POWERS OF THE WIZARD! THE HANGMAN AND I HAVE COME TO TERMS... FROM NOW ON WE SHALL COOPERATE TOGETHER AND LOOT EARTH TO OUR HEART'S DESIRE!
I HAVE RETURNED BOTH OF US TO THIS THREE-DIMENSIONAL WORLD, BUT YOU'LL NEVER LEARN EXACTLY WHERE! WHAT YOU ARE NOW WITNESS-ING ARE MERE ILLUSIONS I HAVE CREATED! AND NOW... HA, HA... FAREWELL, FOOLS!
WE'LL MEET AGAIN, FLY-MAN... AND I'LL PAY YOU BACK FOR OUTWITTING ME!
5.
THE HUGE FACES DISAPPEARED! FRIENDS, AFTER WE'VE RETURNED THE RECOVERED LOOT TO THE LAW, WE MUST CANCEL OUT THE THREAT OF THE WIZARD AND THE HANGMAN!
TOGETHER, WE'LL DEFEAT THEM AND OTHER ULTRA-VILLAINS WHO THREATEN MANKIND!
DON'T MISS THE SENSATION-PACKED NEXT ISSUE OF FLY-MAN!
The End

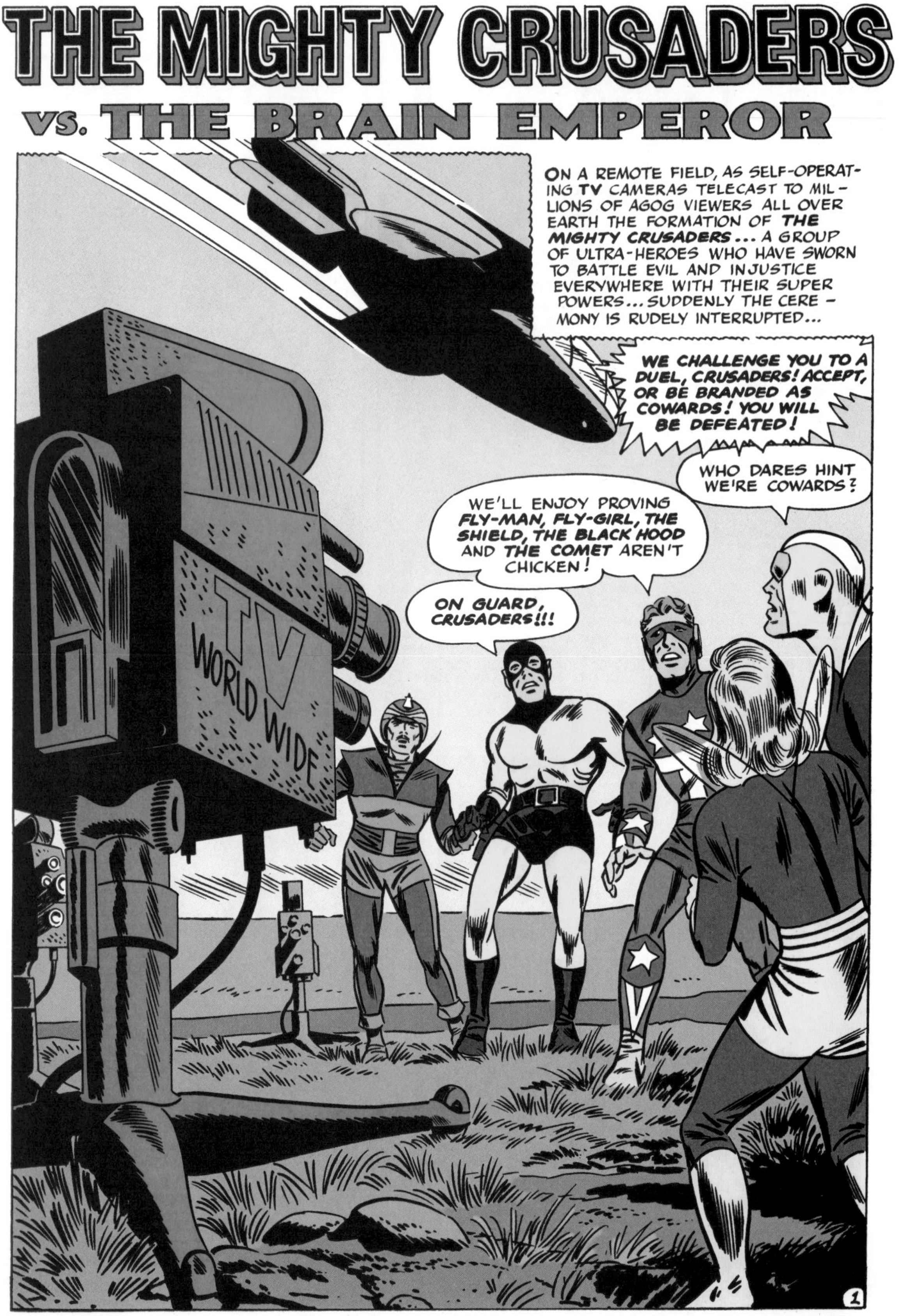
THE MIGHTY CRUSADERS
vs. THE BRAIN EMPEROR
ON A REMOTE FIELD, AS SELF-OPERATING TV CAMERAS TELECAST TO MILLIONS OF AGOG VIEWERS ALL OVER EARTH THE FORMATION OF THE MIGHTY CRUSADERS... A GROUP OF ULTRA-HEROES WHO HAVE SWORN TO BATTLE EVIL AND INJUSTICE EVERYWHERE WITH THEIR SUPER POWERS... SUDDENLY THE CEREMONY IS RUDELY INTERRUPTED...
WE CHALLENGE YOU TO A DUEL, CRUSADERS! ACCEPT, OR BE BRANDED AS COWARDS! YOU WILL BE DEFEATED!
WHO DARES HINT WE'RE COWARDS?
WE'LL ENJOY PROVING FLY-MAN, FLY-GIRL, THE SHIELD, THE BLACK HOOD AND THE COMET AREN'T CHICKEN!
ON GUARD, CRUSADERS!!!
TV WORLD WIDE
1

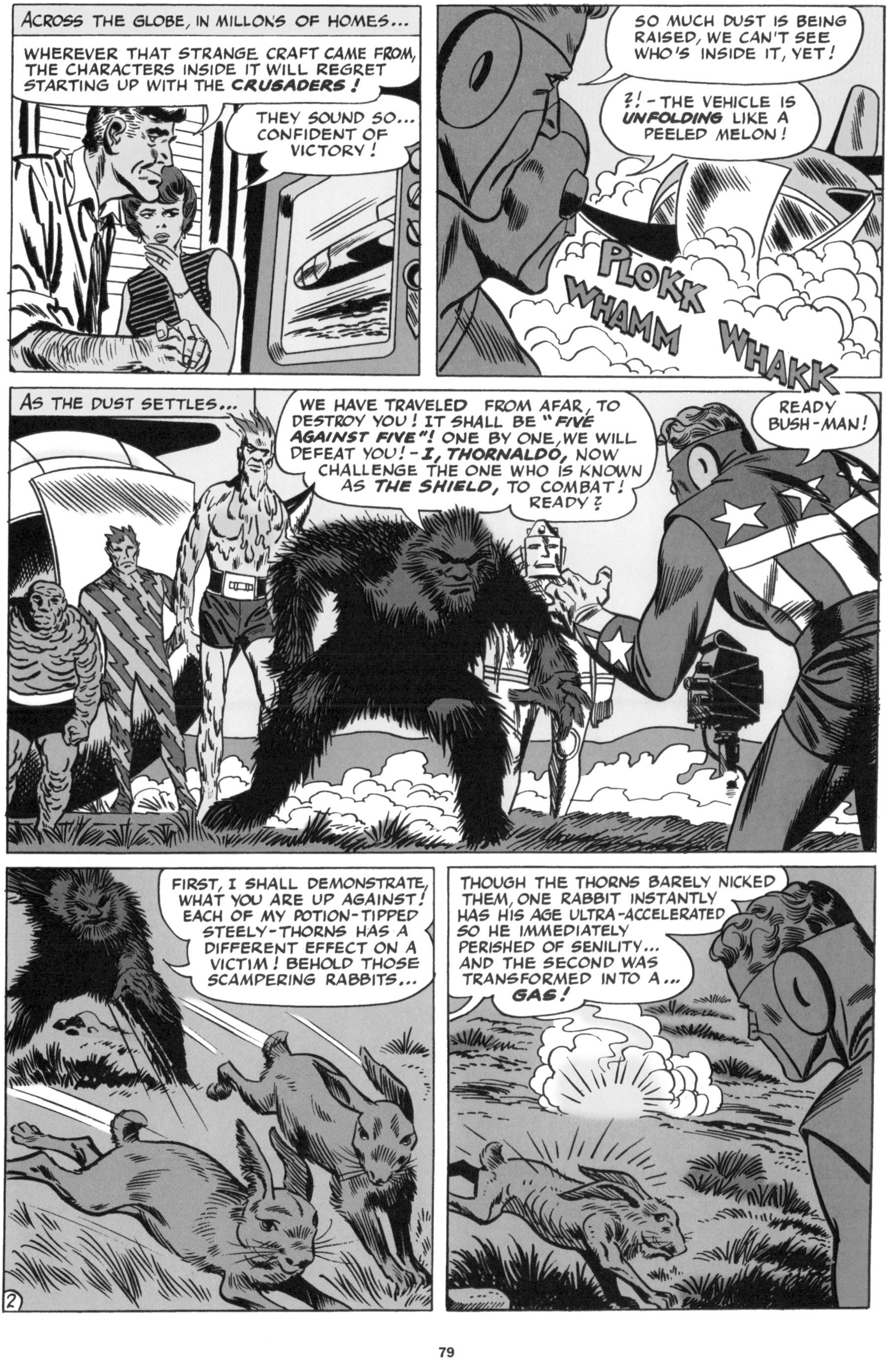
ACROSS THE GLOBE, IN MILLONS OF HOMES...
WHEREVER THAT STRANGE CRAFT CAME FROM, THE CHARACTERS INSIDE IT WILL REGRET STARTING UP WITH THE CRUSADERS!
THEY SOUND SO... CONFIDENT OF VICTORY!
SO MUCH DUST IS BEING RAISED, WE CAN'T SEE WHO'S INSIDE IT, YET!
?! - THE VEHICLE IS UNFOLDING LIKE A PEELED MELON!
PLOKK
WHAMM
WHAKK
AS THE DUST SETTLES...
WE HAVE TRAVELED FROM AFAR, TO DESTROY YOU! IT SHALL BE "FIVE AGAINST FIVE"! ONE BY ONE, WE WILL DEFEAT YOU! - I, THORNALDO, NOW CHALLENGE THE ONE WHO IS KNOWN AS THE SHIELD, TO COMBAT! READY?
READY BUSH-MAN!
FIRST, I SHALL DEMONSTRATE, WHAT YOU ARE UP AGAINST! EACH OF MY POTION-TIPPED STEELY-THORNS HAS A DIFFERENT EFFECT ON A VICTIM! BEHOLD THOSE SCAMPERING RABBITS...
THOUGH THE THORNS BARELY NICKED THEM, ONE RABBIT INSTANTLY HAS HIS AGE ULTRA-ACCELERATED SO HE IMMEDIATELY PERISHED OF SENILITY... AND THE SECOND WAS TRANSFORMED INTO A... GAS!
2

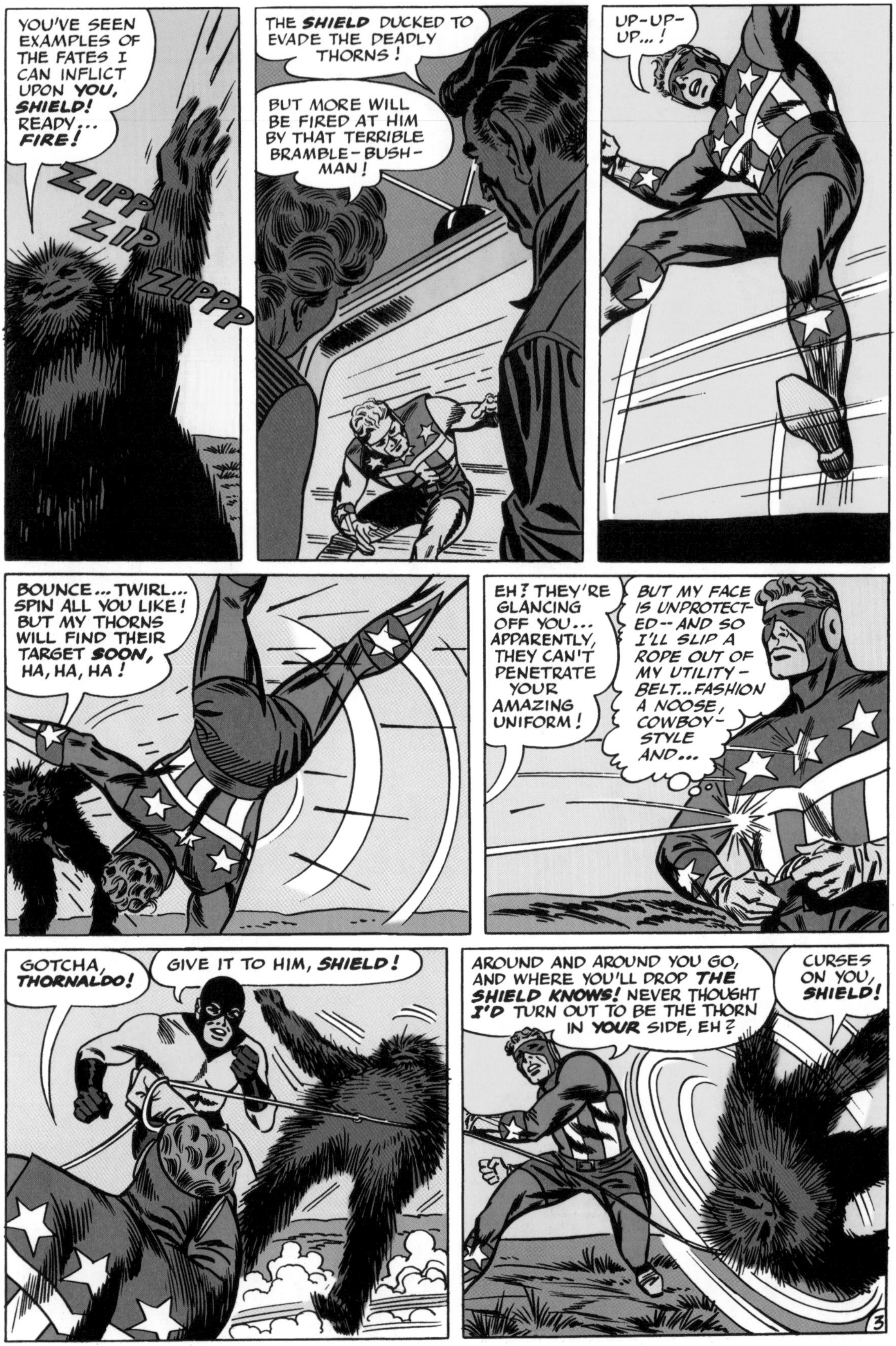
YOU'VE SEEN EXAMPLES OF THE FATES I CAN INFLICT UPON YOU, SHIELD! READY... FIRE!
ZIPP
ZIP
ZIPPP
THE SHIELD DUCKED TO EVADE THE DEADLY THORNS!
BUT MORE WILL BE FIRED AT HIM BY THAT TERRIBLE BRAMBLE-BUSH-MAN!
UP-UP-UP...!
BOUNCE... TWIRL... SPIN ALL YOU LIKE! BUT MY THORNS WILL FIND THEIR TARGET SOON, HA, HA, HA!
EH? THEY'RE GLANCING OFF YOU... APPARENTLY, THEY CAN'T PENETRATE YOUR AMAZING UNIFORM!
BUT MY FACE IS UNPROTECTED-- AND SO I'LL SLIP A ROPE OUT OF MY UTILITY-BELT... FASHION A NOOSE, COWBOY-STYLE AND...
GOTCHA, THORNALDO!
GIVE IT TO HIM, SHIELD!
AROUND AND AROUND YOU GO, AND WHERE YOU'LL DROP THE SHIELD KNOWS! NEVER THOUGHT I'D TURN OUT TO BE THE THORN IN YOUR SIDE, EH?
CURSES ON YOU, SHIELD!
3

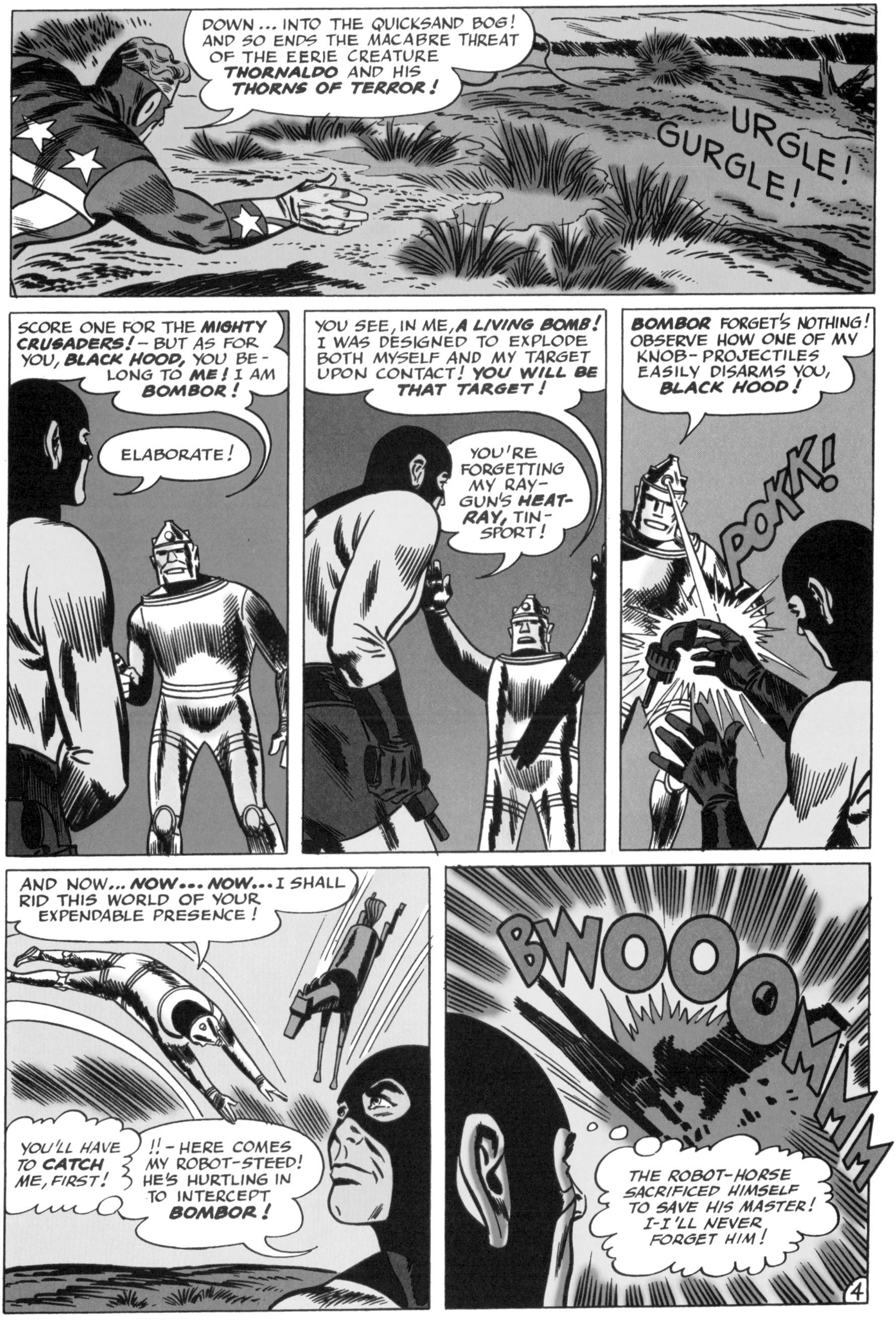
DOWN ... INTO THE QUICKSAND BOG! AND SO ENDS THE MACABRE THREAT OF THE EERIE CREATURE THORNALDO AND HIS THORNS OF TERROR!
URGLE! GURGLE!
SCORE ONE FOR THE MIGHTY CRUSADERS! – BUT AS FOR YOU, BLACK HOOD, YOU BELONG TO ME! I AM BOMBOR!
ELABORATE!
YOU SEE, IN ME, A LIVING BOMB! I WAS DESIGNED TO EXPLODE BOTH MYSELF AND MY TARGET UPON CONTACT! YOU WILL BE THAT TARGET!
YOU'RE FORGETTING MY RAY-GUN'S HEAT-RAY, TIN-SPORT!
BOMBOR FORGET'S NOTHING! OBSERVE HOW ONE OF MY KNOB-PROJECTILES EASILY DISARMS YOU, BLACK HOOD!
POKK!
AND NOW... NOW... NOW... I SHALL RID THIS WORLD OF YOUR EXPENDABLE PRESENCE!
YOU'LL HAVE TO CATCH ME, FIRST!
!! – HERE COMES MY ROBOT-STEED! HE'S HURTLING IN TO INTERCEPT BOMBOR!
BWOOOOMMMM
THE ROBOT-HORSE SACRIFICED HIMSELF TO SAVE HIS MASTER! I-I'LL NEVER FORGET HIM!
4

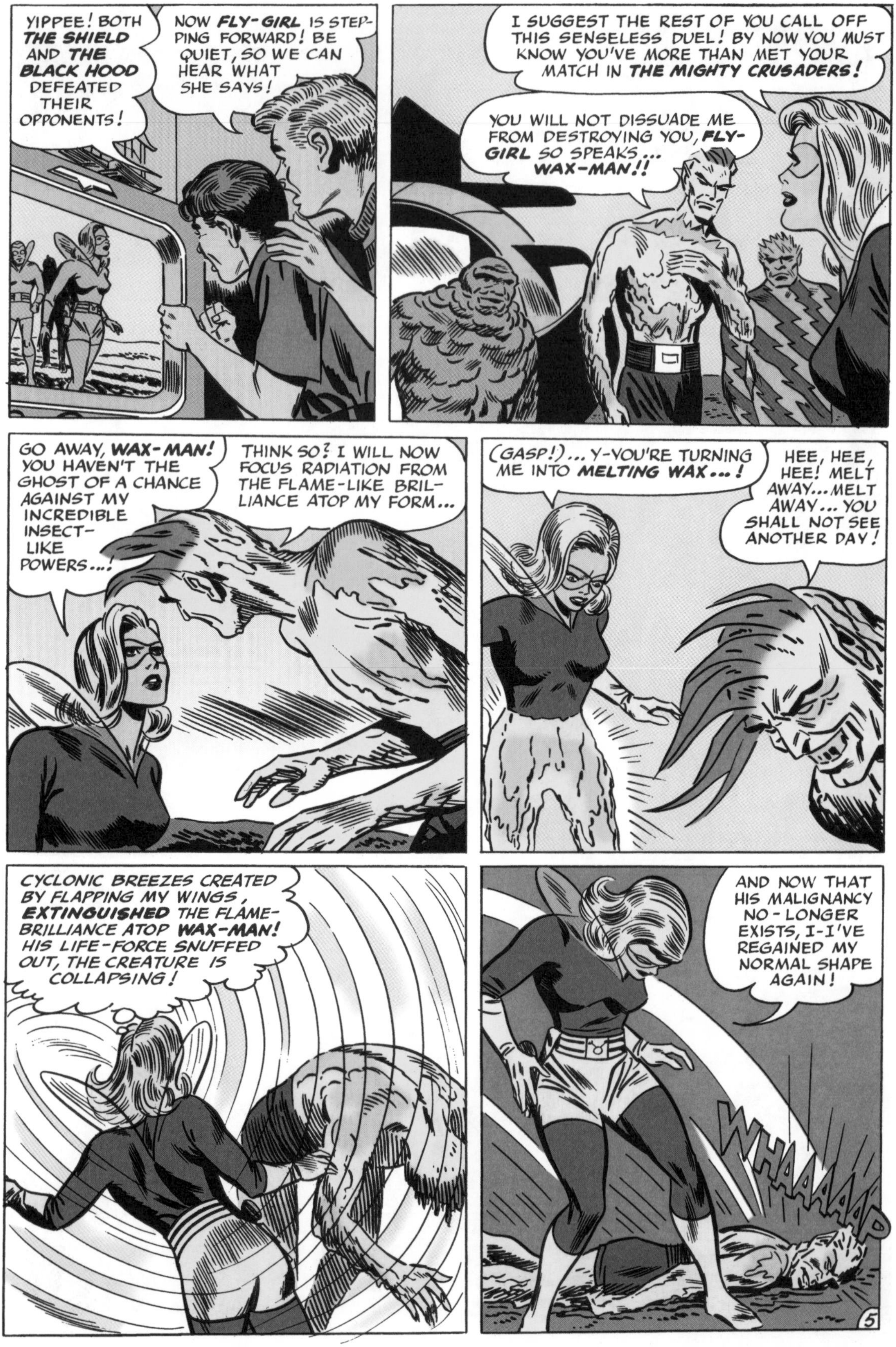
YIPPEE! BOTH THE SHIELD AND THE BLACK HOOD DEFEATED THEIR OPPONENTS!
NOW FLY-GIRL IS STEPPING FORWARD! BE QUIET, SO WE CAN HEAR WHAT SHE SAYS!
I SUGGEST THE REST OF YOU CALL OFF THIS SENSELESS DUEL! BY NOW YOU MUST KNOW YOU'VE MORE THAN MET YOUR MATCH IN THE MIGHTY CRUSADERS!
YOU WILL NOT DISSUADE ME FROM DESTROYING YOU, FLY-GIRL SO SPEAKS... WAX-MAN!!
GO AWAY, WAX-MAN! YOU HAVEN'T THE GHOST OF A CHANCE AGAINST MY INCREDIBLE INSECT-LIKE POWERS...!
THINK SO? I WILL NOW FOCUS RADIATION FROM THE FLAME-LIKE BRILLIANCE ATOP MY FORM...
(GASP!)... Y-YOU'RE TURNING ME INTO MELTING WAX...!
HEE, HEE, HEE! MELT AWAY... MELT AWAY... YOU SHALL NOT SEE ANOTHER DAY!
CYCLONIC BREEZES CREATED BY FLAPPING MY WINGS, EXTINGUISHED THE FLAME-BRILLIANCE ATOP WAX-MAN! HIS LIFE-FORCE SNUFFED OUT, THE CREATURE IS COLLAPSING!
AND NOW THAT HIS MALIGNANCY NO-LONGER EXISTS, I-I'VE REGAINED MY NORMAL SHAPE AGAIN!
WHAAAAAP
5

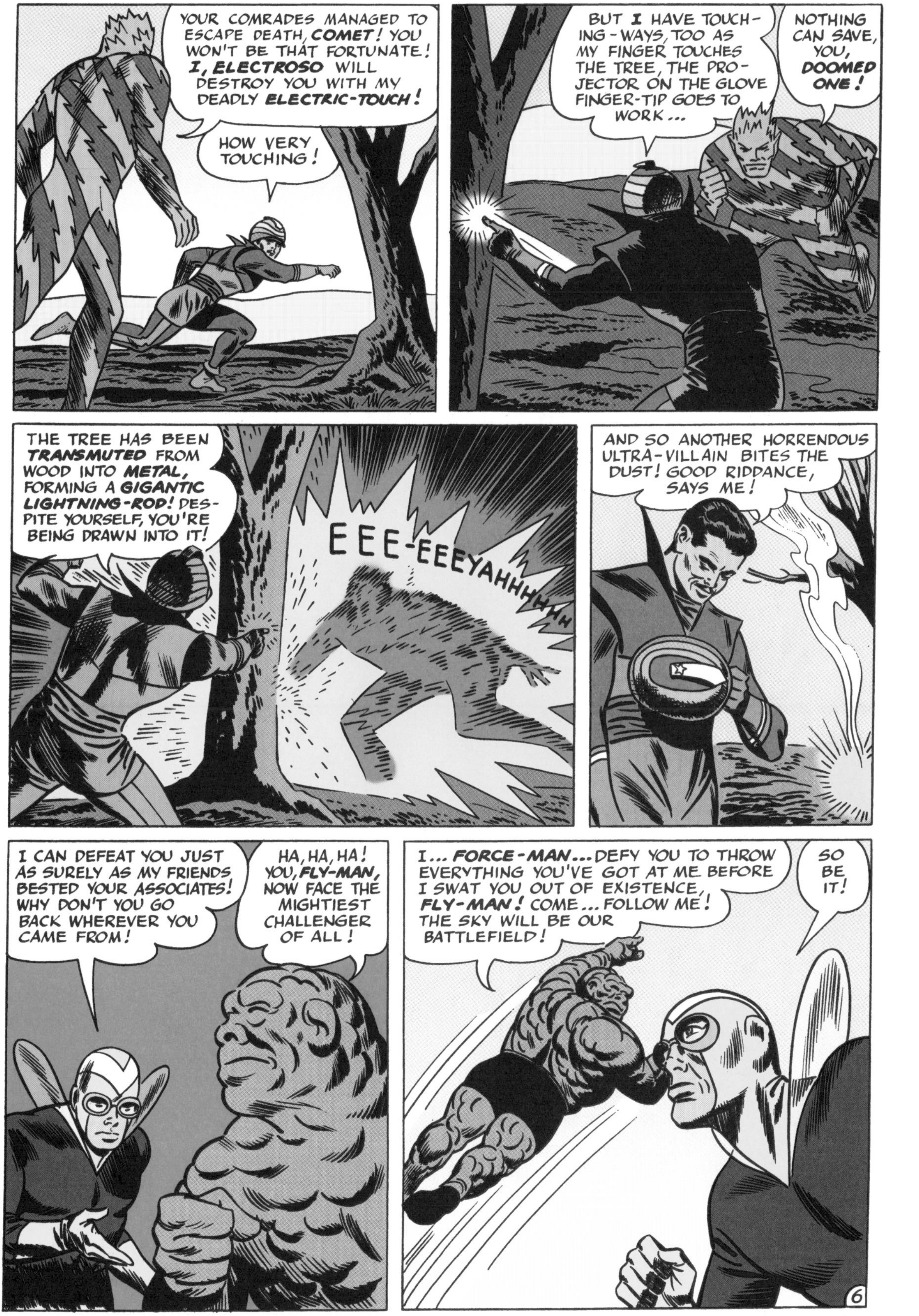
YOUR COMRADES MANAGED TO ESCAPE DEATH, COMET! YOU WON'T BE THAT FORTUNATE! I, ELECTROSO WILL DESTROY YOU WITH MY DEADLY ELECTRIC-TOUCH!
HOW VERY TOUCHING!
BUT I HAVE TOUCHING-WAYS, TOO AS MY FINGER TOUCHES THE TREE, THE PROJECTOR ON THE GLOVE FINGER-TIP GOES TO WORK...
NOTHING CAN SAVE, YOU, DOOMED ONE!
THE TREE HAS BEEN TRANSMUTED FROM WOOD INTO METAL, FORMING A GIGANTIC LIGHTNING-ROD! DESPITE YOURSELF, YOU'RE BEING DRAWN INTO IT!
EEE-EEEYAHHHHHH
AND SO ANOTHER HORRENDOUS ULTRA-VILLAIN BITES THE DUST! GOOD RIDDANCE, SAYS ME!
I CAN DEFEAT YOU JUST AS SURELY AS MY FRIENDS BESTED YOUR ASSOCIATES! WHY DON'T YOU GO BACK WHEREVER YOU CAME FROM!
HA, HA, HA! YOU, FLY-MAN, NOW FACE THE MIGHTIEST CHALLENGER OF ALL!
I... FORCE-MAN... DEFY YOU TO THROW EVERYTHING YOU'VE GOT AT ME BEFORE I SWAT YOU OUT OF EXISTENCE, FLY-MAN! COME... FOLLOW ME! THE SKY WILL BE OUR BATTLEFIELD!
SO BE IT!
6

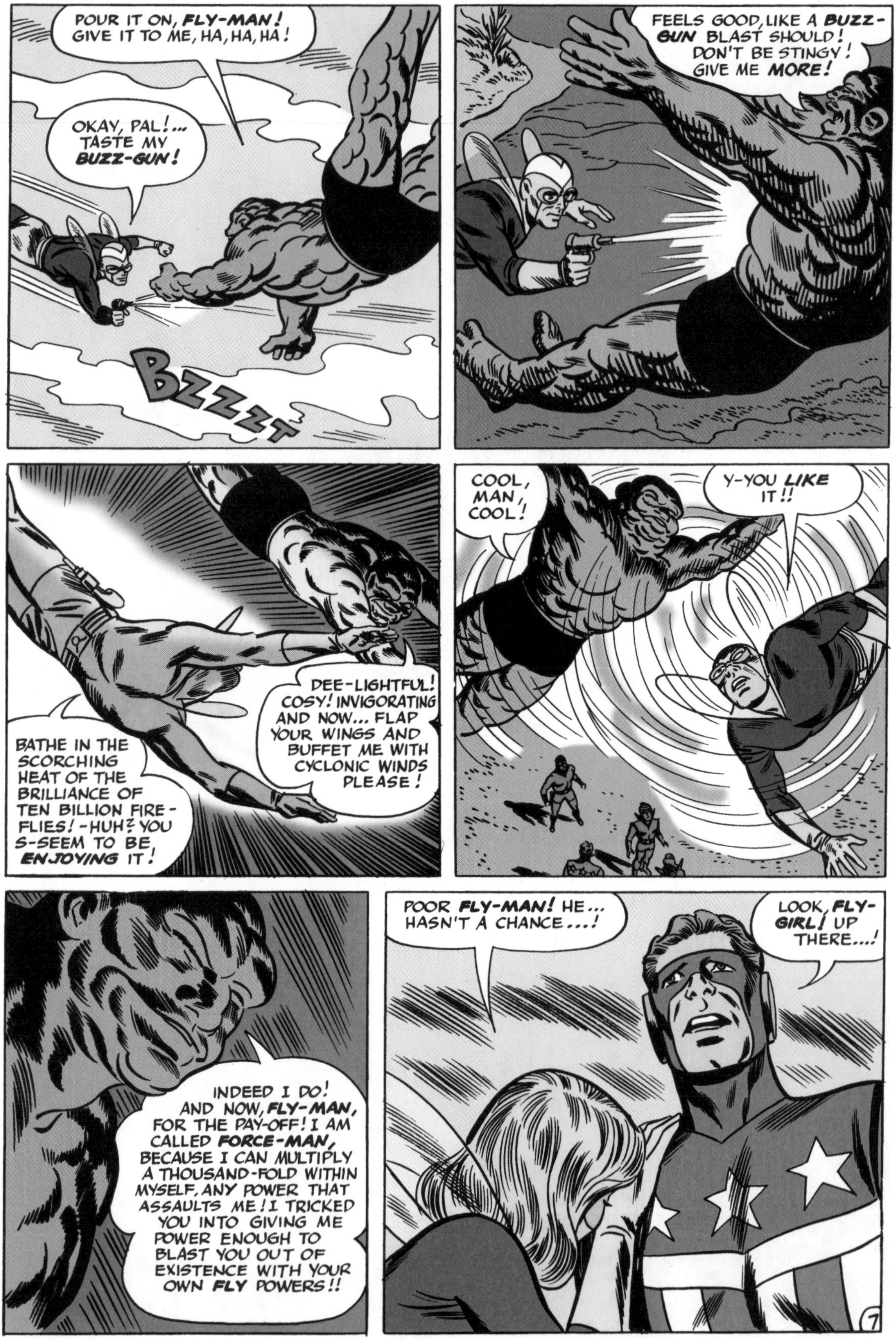
POUR IT ON, FLY-MAN! GIVE IT TO ME, HA, HA, HA!
OKAY, PAL!... TASTE MY BUZZ-GUN!
BZZZZT
FEELS GOOD, LIKE A BUZZ-GUN BLAST SHOULD! DON'T BE STINGY! GIVE ME MORE!
BATHE IN THE SCORCHING HEAT OF THE BRILLIANCE OF TEN BILLION FIRE-FLIES! -HUH? YOU S-SEEM TO BE ENJOYING IT!
DEE-LIGHTFUL! COSY! INVIGORATING AND NOW... FLAP YOUR WINGS AND BUFFET ME WITH CYCLONIC WINDS PLEASE!
COOL, MAN, COOL!
Y-YOU LIKE IT!!
INDEED I DO! AND NOW, FLY-MAN, FOR THE PAY-OFF! I AM CALLED FORCE-MAN, BECAUSE I CAN MULTIPLY A THOUSAND-FOLD WITHIN MYSELF, ANY POWER THAT ASSAULTS ME! I TRICKED YOU INTO GIVING ME POWER ENOUGH TO BLAST YOU OUT OF EXISTENCE WITH YOUR OWN FLY POWERS!!
POOR FLY-MAN! HE... HASN'T A CHANCE...!
LOOK, FLY-GIRL! UP THERE...!
7

FAREWELL, *FLY-MAN!* I SEE THE ERROR OF MY WAYS! I SHALL RETURN WHENCE I CAME!

SO LONG, FELLA!

I DON'T GET IT, *FLY-MAN!* WHY DID *FORCE-MAN* LEAVE AFTER GAINING THE POWER TO DEFEAT YOU??

I TRIED A LONG-SHOT...THAT WORKED...

SINCE *FORCE-MAN* WAS *ABSORBING* EVERYTHING I TOSSED AT HIM, I CONCENTRATED ON IMPARTING TO HIM THE GREATEST FORCE OF ALL... THE POWER FOR *DOING GOOD!* ABSORBING MY GOOD-WILL *THOUGHTS*... GREATLY MAGNIFIED... *REFORMED* HIM!

AROUND THE WORLD, MILLIONS OF TELE-VISION-VIEWERS REJOICE...

BY JOVE! HAVING JOLLY WELL DEFEATED THE INVADERS, THE ULTRA-HEROES ARE GOING TO FINISH THE INTER-*MIGHTY CRUSADERS* FORMATION CEREMONIES!

I SAY! GOOD SHOW!

BUT ONCE AGAIN THE CEREMONY IS INTERRUPTED...

DON'T JOIN, *FLY-GIRL!* ONE PERSON WITH *FLY-*POWERS IS ENOUGH IN THIS COMBO!

NO! *YOU* QUIT!

YOU KNOW SOMETHING, *SHIELD?* WITHOUT YOUR AMAZING UNIFORM, YOU'RE *NOTHING!*

HOW'D YOU LIKE SOME BLACK *EYES,* TO MATCH YOUR BLACK *HOOD?*

YOU *ALL* SICKEN ME!

SEE *PART II* IN THIS ISSUE FOR THE START-LING CONCLUSION OF THIS ASTOUNDING TALE!

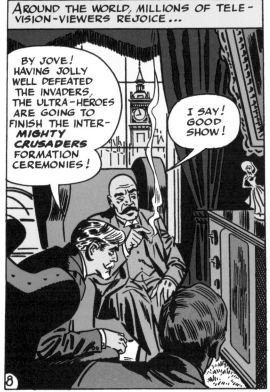

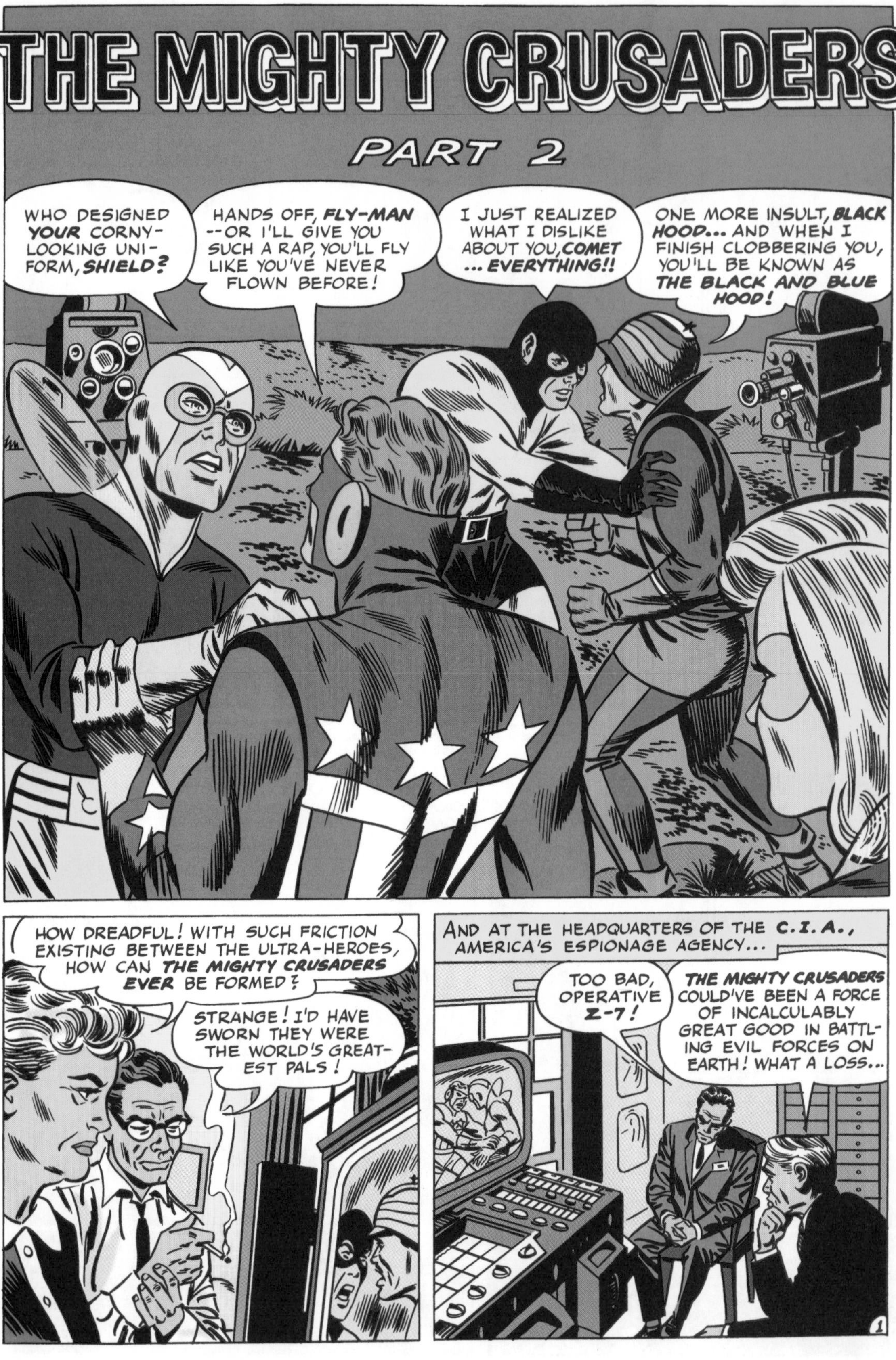
THE MIGHTY CRUSADERS
PART 2
WHO DESIGNED YOUR CORNY-LOOKING UNI-FORM, SHIELD?
HANDS OFF, FLY-MAN --OR I'LL GIVE YOU SUCH A RAP, YOU'LL FLY LIKE YOU'VE NEVER FLOWN BEFORE!
I JUST REALIZED WHAT I DISLIKE ABOUT YOU, COMET ... EVERYTHING!!
ONE MORE INSULT, BLACK HOOD... AND WHEN I FINISH CLOBBERING YOU, YOU'LL BE KNOWN AS THE BLACK AND BLUE HOOD!
HOW DREADFUL! WITH SUCH FRICTION EXISTING BETWEEN THE ULTRA-HEROES, HOW CAN THE MIGHTY CRUSADERS EVER BE FORMED?
STRANGE! I'D HAVE SWORN THEY WERE THE WORLD'S GREAT-EST PALS!
AND AT THE HEADQUARTERS OF THE C.I.A., AMERICA'S ESPIONAGE AGENCY...
TOO BAD, OPERATIVE Z-7!
THE MIGHTY CRUSADERS COULD'VE BEEN A FORCE OF INCALCULABLY GREAT GOOD IN BATTL-ING EVIL FORCES ON EARTH! WHAT A LOSS...
1

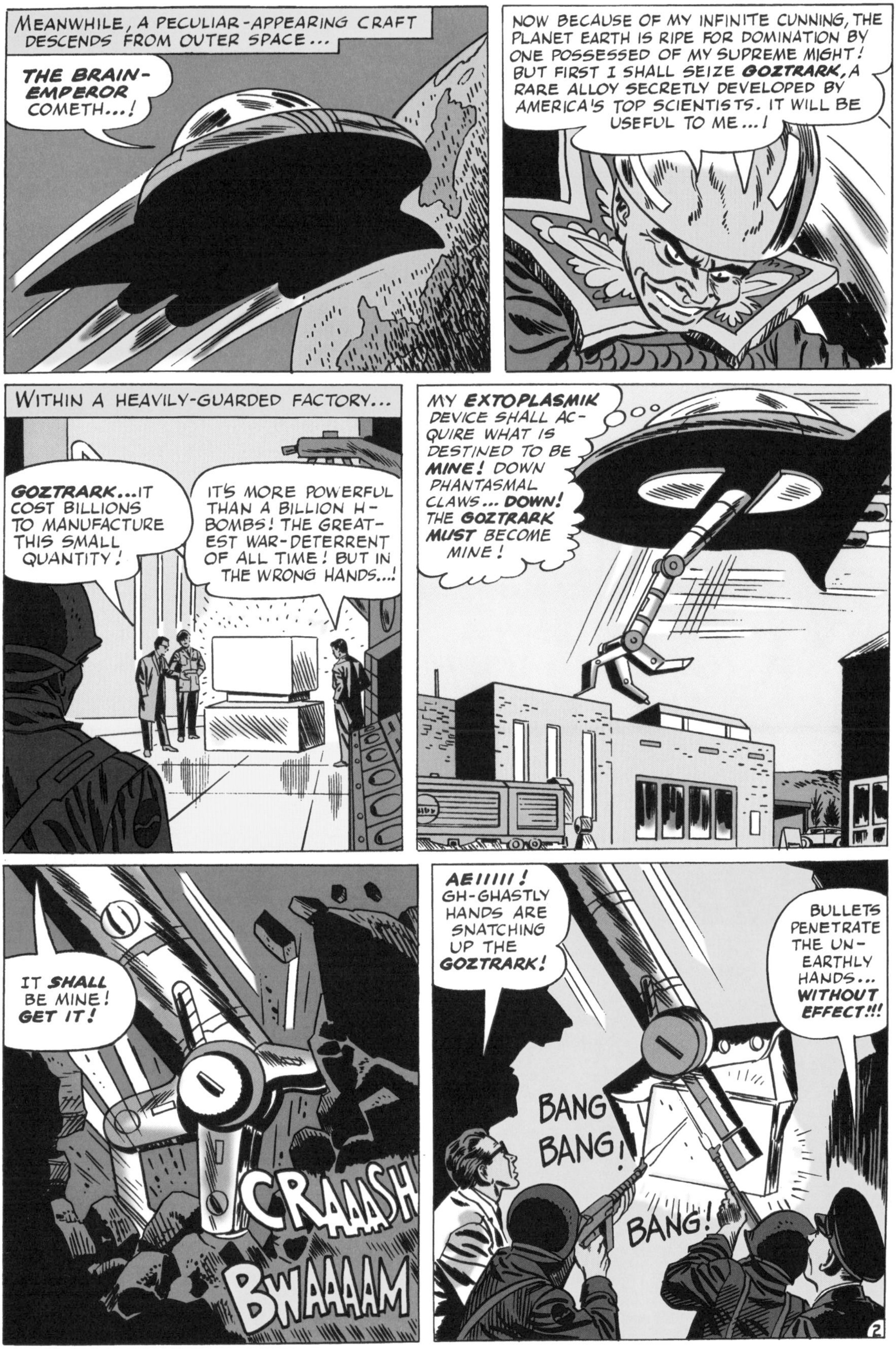
MEANWHILE, A PECULIAR-APPEARING CRAFT DESCENDS FROM OUTER SPACE...
THE BRAIN-EMPEROR COMETH...!
NOW BECAUSE OF MY INFINITE CUNNING, THE PLANET EARTH IS RIPE FOR DOMINATION BY ONE POSSESSED OF MY SUPREME MIGHT! BUT FIRST I SHALL SEIZE GOZTRARK, A RARE ALLOY SECRETLY DEVELOPED BY AMERICA'S TOP SCIENTISTS. IT WILL BE USEFUL TO ME...!
WITHIN A HEAVILY-GUARDED FACTORY...
GOZTRARK...IT COST BILLIONS TO MANUFACTURE THIS SMALL QUANTITY!
IT'S MORE POWERFUL THAN A BILLION H-BOMBS! THE GREATEST WAR-DETERRENT OF ALL TIME! BUT IN THE WRONG HANDS...!
MY EXTOPLASMIK DEVICE SHALL ACQUIRE WHAT IS DESTINED TO BE MINE! DOWN PHANTASMAL CLAWS... DOWN! THE GOZTRARK MUST BECOME MINE!
IT SHALL BE MINE! GET IT!
CRAAASH
BWAAAAM
AEIIIII! GH-GHASTLY HANDS ARE SNATCHING UP THE GOZTRARK!
BULLETS PENETRATE THE UN-EARTHLY HANDS... WITHOUT EFFECT!!!
BANG
BANG!
BANG!
2

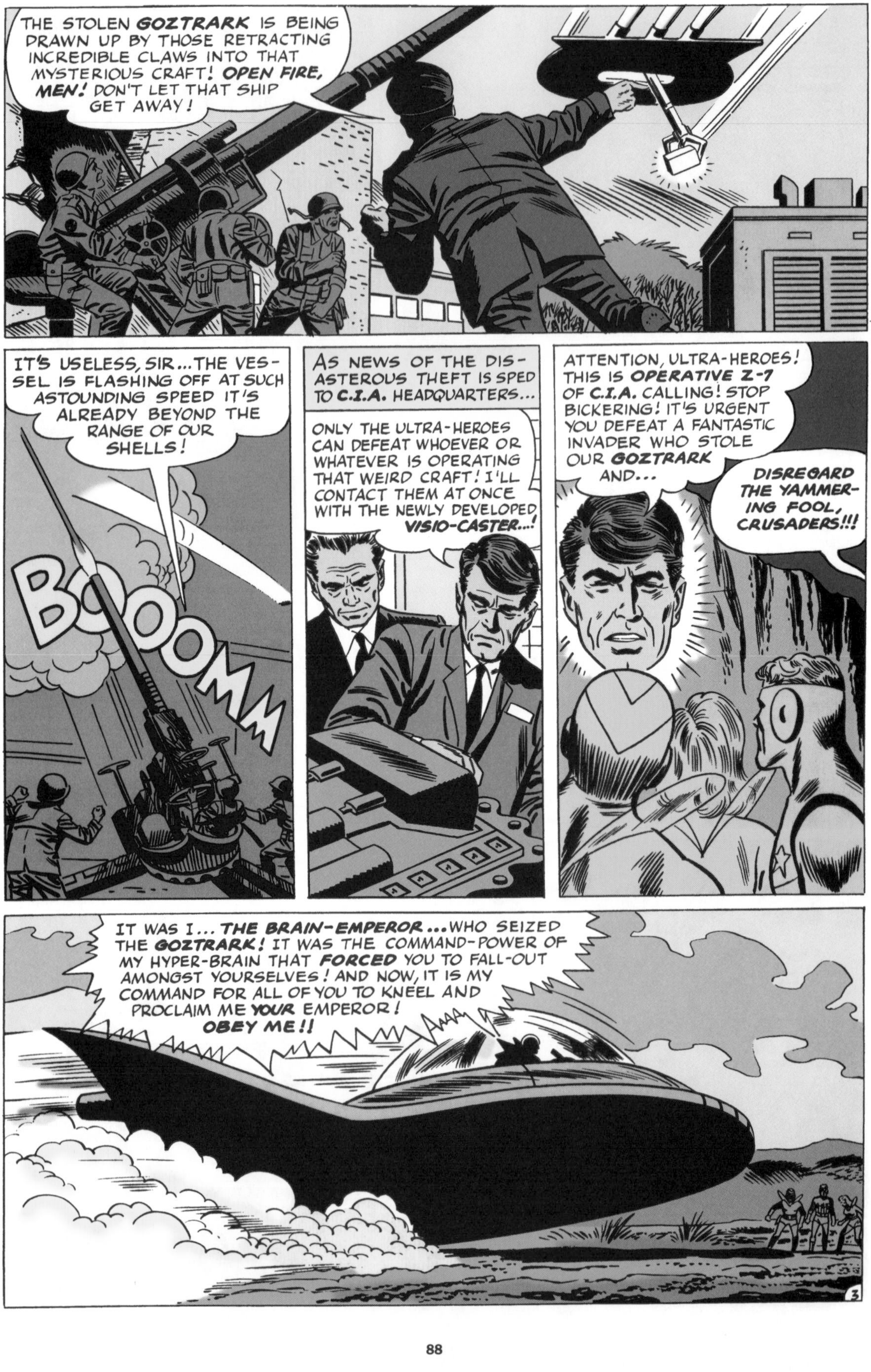
THE STOLEN GOZTRARK IS BEING DRAWN UP BY THOSE RETRACTING INCREDIBLE CLAWS INTO THAT MYSTERIOUS CRAFT! OPEN FIRE, MEN! DON'T LET THAT SHIP GET AWAY!
IT'S USELESS, SIR...THE VESSEL IS FLASHING OFF AT SUCH ASTOUNDING SPEED IT'S ALREADY BEYOND THE RANGE OF OUR SHELLS!
BOOOMM
AS NEWS OF THE DISASTEROUS THEFT IS SPED TO C.I.A. HEADQUARTERS...
ONLY THE ULTRA-HEROES CAN DEFEAT WHOEVER OR WHATEVER IS OPERATING THAT WEIRD CRAFT! I'LL CONTACT THEM AT ONCE WITH THE NEWLY DEVELOPED VISIO-CASTER...!
ATTENTION, ULTRA-HEROES! THIS IS OPERATIVE Z-7 OF C.I.A. CALLING! STOP BICKERING! IT'S URGENT YOU DEFEAT A FANTASTIC INVADER WHO STOLE OUR GOZTRARK AND...
DISREGARD THE YAMMERING FOOL, CRUSADERS!!!
IT WAS I... THE BRAIN-EMPEROR...WHO SEIZED THE GOZTRARK! IT WAS THE COMMAND-POWER OF MY HYPER-BRAIN THAT FORCED YOU TO FALL-OUT AMONGST YOURSELVES! AND NOW, IT IS MY COMMAND FOR ALL OF YOU TO KNEEL AND PROCLAIM ME YOUR EMPEROR! OBEY ME!!
3

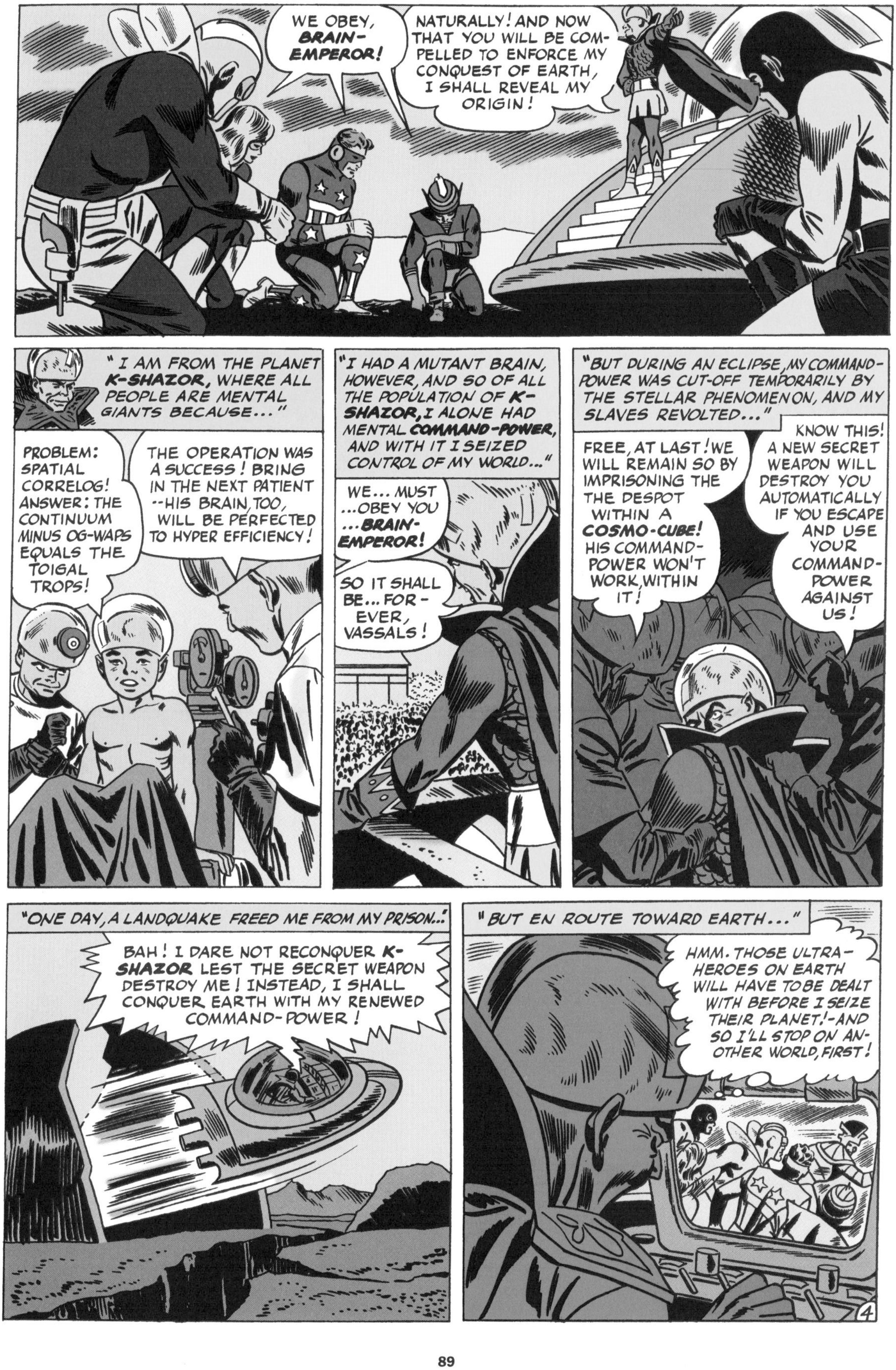
WE OBEY, BRAIN-EMPEROR!
NATURALLY! AND NOW THAT YOU WILL BE COMPELLED TO ENFORCE MY CONQUEST OF EARTH, I SHALL REVEAL MY ORIGIN!
"I AM FROM THE PLANET K-SHAZOR, WHERE ALL PEOPLE ARE MENTAL GIANTS BECAUSE..."
PROBLEM: SPATIAL CORRELOG! ANSWER: THE CONTINUUM MINUS OG-WAPS EQUALS THE TOIGAL TROPS!
THE OPERATION WAS A SUCCESS! BRING IN THE NEXT PATIENT --HIS BRAIN, TOO, WILL BE PERFECTED TO HYPER EFFICIENCY!
"I HAD A MUTANT BRAIN, HOWEVER, AND SO OF ALL THE POPULATION OF K-SHAZOR, I ALONE HAD MENTAL COMMAND-POWER, AND WITH IT I SEIZED CONTROL OF MY WORLD..."
WE... MUST ...OBEY YOU ...BRAIN-EMPEROR!
SO IT SHALL BE... FOR-EVER, VASSALS!
"BUT DURING AN ECLIPSE, MY COMMAND-POWER WAS CUT-OFF TEMPORARILY BY THE STELLAR PHENOMENON, AND MY SLAVES REVOLTED..."
FREE, AT LAST! WE WILL REMAIN SO BY IMPRISONING THE THE DESPOT WITHIN A COSMO-CUBE! HIS COMMAND-POWER WON'T WORK, WITHIN IT!
KNOW THIS! A NEW SECRET WEAPON WILL DESTROY YOU AUTOMATICALLY IF YOU ESCAPE AND USE YOUR COMMAND-POWER AGAINST US!
"ONE DAY, A LANDQUAKE FREED ME FROM MY PRISON..."
BAH! I DARE NOT RECONQUER K-SHAZOR LEST THE SECRET WEAPON DESTROY ME! INSTEAD, I SHALL CONQUER EARTH WITH MY RENEWED COMMAND-POWER!
"BUT EN ROUTE TOWARD EARTH..."
HMM. THOSE ULTRA-HEROES ON EARTH WILL HAVE TO BE DEALT WITH BEFORE I SEIZE THEIR PLANET!-AND SO I'LL STOP ON ANOTHER WORLD, FIRST!
4

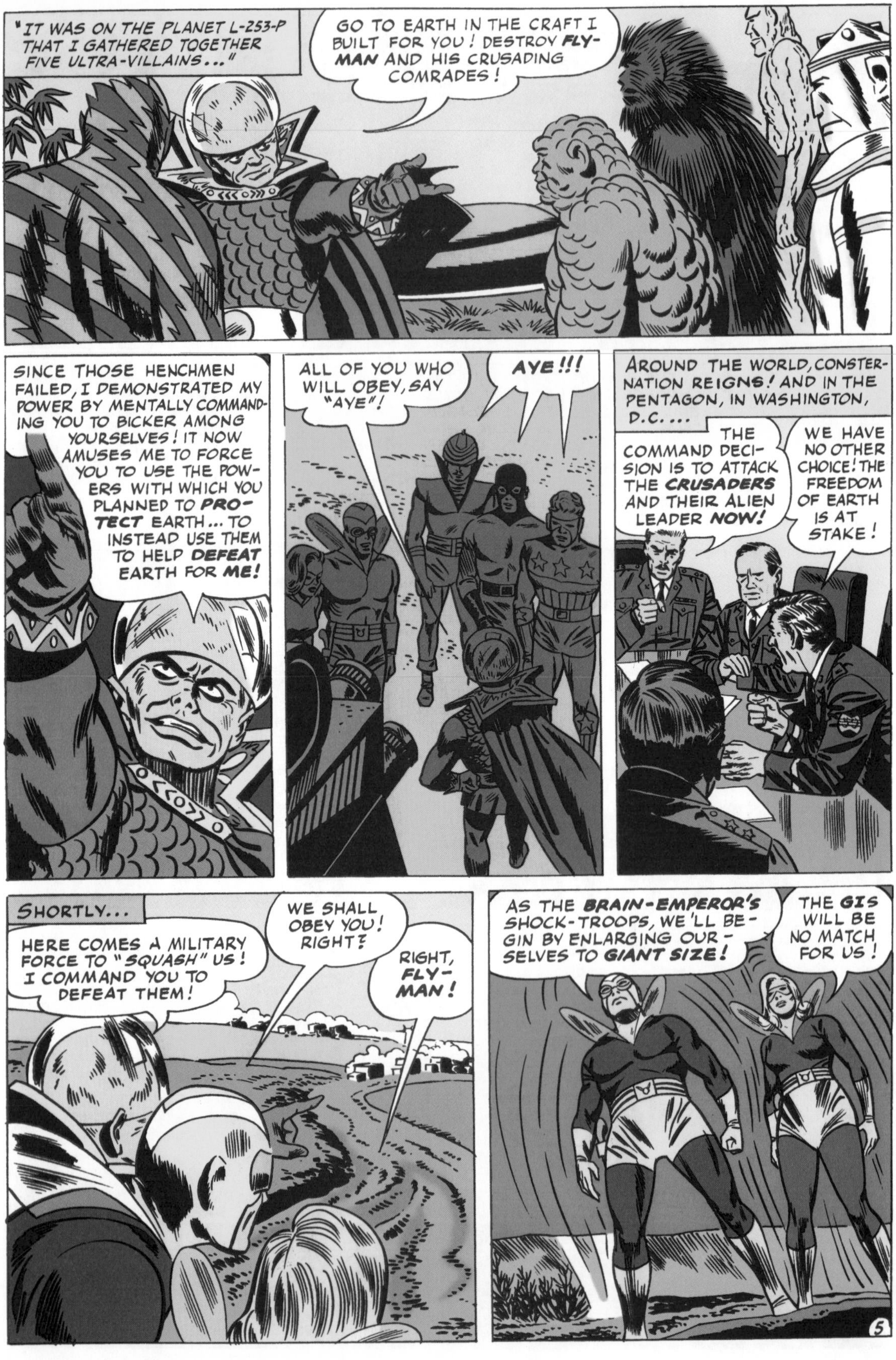
"IT WAS ON THE PLANET L-253-P THAT I GATHERED TOGETHER FIVE ULTRA-VILLAINS..."
GO TO EARTH IN THE CRAFT I BUILT FOR YOU! DESTROY FLY-MAN AND HIS CRUSADING COMRADES!
SINCE THOSE HENCHMEN FAILED, I DEMONSTRATED MY POWER BY MENTALLY COMMANDING YOU TO BICKER AMONG YOURSELVES! IT NOW AMUSES ME TO FORCE YOU TO USE THE POWERS WITH WHICH YOU PLANNED TO PROTECT EARTH... TO INSTEAD USE THEM TO HELP DEFEAT EARTH FOR ME!
ALL OF YOU WHO WILL OBEY, SAY "AYE"!
AYE!!!
AROUND THE WORLD, CONSTERNATION REIGNS! AND IN THE PENTAGON, IN WASHINGTON, D.C....
THE COMMAND DECISION IS TO ATTACK THE CRUSADERS AND THEIR ALIEN LEADER NOW!
WE HAVE NO OTHER CHOICE! THE FREEDOM OF EARTH IS AT STAKE!
SHORTLY...
HERE COMES A MILITARY FORCE TO "SQUASH" US! I COMMAND YOU TO DEFEAT THEM!
WE SHALL OBEY YOU! RIGHT?
RIGHT, FLY-MAN!
AS THE BRAIN-EMPEROR'S SHOCK-TROOPS, WE'LL BEGIN BY ENLARGING OURSELVES TO GIANT SIZE!
THE GIS WILL BE NO MATCH FOR US!
5

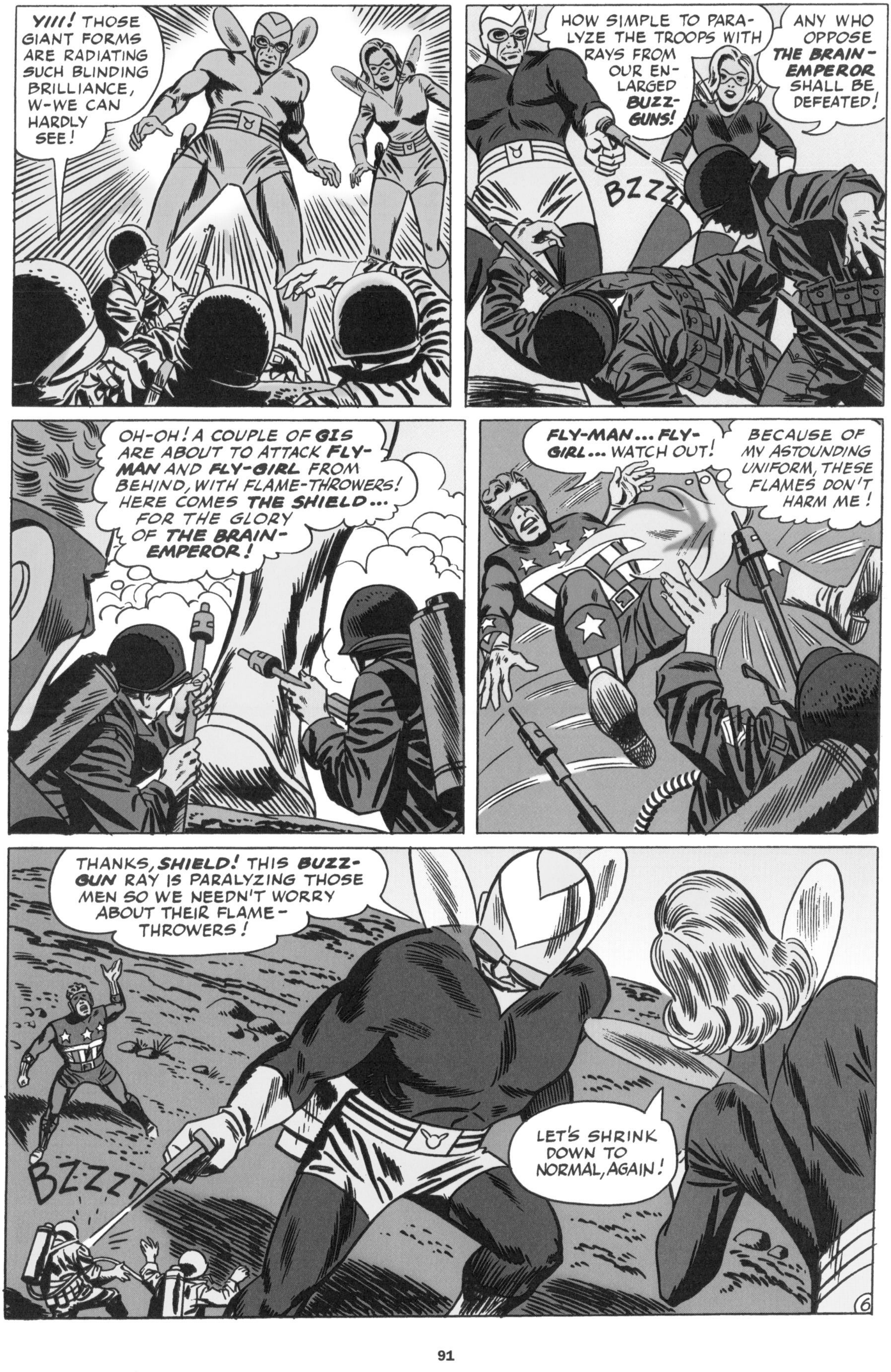
YIII! THOSE GIANT FORMS ARE RADIATING SUCH BLINDING BRILLIANCE, W-WE CAN HARDLY SEE!
HOW SIMPLE TO PARALYZE THE TROOPS WITH RAYS FROM OUR ENLARGED BUZZ-GUNS!
ANY WHO OPPOSE THE BRAIN-EMPEROR SHALL BE DEFEATED!
BZZZT
OH-OH! A COUPLE OF GIS ARE ABOUT TO ATTACK FLY-MAN AND FLY-GIRL FROM BEHIND, WITH FLAME-THROWERS! HERE COMES THE SHIELD... FOR THE GLORY OF THE BRAIN-EMPEROR!
FLY-MAN... FLY-GIRL... WATCH OUT!
BECAUSE OF MY ASTOUNDING UNIFORM, THESE FLAMES DON'T HARM ME!
THANKS, SHIELD! THIS BUZZ-GUN RAY IS PARALYZING THOSE MEN SO WE NEEDN'T WORRY ABOUT THEIR FLAME-THROWERS!
LET'S SHRINK DOWN TO NORMAL, AGAIN!
BZZZT
6

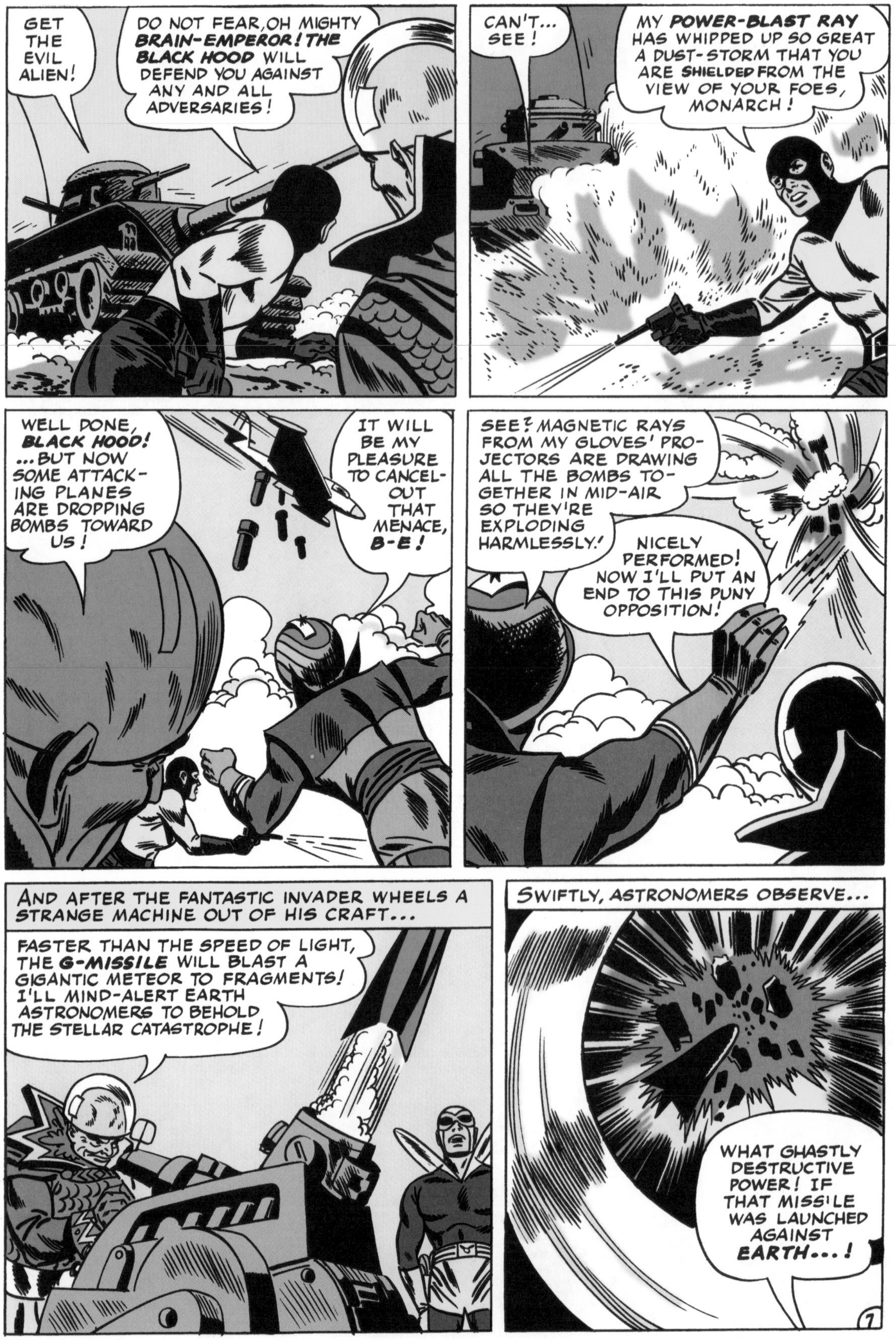
GET THE EVIL ALIEN!
DO NOT FEAR, OH MIGHTY BRAIN-EMPEROR! THE BLACK HOOD WILL DEFEND YOU AGAINST ANY AND ALL ADVERSARIES!
CAN'T... SEE!
MY POWER-BLAST RAY HAS WHIPPED UP SO GREAT A DUST-STORM THAT YOU ARE SHIELDED FROM THE VIEW OF YOUR FOES, MONARCH!
WELL DONE, BLACK HOOD! ...BUT NOW SOME ATTACKING PLANES ARE DROPPING BOMBS TOWARD US!
IT WILL BE MY PLEASURE TO CANCEL-OUT THAT MENACE, B-E!
SEE? MAGNETIC RAYS FROM MY GLOVES' PROJECTORS ARE DRAWING ALL THE BOMBS TOGETHER IN MID-AIR SO THEY'RE EXPLODING HARMLESSLY!
NICELY PERFORMED! NOW I'LL PUT AN END TO THIS PUNY OPPOSITION!
AND AFTER THE FANTASTIC INVADER WHEELS A STRANGE MACHINE OUT OF HIS CRAFT...
FASTER THAN THE SPEED OF LIGHT, THE G-MISSILE WILL BLAST A GIGANTIC METEOR TO FRAGMENTS! I'LL MIND-ALERT EARTH ASTRONOMERS TO BEHOLD THE STELLAR CATASTROPHE!
SWIFTLY, ASTRONOMERS OBSERVE...
WHAT GHASTLY DESTRUCTIVE POWER! IF THAT MISSILE WAS LAUNCHED AGAINST EARTH...!
7

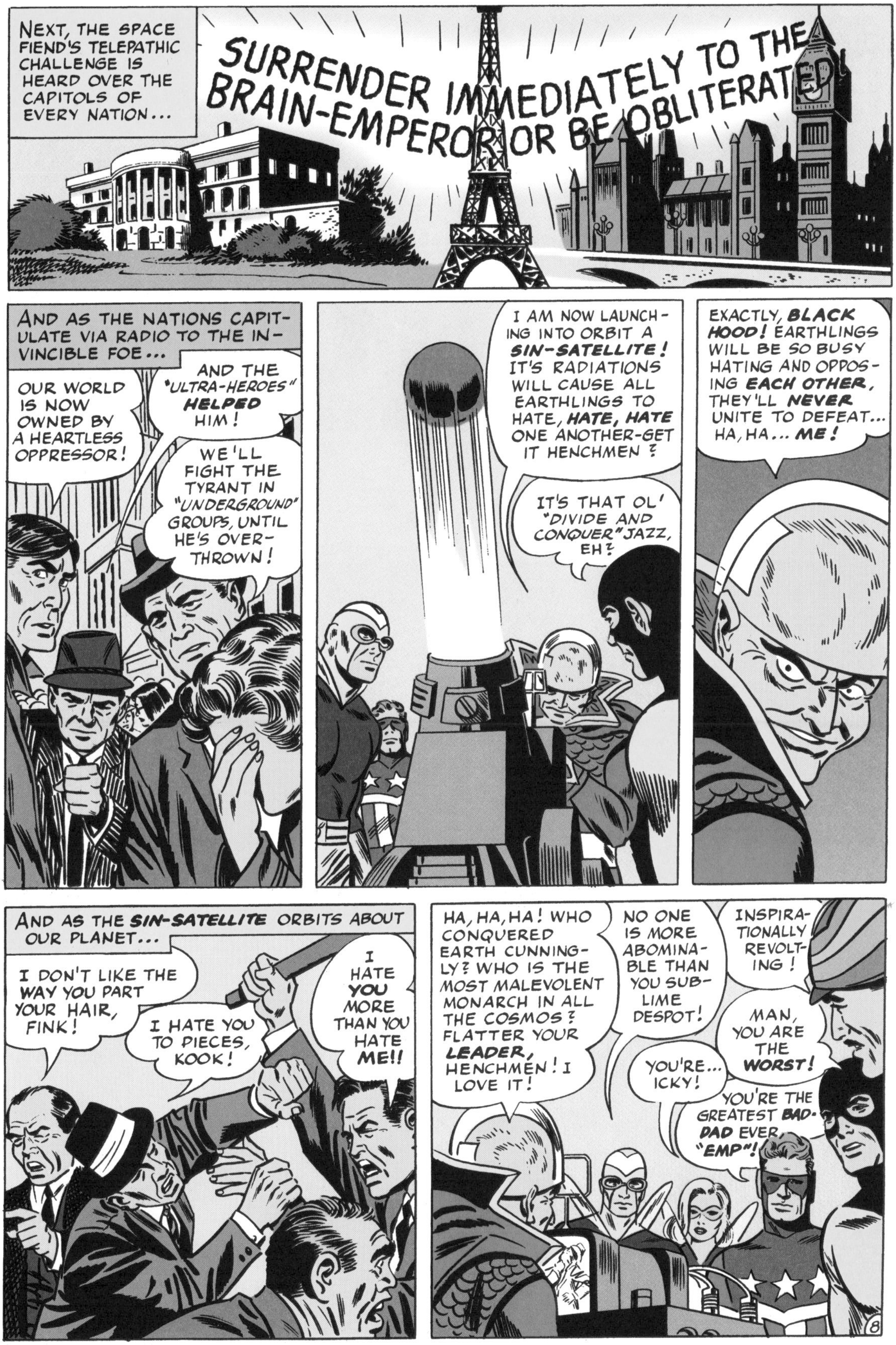
NEXT, THE SPACE FIEND'S TELEPATHIC CHALLENGE IS HEARD OVER THE CAPITOLS OF EVERY NATION...
SURRENDER IMMEDIATELY TO THE BRAIN-EMPEROR OR BE OBLITERATED!
AND AS THE NATIONS CAPITULATE VIA RADIO TO THE INVINCIBLE FOE...
OUR WORLD IS NOW OWNED BY A HEARTLESS OPPRESSOR!
AND THE "ULTRA-HEROES" HELPED HIM!
WE'LL FIGHT THE TYRANT IN "UNDERGROUND" GROUPS, UNTIL HE'S OVERTHROWN!
I AM NOW LAUNCHING INTO ORBIT A SIN-SATELLITE! IT'S RADIATIONS WILL CAUSE ALL EARTHLINGS TO HATE, HATE, HATE ONE ANOTHER-GET IT HENCHMEN?
IT'S THAT OL' "DIVIDE AND CONQUER" JAZZ, EH?
EXACTLY, BLACK HOOD! EARTHLINGS WILL BE SO BUSY HATING AND OPPOSING EACH OTHER, THEY'LL NEVER UNITE TO DEFEAT... HA, HA... ME!
AND AS THE SIN-SATELLITE ORBITS ABOUT OUR PLANET...
I DON'T LIKE THE WAY YOU PART YOUR HAIR, FINK!
I HATE YOU TO PIECES, KOOK!
I HATE YOU MORE THAN YOU HATE ME!!
HA, HA, HA! WHO CONQUERED EARTH CUNNINGLY? WHO IS THE MOST MALEVOLENT MONARCH IN ALL THE COSMOS? FLATTER YOUR LEADER, HENCHMEN! I LOVE IT!
NO ONE IS MORE ABOMINABLE THAN YOU SUBLIME DESPOT!
INSPIRATIONALLY REVOLTING!
MAN, YOU ARE THE WORST!
YOU'RE... ICKY!
YOU'RE THE GREATEST BAD-DAD EVER, "EMP"!
8

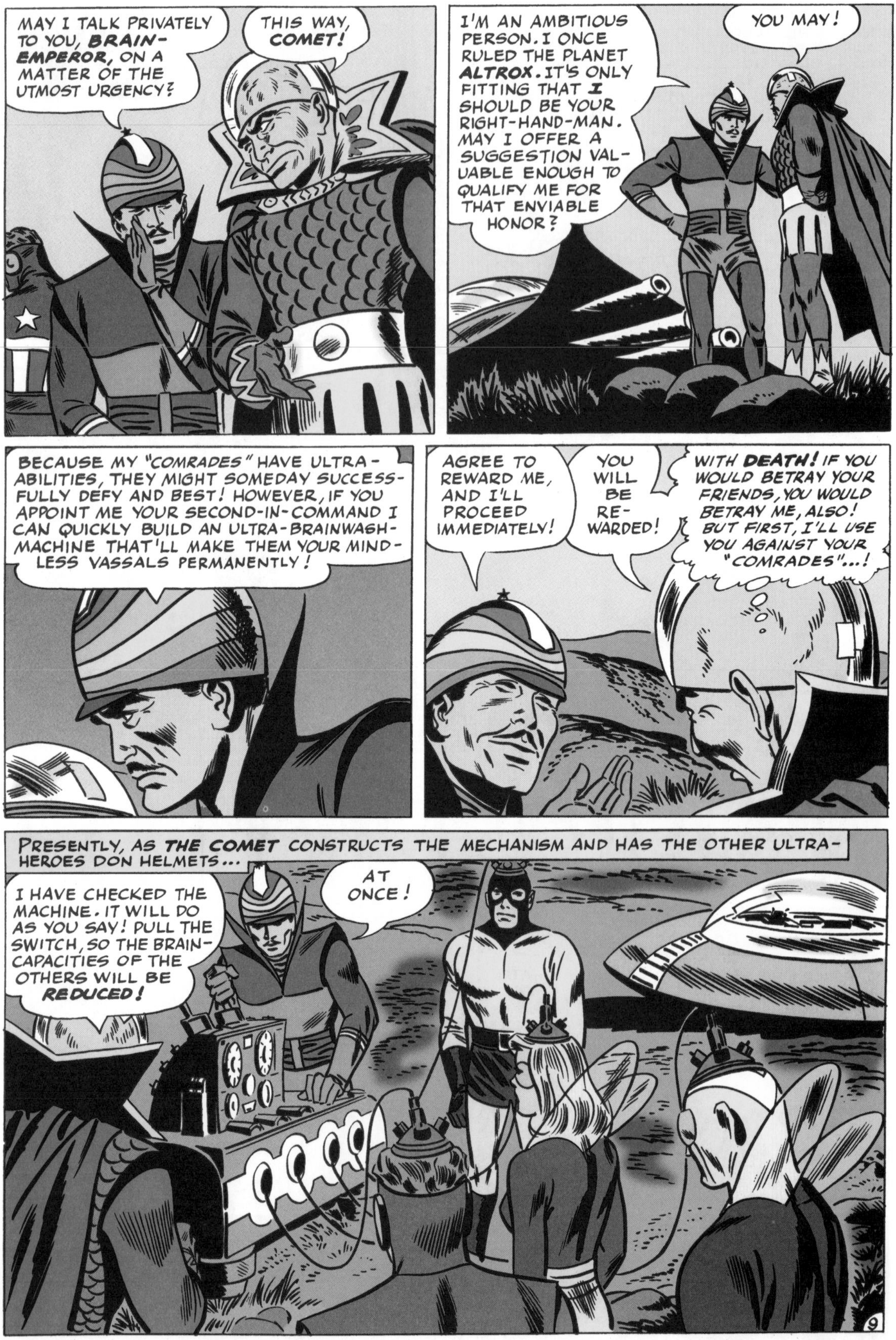
MAY I TALK PRIVATELY TO YOU, BRAIN-EMPEROR, ON A MATTER OF THE UTMOST URGENCY?
THIS WAY, COMET!
I'M AN AMBITIOUS PERSON. I ONCE RULED THE PLANET ALTROX. IT'S ONLY FITTING THAT I SHOULD BE YOUR RIGHT-HAND-MAN. MAY I OFFER A SUGGESTION VAL-UABLE ENOUGH TO QUALIFY ME FOR THAT ENVIABLE HONOR?
YOU MAY!
BECAUSE MY "COMRADES" HAVE ULTRA-ABILITIES, THEY MIGHT SOMEDAY SUCCESS-FULLY DEFY AND BEST! HOWEVER, IF YOU APPOINT ME YOUR SECOND-IN-COMMAND I CAN QUICKLY BUILD AN ULTRA-BRAINWASH-MACHINE THAT'LL MAKE THEM YOUR MIND-LESS VASSALS PERMANENTLY!
AGREE TO REWARD ME, AND I'LL PROCEED IMMEDIATELY!
YOU WILL BE RE-WARDED!
WITH DEATH! IF YOU WOULD BETRAY YOUR FRIENDS, YOU WOULD BETRAY ME, ALSO! BUT FIRST, I'LL USE YOU AGAINST YOUR "COMRADES"...!
PRESENTLY, AS THE COMET CONSTRUCTS THE MECHANISM AND HAS THE OTHER ULTRA-HEROES DON HELMETS...
I HAVE CHECKED THE MACHINE. IT WILL DO AS YOU SAY! PULL THE SWITCH, SO THE BRAIN-CAPACITIES OF THE OTHERS WILL BE REDUCED!
AT ONCE!
9

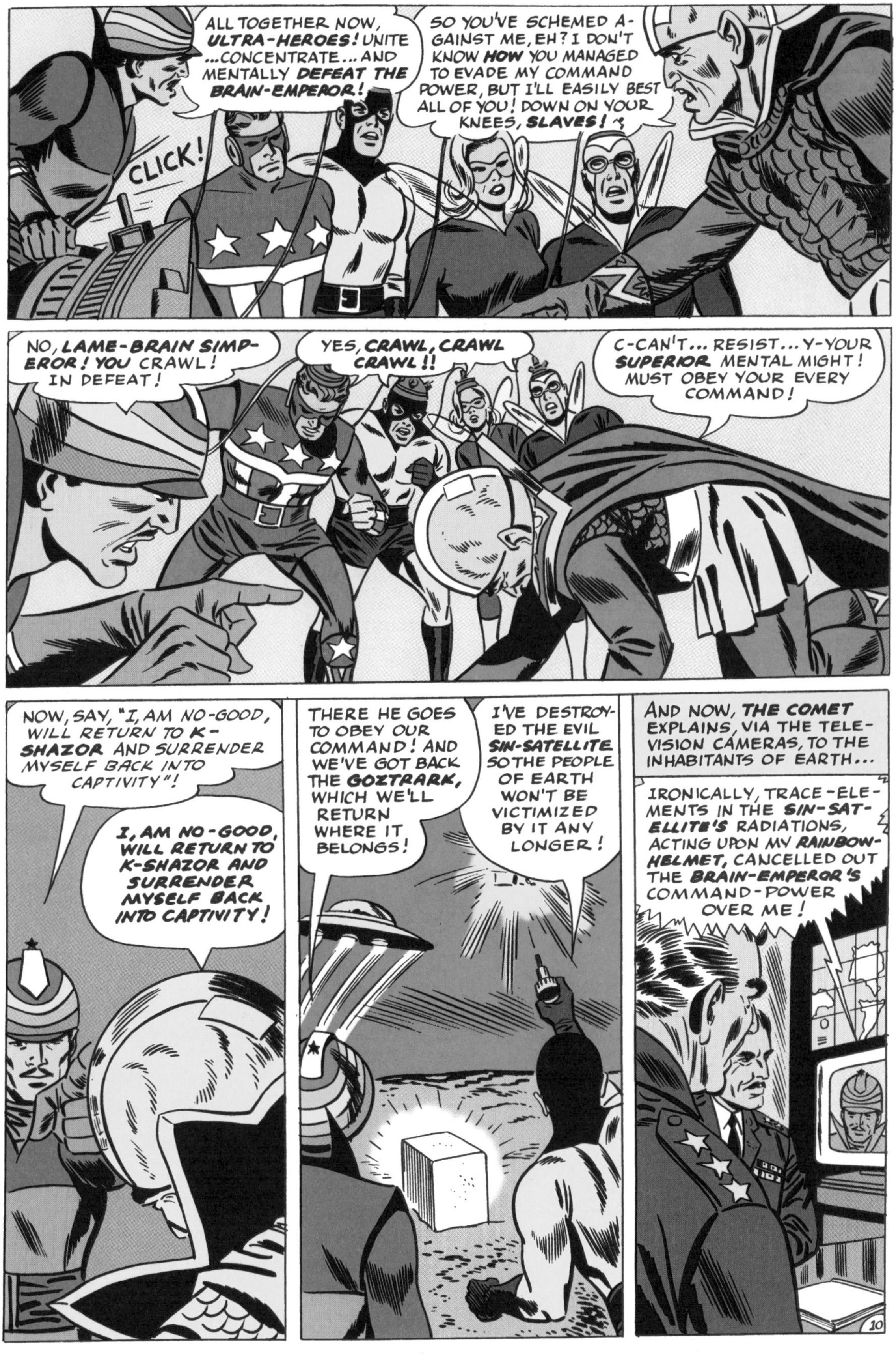
ALL TOGETHER NOW, ULTRA-HEROES! UNITE ...CONCENTRATE... AND MENTALLY DEFEAT THE BRAIN-EMPEROR!
SO YOU'VE SCHEMED AGAINST ME, EH? I DON'T KNOW HOW YOU MANAGED TO EVADE MY COMMAND POWER, BUT I'LL EASILY BEST ALL OF YOU! DOWN ON YOUR KNEES, SLAVES!
CLICK!
NO, LAME-BRAIN SIMPEROR! YOU CRAWL! IN DEFEAT!
YES, CRAWL, CRAWL CRAWL!!
C-CAN'T... RESIST... Y-YOUR SUPERIOR MENTAL MIGHT! MUST OBEY YOUR EVERY COMMAND!
NOW, SAY, "I, AM NO-GOOD, WILL RETURN TO K-SHAZOR AND SURRENDER MYSELF BACK INTO CAPTIVITY"!
I, AM NO-GOOD, WILL RETURN TO K-SHAZOR AND SURRENDER MYSELF BACK INTO CAPTIVITY!
THERE HE GOES TO OBEY OUR COMMAND! AND WE'VE GOT BACK THE GOZTRARK, WHICH WE'LL RETURN WHERE IT BELONGS!
I'VE DESTROYED THE EVIL SIN-SATELLITE SO THE PEOPLE OF EARTH WON'T BE VICTIMIZED BY IT ANY LONGER!
AND NOW, THE COMET EXPLAINS, VIA THE TELEVISION CAMERAS, TO THE INHABITANTS OF EARTH...
IRONICALLY, TRACE-ELEMENTS IN THE SIN-SAT-ELLITE'S RADIATIONS, ACTING UPON MY RAINBOW-HELMET, CANCELLED OUT THE BRAIN-EMPEROR'S COMMAND-POWER OVER ME!
10

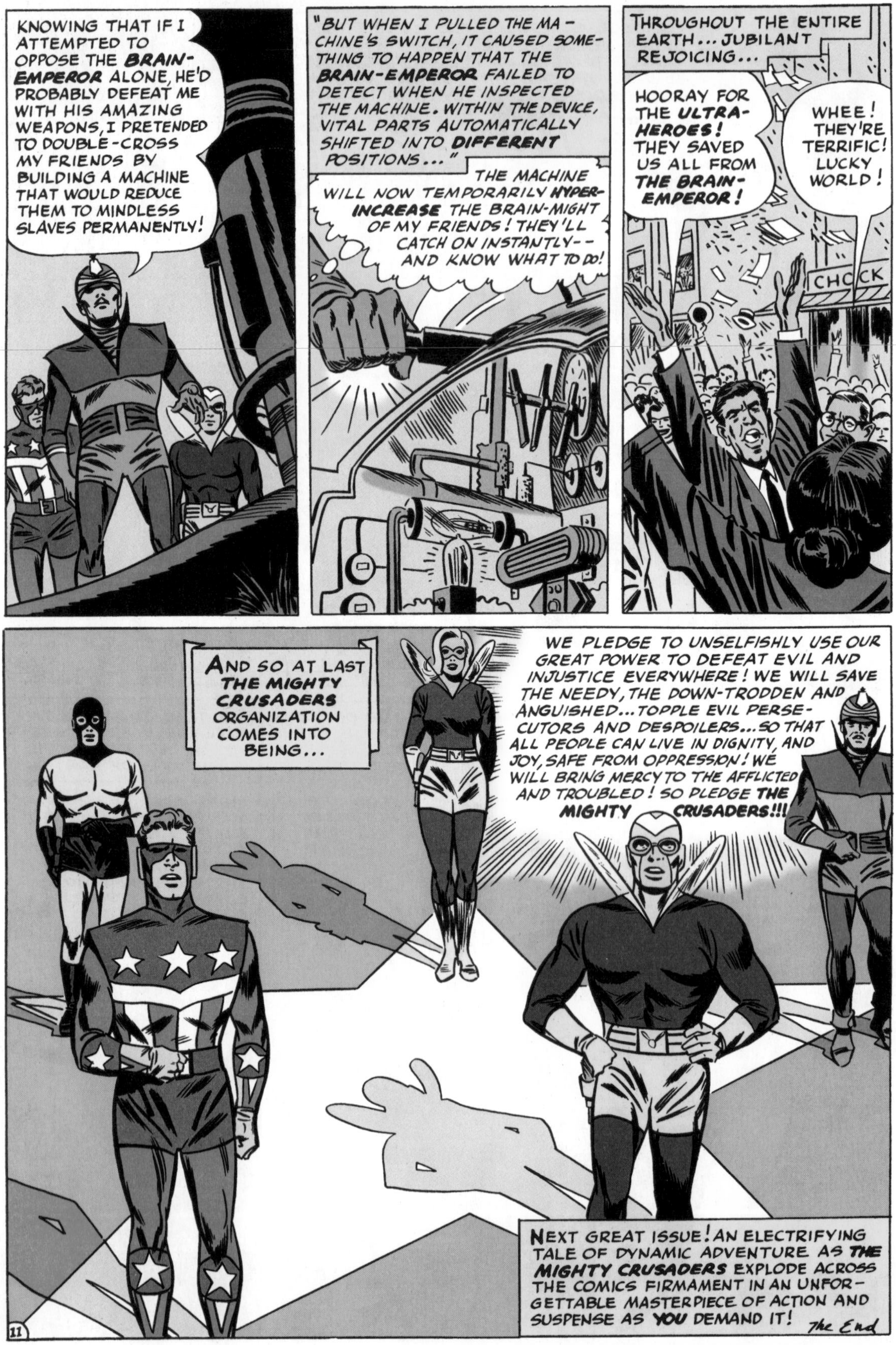
KNOWING THAT IF I ATTEMPTED TO OPPOSE THE BRAIN-EMPEROR ALONE, HE'D PROBABLY DEFEAT ME WITH HIS AMAZING WEAPONS, I PRETENDED TO DOUBLE-CROSS MY FRIENDS BY BUILDING A MACHINE THAT WOULD REDUCE THEM TO MINDLESS SLAVES PERMANENTLY!
"BUT WHEN I PULLED THE MACHINE'S SWITCH, IT CAUSED SOMETHING TO HAPPEN THAT THE BRAIN-EMPEROR FAILED TO DETECT WHEN HE INSPECTED THE MACHINE. WITHIN THE DEVICE, VITAL PARTS AUTOMATICALLY SHIFTED INTO DIFFERENT POSITIONS..."
THE MACHINE WILL NOW TEMPORARILY HYPER-INCREASE THE BRAIN-MIGHT OF MY FRIENDS! THEY'LL CATCH ON INSTANTLY--AND KNOW WHAT TO DO!
THROUGHOUT THE ENTIRE EARTH... JUBILANT REJOICING...
HOORAY FOR THE ULTRA-HEROES! THEY SAVED US ALL FROM THE BRAIN-EMPEROR!
WHEE! THEY'RE TERRIFIC! LUCKY WORLD!
CHOCK
AND SO AT LAST THE MIGHTY CRUSADERS ORGANIZATION COMES INTO BEING...
WE PLEDGE TO UNSELFISHLY USE OUR GREAT POWER TO DEFEAT EVIL AND INJUSTICE EVERYWHERE! WE WILL SAVE THE NEEDY, THE DOWN-TRODDEN AND ANGUISHED... TOPPLE EVIL PERSECUTORS AND DESPOILERS... SO THAT ALL PEOPLE CAN LIVE IN DIGNITY, AND JOY, SAFE FROM OPPRESSION! WE WILL BRING MERCY TO THE AFFLICTED AND TROUBLED! SO PLEDGE THE MIGHTY CRUSADERS!!!
NEXT GREAT ISSUE! AN ELECTRIFYING TALE OF DYNAMIC ADVENTURE AS THE MIGHTY CRUSADERS EXPLODE ACROSS THE COMICS FIRMAMENT IN AN UNFORGETTABLE MASTERPIECE OF ACTION AND SUSPENSE AS YOU DEMAND IT!
The End
11